Lindisfarne
The Cradle Island

LINDISFARNE
THE CRADLE ISLAND

by

Magnus Magnusson

illustrated by

Sheila Mackie

Consultant

David O'Connor
Warden of Lindisfarne

ORIEL PRESS
STOCKSFIELD
BOSTON, MELBOURNE, HENLEY, LONDON

Lindisfarne, The Cradle Island

© 1984, Text, Magnus Magnusson
Pictures, Sheila Mackie

First published in 1984
by Oriel Press Limited
Stocksfield, Northumberland,
England, NE43 7NA.
9 Park Street, Boston,
Mass. 02108, U.S.A. and
6th Floor, 464 St. Kilda Road,
Melbourne, Victoria 3004, Australia.

Set in Baskerville and
printed by Knight & Forster, Leeds.

Trade enquiries to
Routledge & Kegan Paul PLC
Broadway House, Newtown Road,
Henley-on-Thames, Oxon, RG9 1EN.

First published as a paperback in 1985
ISBN 0-85362-223-X

ISBN 0 85362 210 8

Contents

v

vi

1 The Cradle Island

Journeying to Lindisfarne is to make pilgrimage, a voyage of discovery: discovering an island of astonishing charm and endless variety, a windswept little island deep-hallowed by age-old associations from and with the past, a present community steadfastly locked into its own traditions and its own contented insularity. Above all, for some it's a place where you discover yourself.

Lindisfarne: what a lovely, sensuous name it is. It reflects a marriage between Old English and Celtic elements, although they cannot now be identified with any certainty. Some say that *farne* is a Celtic word meaning 'land', and *lindis* came from the name of some stream associated with the island; others suggest a derivation from Scots-Celtic *linn*, meaning 'torrent' or 'cascade'. For myself, I prefer to believe that *Lindis* comes from the Old English *lind* in its meaning of 'shield' (from the lime trees whose wood was used to make Anglo-Saxon bucklers). Who can be sure? I only know that 'Shield-land' would be a happily appropriate designation for the Lindisfarne of then and now.

But Lindisfarne has two fine names, not one; for when the Normans re-established ecclesiastical life on the island with a Priory and Church, late in the 11th century, they accorded it the official name of *Insula Sacra*, Holy Island, in honour of the early Celtic saints who lived and worked there. Both names are interchangeable to this day; taken together — 'The Holy Island of Lindisfarne' — they have the chime and resonance of church bells in tongue.

It may seem extravagant to bestow a third name upon it, but I always think of it as the Cradle Island, for such it has been since history began. It was here on these unshielded acres that the lantern of Celtic Christianity was first lit, away back in the 7th century, illumining the Dark Ages for the northern kingdoms of England. Here St Aidan, Irish-born, Iona-trained, founded in 635 a church and monastery that became the Mother Church of Northumbria. Here was fostered a place of worship, both simple and profound, that lives on still in the annals of the spirit. Here was a great school of religious discipline, an inspired

1

power-house of culture and learning, a seminary of the soul whose missionary graduates would carry the torch of Christianity far afield over Britain and the Continent. Nine saints were associated with this Christian cradle, and sixteen bishops had their see here, of whom the sixth, St Cuthbert, would earn the greatest' fame.

It's almost as if Nature had deliberately created Lindisfarne as a holy, hallowed place, a gospel shield, a place of sanctuary. Sanctuary it has certainly always been for the countless birds whose very lives depend on winter feeding from its broad and generous estuaries and mud-flats; and cradle-sanctuary, too, for the thousands of Grey Seals (Atlantic seals, we used to call them) which gather in its seas to mate, and pup, and mate again. Sanctuary it will be for evermore, now that Lindisfarne has become a National Nature Reserve.

On the map, Lindisfarne looks in outline not unlike a rusty old axe-head, with a knobbly shaft lying west-to-east and the blade itself, chunky and hard-bitten, pointing south. The axe-head measures roughly about a mile square, with the peninsular haft reaching out a further mile and a half towards the mainland. The total area is something over a thousand acres; the total population now only about 170 souls.

It lies about a mile off the Northumberland coast, off the cold shoulder of north-eastern England. The nearest mainland settlement is the hamlet of Beal, about a mile inland. The town of Berwick-upon-Tweed, hard upon the Scottish border, lies some eight miles to the north; the formidable fortress of Bamburgh Castle rears dramatically proud of the skyline about the same distance away to the south.

On the island itself, the whole of the northern landscape is a range of brawling, shifting sand-dunes, battened down against the wind and sea by a covering of tough, resilient Marram grass, especially on the long shaft of the Snook, to the west. Sometimes you feel that the whole island is held together by Marram grass and little else. The northern coast is ramparted with splendid rocky cliffs whose roots stretch treacherously out to sea; but in between are golden sandy bays, like Sandham Bay and Coves Haven, of remarkable and unexpected beauty and serenity. The east coast is similarly bastioned with rocky walls and red shingly earthworks, while the interior is flat farmland untenanted by trees but quartered by fencing. Two trackways across it — the Straight Lonnen and the Crooked Lonnen — are lined with stubborn hawthorn hedge, buffeted and bowed, which offers merciful haven to hosts of little migrants making landfall at the edge of their endurance.

The most striking features of the island are two arrogant outcrops of dolerite rock that have thrust their way brusquely out of the bed of limestone on which the island lies. These are the Heugh (onomatopoeia set in stone), which shelters the village from the south, and Beblowe Crag, superintended now by a piled-up castle straight from fairy-tale.

All the human settlement huddles together for company in this southern segment of the island: the harbour and its attendant beach of fishery bits and pieces, the sombre ruins of the Norman Priory and Church, the island's two farms (Beblowe and St Coomb's, named after St Columba, the founding father of Celtic Christianity on that other Holy Isle, Iona in the Hebrides), and the village itself.

Today the village is a close cluster of sensible homes hugging themselves against the wind. Whatever street-plan it may once have had in medieval times is all but forgotten; lanes swerve and wriggle from the Market Place through ranks of sturdy houses rooted to their age-old sites, home-grown of fine Northumbrian stone to hold their own against the seasoned wind, one-storey, two-storey, pantile roofs and small-paned windows peeping out from lowered lids. Most of them are modernised within, warm setts of unassuming domesticity; the new are tailored carefully to fit the cut of the old. The place-names speak with blurred memory of former people and pre-occupations — Lilburn's Cottage, Piet Hill, Jenny Bell's Well, Willy Potts' Rock, Bigg (for barley) Close, Pally (for some imagined Bishop's Palace) Hill, Mustard (for minster) Close, Cuddy (for Cuthbert) Walls, Sanctuary Close. There's a shop or two, a pub or two (well, three actually), hotels and boarding-houses for the visitor trade, a factory for making Lindisfarne Mead, no less; and a summer fish-and-chip van.

What gives Lindisfarne its geographical distinction is the fact that it is only a half-time island — a tidal island in reality. The area between island and mainland is a broad reach of sand-bank and mud-flat, riven by streams and runnels, totally submerged by the tide for some five hours twice a day. The Venerable Bede, father of English history, described the phenomenon succinctly and well as long ago as the middle of the eighth century, in Book III of his *Ecclesiastical History of the English People*:

> As the tide ebbs and flows, this place is surrounded twice daily by the waves of the sea like an island, and twice, when the sands are dry, it becomes again attached to the mainland.

Sir Walter Scott, the arch-romantic, conjured up a more poetic image in his long narrative poem, *Marmion* (II, 9):

> For, with the flow and ebb its stile
> Varies from continent to isle;
> Dry-shod, o'er sands, twice every day,
> The pilgrims to the shrine find way:
> Twice every day, the waves efface
> Of staves and sandaled feet the trace.

This tidal semi-moat is now traversed by a metalled Causeway, connecting to the underbelly of the island like a stretched umbilical; but this, too, is drowned at high tide to a depth of several feet and made totally impassable.

It gives the island a curious sense of timelessness, of being *in* time but not entirely *of* it: a powerfully atmospheric impression of reserved isolation, a place where history and legend can still inform the here and now, a place where unreality softly tones the drabber colours of reality. This welcomed isolation has always been part of the Lindisfarne experience, and is so to this day. In the early days of settlement, when Aidan chose this site for hallowed work, it was this ambiguous insularity that must have helped inspire its election — this being of the mainland but not on it, this being of the world but not worldly, this being a retreat but not a hideaway.

The eternal rhythm of the tide, girdling the island twice a day, governs all. It governs the lives of wildfowl and waders, scurrying for food before the incoming surge and chasing it out again on the ebb. It is the tide that summons out from their warm beds the fishermen, the winkle-pickers, the mussel-gatherers, at whatever time of night or state of mind. It is the tide that governs transit, that draws the surging floods of tourist-trippers as the summer mounts — half a million of them now, at least, a running rush on the fall, a draining on the rise, leaving their daily tide-mark of quickly-cleared paper bags and cans. No staves or sandaled feet these days, except for the odd occasion of self-conscious historical formality; but nonetheless the difference, the obstacle, the air of excursion and adventure, give them all a subtle sense of pilgrimage.

And when did all this begin, this daily, lunar, seasonal, everlasting round of action and reaction, of cradle and creation, of coming and of going? The answer is we do not know, and can barely even guess. The prehistory of Lindisfarne is shrouded in the darkness of the past, and all but buried in the endlessly shifting sands of the island's dunes. Some fragmentary echoes of this past are in the Museum of Antiquities of the University of Newcastle upon Tyne: a Bronze Age spear-head, with a

TIME AND TIDE

They look so incredibly ancient, primeval even, the creatures that lurk and loiter on the bed of the seas around Lindisfarne; they seem old as time itself . . .

Globular spiny Sea-urchins with their shells of calcareous plates, animated burrs the size of tennis-balls — and inside them, a marvellously intricate apparatus of struts and muscles to operate its teeth, known as 'Aristotle's lantern'. Tiny Tellins like miniature Cockles, cowering in their thousands in the mud. Mussels anchored to each other and the ground, their shells dotted with barnacles like a lunar landscape. Crabs that scurry sideways into hiding as the tide recedes, seeking urgent cover from the probing beaks of hungry waders. And the doyen of them all, the mighty Lobster, purple-blue and speckled white, the dinosaur of the sea-bed, long red antennae constantly in motion like early-warning radar scanners.

They're such fascinating creatures, lobsters. And those great claws! One is a powerful pincer for grabbing hold (and a fearsome nip you can get from it), the other is for tearing and shredding food. Both are used for attacking and defending alike. And if the struggle goes against it, if a limb is trapped or crushed, the lobster sheds its claw or limbs — cutting its losses, so to speak, tearing it off along a predestined break-line like a perforated stamp. It's an automatic thing, a reflex muscular spasm when the limb is broken; and in time, another will grow to take its place.

Man has always lived off these extraordinary denizens of the inshore sea-bed, from early prehistoric times. Today the lordly lobster is the backbone of Lindisfarne's fishing economy. There's a huge mussel-bed on Oyster Scap, south of the harbour, which is regularly cropped and re-seeded by the island fishermen. Winkles are also gathered from the shores at low water — a miserably cold and numbing task, but one that must be done when other sources fail.

Time and tide — they are what Lindisfarne is made of.

tiny piece of ash-wood still in the socket, found on the shoreline below the Heugh a few years ago; a polished Neolithic axe-head made of dolerite and found in the 1920s; a worked flint arrow-head found at the base of Beblowe Crag in the 1930s; a small box-full of other assorted flints. Not much of a haul from the silent millennia of man's prehistory.

There must be more, of course. Stone Age man must surely have frequented these inviting shores to gather shellfish — mussels and winkles and cockles in abundance — or to capture fish and fowl and eggs. Ernie Evans, for instance, a part-time local guide and full-time enthusiast for all things island, old and new, is the pleased possessor of two little artefacts of seemingly great antiquity that he picked up near Coves Haven — a broken flint spear-head, and a curiously-shaped lump of dolerite that may well have been used as a scraper.

And now another accidental find may lead to real illumination. In September, 1983, a joint team from the Department of Archaeology at Leicester University and the Archaeology Unit at St David's University College, Lampeter, carried out a full-scale survey of a large area of claggy, sandy duneland near the old quarry at Ness-end, in the north of the island. It came about because two members of the team, Dr Robert Young from Lampeter and Deirdre O'Sullivan of Leicester had found pieces of worked flint by chance there during a bout of preliminary fieldwork in 1980. The chosen area measured 250 metres by 70; and from the soil they sieved and riddled no fewer than 1300 pieces of struck flint, chert, quartz and chalcedony — a broad range of artefacts spanning the Mesolithic (Middle Stone Age), Neolithic (New Stone Age) and Early Bronze Age periods: 7,000 years or more from around 8,000 to 1,000 BC.

Of settlement as such there is as yet no trace — no sign of habitation in the caves of Coves Haven, no shadowy imprint of some ancient hearth. But that may come. Who knows what patterns of living and working, hunting and gathering, perhaps even of trade and barter, might be pieced together by Lampeter and Leicester? A long programme of detailed survey work and excavation is planned with the eventual aim of producing a detailed study of the early settlement history of the island.

2 The Making of the British

For many centuries after those fugitive visitations by occasional hunters or hunted in remote prehistoric times, the little island of Lindisfarne slept a dreamless sleep, basking undisturbed by man, alternately at anchor or aground in its offshore waters. Then, as now, it was sanctuary for myriads of seabirds, wildfowl and waders, for moths and butterflies, for blossoms and grasses, mosses and lichens, and all the astonishingly complex and teeming life of the sands and seashore. There is nothing in the archaeological record, threadbare as it is, to indicate any form of human occupation to interrupt the rhythmic cycle of the seasons. Nature alone regulated the eternal springs and falls of life.

But on the mainland, barely a mile away, history was beginning to march inexorably in its hobnailed boots over the lives of peasants and princes alike. The Mesolithic (Middle Stone Age) with its meagre population of scattered bands of nomadic hunter-gatherers gave way, around 4,000 BC, to the Neolithic (New Stone Age). This was the crucial stage in human progress; it has been called the most important single advance ever made by man — when invaders or infiltrators from the Continent introduced the idea of farming and stock-rearing, of harvesting the land. It marked a major revolution in the life-style of man, because it enabled him to settle permanently in once place, by imposing a measure of control over the processes of Nature instead of being totally subservient to them. Mesolithic mobility coagulated into Neolithic stability. Plots and pastures were cleared for cultivation and animal husbandry, pottery vessels for cooking or storage made their first appearance. Adam delved, and Eve span. Massive construction works were built — causewayed camps, long-barrows for family or tribal burials, massive megalithic ('great stone') tombs. But magnificent burial chambers like Maes Howe in the Orkneys, now dated to around 2,700 BC, did not simply happen; they were the culmination of a long architectural apprenticeship. They needed planning and skill and organisation, and a large, well-disciplined labour force. They needed, in a word, authority.

S.G.M.

8

This authority was made possible by the Neolithic Revolution. Land cultivation meant better food supplies, and led to larger populations; food surpluses allowed the development of craft specialisation, like flint-mining and stone-quarrying; having a place of one's own encouraged the accumulation of personal possessions, and stimulated mutual barter with other groups — as well as the envy of neighbours. Wealth required as careful husbanding as cattle or kinsmen. Wealth meant power and authority — the authority to harness surplus energy into communal projects, and the wealth to finance them with surplus produce. For the first time, fleeting groups of nomads began to assume viable and lasting identities as rooted social settlements.

It has long been the custom for archaeologists to partition the course of human progress in terms of the so-called 'Three Age System' of Stone, Bronze and Iron; and round about 2,000 BC, Britain was convulsed once again by the introduction, forcibly and forcefully, of a second far-reaching innovation from the Continent — bronze. Bronze is an alloy of copper and tin — about nine parts of copper to one part tin. Copper had been one of the first natural metals to be exploited by man, at first by simple cold-hammering (like gold) and later by smelting and casting. Metallurgy had been developing steadily in the Balkans and the Middle East for a long time; pottery techniques had reached astounding heights of industrial sophistication, with kilns capable of firing clay at 1,100° Centigrade. Able, questing minds — no less questing or able than ours are today — were constantly experimenting, constantly seeking new products or refining old ones. One result of this ceaseless experimentation was bronze: harder than copper, but easier to smelt and to cast. It could be used for making high-prestige ceremonial objects — and, more to the point, weapons that were sharper and more versatile than the relatively clumsy axes of the Neolithic.

In Britain, the Bronze Age began around 2,000 BC with the influx of a robust and big-boned warrior race from the Continent: the Beaker Folk, as they have been dubbed from their distinctively-shaped pottery. They laid about them with a will, ruthlessly dispossessing or absorbing the 'native' Neolithics. The tin-mines of south-west England may have been the magnet that drew the first invaders, for tin was scarce while copper was plentiful, and whoever monopolized the tin-trade cornered the bronze market. Now we see truly conspicuous wealth developing, expressed in magnificent ornaments of bronze and gold and jet, both the cause and the effect of intense craft specialisation and entrepreneurial commerce. Well-made, aesthetically attractive objects became desirable possessions in their own right.

All conspicuous wealth, however, needs conspicuous force to defend it, or accumulate it. Around 1,700 BC another wave of bronze-clad warriors came pouring across the Channel from Brittany, even better armed than the first. We can now begin to guess at the hazy beginnings of formal chiefdoms; and under their protective authority the south of England in particular enjoyed a long period of stability and economic prosperity, built on skilled land management and expressed in industrial and artistic enterprise.

The start of the third technological break-through in prehistory — the Iron Age — is conventionally dated, as far as Britain is concerned, around 500 BC. Once again, it was spawned amongst the Celtic tribes in the cockpit of central Europe and spread rapidly westward and northward. Their culture (named Hallstat after the seminal find-site, near Salzburg) is identified by spacious timber round-houses, fortified hill-top strongholds and, in particular, long iron swords. Iron had originally been developed by Hittite metallurgists for ornamental purposes around 1,500 BC, but they managed to keep the process secret (there is nothing new about the fear of industrial espionage!) until the overthrow of the Hittite empire in Anatolia by the Sea-Peoples (Philistines) around 1200 BC; then the race was on in earnest to develop a commercially viable technique for the mass-production of iron. Iron was much harder than bronze; iron ore was much more plentiful than tin or even copper; and because meteoric 'natural' iron came, observably and literally, from the heavens, it was much prized for its assumed magical properties.

These Hallstat Celts began their take-over of the British Isles around 600 BC with infiltrations into the north-east of Scotland. The mass settlement wave came from France and the Low Countries; and then one of the main targets was the east coast of Yorkshire and, either directly or indirectly, Ireland. Two centuries later, around 250 BC, another wave gathered itself in northern France and broke over the south and east coasts of England; these were Celts of the so-called La Tène culture (named after a huge deposit of votive offerings found in Lake Neuchâtel in Switzerland). And with the La Tène people, we begin to recognise, in outline at least, the features of the British, of native Britons as we come to know them from historical sources.

What distinguished these newcomers was an inordinate love of luxury ornaments. They were an extremely wealthy warrior

BEACON POINT

It could be at the ends of the earth — the sandy wastes of dune-land, the lonely beacon on a farthest shore. And as it happens, it was the end of the line for many a life and many a brave ship. For this is Emmanuel Head, the north-eastern extremity of Lindisfarne; and on its rocky coast, a scatter of rusting plates and rotting timbers marks their last resting-places.

It's always been a hazardous coastline, this, especially in the days of sail. There has always been a lot of traffic up and down this coast — the Firth of Forth lies to the north, Tynemouth to the south. Just to the west, across Sandham Bay, is the rocky promontory of Ness-end; from it runs out to sea a wicked line of unseen reefs that would tear the bottom out of any ship.

On Admiralty charts, Ness-end is marked as 'False Emmanuel Head', because so many ships and lives were lost when helmsmen mistook the Ness-end for Emmanuel Head, and turned their vessels south — straight onto the hidden rocks. And so, in 1828, Trinity House, the organization responsible for lighthouses and the like, erected a high stone pyramid to mark the true Emmanuel Head, painted a dazzling white, to help mariners clear the point in safety. There are other markers now, all maintained by Trinity House, on prominent points like the Heugh, the Plough Rock off the east coast, and the beacons on the northern end of Old Law, on the mainland, which provide the only bearing for a safe entry into Holy Island anchorage.

The obelisk on Emmanuel Head also makes its point for landlubbers, a reference and waymark for ramblers in the National Nature Reserve. In that undulating sea of sand-dunes which makes up the northern half of the island, it isn't hard to lose one's bearings. It's a fine place to sit and rest, sheltered from the wind from any airt, to watch the ships go safely by, to admire the gannets plunging for their prey, and listen to the siren song of seals on False Emmanuel Head.

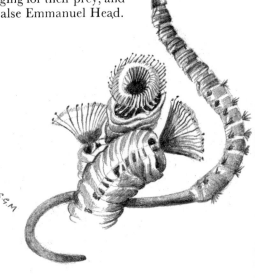

12

aristocracy, who introduced to the British Isles the two-wheeled war-chariot drawn by a pair of specially bred horses the size of the modern Welsh pony. Their art-work was as flamboyant and rumbustious as they themselves were, initially inspired by the southern decorative motifs on the flagons of wine they imported in huge quantities. But they also brought with them an ideal of the 'heroic' way of life that would later find memorable expression in early Irish literature, in all those stirring tales of Cú Chulainn and other champions of yore. And they may well have introduced the Druid priesthood to preside over their ferocious religious rites in blood-spattered sacred groves. They struck deep roots in Britain, particularly in Yorkshire, creating a heroic, privileged, restless, brawling, cattle-rustling nobility in which women, incidentally, seem to have been held in high honour and respect.

They in their turn were followed, around 100 BC, by an influx of Belgic tribes from Gaul who, squeezed by the advancing frontiers of Imperial Rome, overflowed into southern Britain. With them, we emerge from the mists of prehistory into the dawning light of written history from the pens of Roman commentators and historians. In Britain, the Belgae developed the embryo La Tène townships into formidable *oppida* — heavily fortified towns of sprawling settlements of huddled homes and workshops, the first towns in Britain, which served as the capitals of independent and frequently warring tribal territories. They may all have been Belgae, but they all wanted a place in the sun for themselves. They brought with them the ancestral gods and ancestral cult symbols they had revered in Gaul, and they kept up close political contacts with their kin and kith in Gaul. Britain, in fact, became a sanctuary for refugee Gauls and a breeding-ground for counter-insurgency against the Roman occupation — so much so that Julius Caesar was provoked into an abortive punitive expedition against the British in 55 BC, and a much more determined attempt at subjugation in 54 BC. His main objective was to crush the most powerful of the Belgic tribes, the Catuvellauni, who controlled large territories north of the Thames under their vigorous king, Cassivellaunus. Apprehensive of his growing power, the neighbouring tribe of the Trinovantes in Essex were only too glad to collaborate with the Roman invaders. Caesar's legions had little difficulty in overrunning Cassivellaunus' capital *oppidum* at Wheathampstead, near Welwyn in Hertfordshire (stretches of the great defensive ditch and bank are still visible there to this day). Cassivellaunus, however, and

13

the bulk of his army, escaped to fight another day, but in the event did not require to do so: he made terms with Caesar, promising not to molest the Trinovantes, whose territory in future would be protected by a 'guarantee' from Rome. With that, his ruffled pride somewhat preened, Caesar went back to Gaul, never to return to Britain.

For almost a century, Rome left Britain alone, apart from fixing political alliances with several of the minor tribes, and actively promoting trade with Britain. The aggressive Catuvellauni made good use of this respite by swallowing up their weaker tribal neighbours; and in 7 AD, just after the birth of Christ in far-off Palestine, the great Catuvellaunian king, Cunobelinus (Shakespeare's Cymbeline), felled the Trinovantes by conquering and annexing their capital, Camulodium (Colchester) in Essex — the key centre for the lucrative Roman trade.

The Catuvellauni were now the dominant super-tribe in southern Britain. They had introduced their own gold coinage, replacing the former native currency of iron bars; by their own standards they were 'civilised' in the strict sense of being urbanised. They controlled the whole of south-eastern England, and were pushing relentlessly westward, storming with apparent ease even the most formidable strongholds like Maiden Castle in Dorset. By the end of his life, around 40 AD, Cunobelinus had forged a Belgic empire that came close to being Britain's first 'national' centralised state.

But Rome had simply been biding its time, waiting for the Catuvellauni to over-reach themselves. The Imperial throne was now occupied by the unlikely person of Claudius, the stammering cripple who had been unexpectedly elevated to the purple by the army after the assassination of his monstrous nephew, Caligula. Claudius desperately needed a spectacular military 'triumph' to consolidate his throne; a Belgic tribe threatened by the Catuvellauni desperately needed help, and appealed to Rome for military support. Claudius responded with alacrity — a nice and easy Conquest of Britain would breathe life into his lacklustre laurels. In 43 AD he launched a massive invasion.

Meanwhile, those chieftains who had feared or resented the encroachments of Cunobelinus and his strapping sons, and feared the power of Rome even more, had fled to the north, to Northumberland and the Lowlands of Scotland, there to establish themselves as tough and stubborn opponents of both the Roman Conquest and, later, the insistent incursions of the Anglo-Saxons whose Germanic culture would eventually swamp the Celtic culture of the British.

SCHOONER AHOY

Far to the north of Snook Point, far, far away across an astonishing expanse of tawny golden sands known as the Sand Ridge, an old wooden schooner lies at anchor for ever-more, its sailing days long since past. It's the wreck of a 40-foot boat that came to grief on this innocent-looking sand-bank so long ago that no one now remembers exactly when it was.

There isn't much left of it now — just the stumps of its timbers sticking up like rotting teeth. Its only cargo is the shifting sand that fills it to the gunwales. But it has become an important landmark to the fishermen who ply their craft in the shoaling sea to the north — so important that a marker board has been erected on a long metal pole to give the fishermen their bearings on it.

It's an integral part of the shore-scene now. One day, perhaps, it will form the nucleus of a new raised islet of sand and debris bound together by Marram grass; but such is the restless energy of the spring tides that come flooding in over the sands that it could disappear again overnight.

Meanwhile it offers shelter and a nesting site to various small waders, when the weather stays kind. A Mallard duck has nested in the lee of its decaying timbers. It looks an alarmingly exposed site, in the middle of such an open area; but at least no predator can creep up on the sitting bird unnoticed.

The predators aren't far to seek. On the new-washed sand, now as feathery as powdered snow, the tell-tale footprints of a fox come meandering over. He has cocked his leg against the bow-post and stern-post, marking the schooner as part of his hunting territory. Yes, and in the lee of one of the wooden baulks he has curled himself up for a doze in the safe afternoon sunshine; it's slack-tide, and there's no point in going hunting. In the distance, the sea crisps vividly blue and white on the tide-line. All's well with the world, aboard the schooner that will never sail again.

For the time being.

3 Roman Britain

It took the Romans a full forty years of gradual advance and consolidation to become masters of the province of Britannia. In the course of those four decades, they suffered some desperate setbacks — including the ferocious uprising of the Iceni tribe of Norfolk and Suffolk under their redoubtable warrior queen, Boudicca (*Boadicea* in Latin), in 60 AD. It was an object lesson to the Romans — to all occupying forces anywhere, indeed — on how not to treat the local population of a conquered territory.

The Iceni were a fierce warrior tribe of exceptional wealth and martial ability. Their goldsmiths produced superb neck-rings, such as those unearthed in the hoard-finds at Snettisham, and magnificent trappings for their horses and chariots. At the time of the Invasion, the Iceni had cannily made a treaty of non-belligerence with Rome; but in 60 AD, perhaps to protect their newly-founded *colonia* of Camulodunum (Colchester) in Essex while they pushed northward into the inhospitable territory of the Brigantes, the Romans decided to incorporate the kingdom of the Iceni willy-nilly into the growing Province. They carried it out with unbelievable stupidity and insensitivity; Boudicca, widow of the last king of the Iceni, was brutally flogged by greedy Roman tax-collectors, and her daughters raped. In his *Annals*, the historian Tacitus, son-in-law of the future governor of Britain, Agricola, makes no bones about the fact that the ensuing rebellion was entirely Rome's own fault.

The fury of the dispossessed Iceni and their neighbours, the Trinovantes, knew no bounds. With a huge army of warriors accompanied by their families and camp-followers, Boudicca swept down on the hated *colonia* at Colchester, only 80 miles away, where Roman ex-soldiers had been 'planted' on tribal lands. Colchester was overrun and razed to the ground; the detested colonists, who had taken refuge in the huge new Temple of Claudius, were massacred to a man. From Colchester the rebels went swarming down to Londinium (London), which they sacked, then swung north up Watling Street and engulfed Verulamium (St Albans) in a storm of fire. According to

Tacitus, as many as 70,000 Romans and provincials perished in the terrible vengeance of Boudicca.

The whole future of Roman Britain was now trembling in the balance. The Romans were reeling from the savagery of the tribal onslaught. Their legions were scattered and disorientated. But somehow the Romans recovered. The provincial governor, Suetonius Paulinus, came racing back from Wales and, after abandoning London and St Albans to their fate, regrouped his depleted forces in an unidentified valley somewhere in the Midlands, there to await Boudicca's rampaging hordes and the crucial battle that would decide the fate of Britain:

> Suetonius drew up his regular troops in close order, with the light-armed auxiliaries at their flanks, and the cavalry massed on the wings. On the British side, cavalry and infantry bands seethed over a wide area. Their numbers were unprecedented, and they had confidently brought their wives to see the victory, installing them in carts stationed at the edge of the battlefield.

(Tacitus, *Annals*)

Despite their unprecedented numbers and their reckless bravery, however, the British were no match for steely Roman battle-discipline and superior weaponry. In the ensuing massacre some 80,000 Britons were reported to have died, for a loss of only 400 on the Roman side. Boudicca herself is reputed to have taken poison to avoid capture.

The tribal terror of the Iceni uprising gave the Romans pause for a while. It was not until shortly after 70 AD that they managed to 'pacify' the north of England, where the Brigantes held sway both east and west of the Pennines, after a dour three-year campaign. To consolidate their gains, the Romans built a huge legionary fortress for the Ninth Legion at Eboracum (York) in 71 AD. With the north-east secure at last, the Romans now turned their attention to the British tribes in Wales — the Silures under their gallant leader Caractacus, and the Ordovices in north Wales, both of them durable guerrilla-fighters and implacable enemies of the Romans. Eventually, after the establishment of further legionary fortressses, at Isca Silurum (Caerleon) near Newport in Gwent, and then Deva (Chester) to control northern Wales and the Pennines, the Welsh succumbed. By 79 AD, England and Wales were firmly under Roman occupation.

Now only the far north remained — the Lowlands and Highlands of Scotland. This was *terra incognita* to the Romans; unreconnoitred bad-lands. But Agricola, by now appointed provincial governor, drove in hard and ruthlessly. By 81 AD he had subjugated the Lowlands of

19

DAINTIEST DISH

According to that genial 17th century essayist, Sir Thomas
Browne, Godwits were once accounted 'the daintiest dish in
England;and I think, for the bigness, of the biggest price'.
They are no longer prized for the table; but they are still
much admired for their elegant, slender stance, and for their
twirling, sweeping, whirling flight. For Richard Perry, the
naturalist, the angular Bar-tailed Godwit *(Limosa lapponica)*
with its long tip-tilted bill was the master-flier of all the
myriad waders on the winter shores of Lindisfarne. Their
feedings habits delighted him, too:

> From end to end the sands are interlaced with the
> Godwit's trident prints, and are pitted, here and there,
> with awl-shaped holes, an inch across, where they have
> pivoted round 360° on boring bills. Their method of
> feeding is ever a delight to me, and it is amusing to
> watch them . . . pacing all along the sand, swallowing
> up the thin lug-worms with their long retroussé bills.
> Those feeding in shallow pools in the lagoons shove
> their heads right under water, stabbing the ooze viol-
> ently, frequently raising their heads and elevating pink
> bills to swallow some morsel.

These morsels consist of just about anything that lives and
moves on the shore: shrimps, snails, small shellfish, lugworms, sandhoppers. Lugworms in particular provide a
hearty mouthful; they're sturdy creatures, usually larger
than garden worms, and diligently hunted by birds and
human fishermen alike. You can tell a lugworm's presence
by its worm-casts. It lives in a U-shaped burrow a few inches
deep, which it creates by eating its way downwards, then
lying at the bottom of the bend for 40 minutes or so digesting
whatever organic matter was in the sand, before resurfacing
to excrete the debris in conical deposits. Godwits have sensitive pressure receptors at the end of their bills to help them
locate a moving worm.

But the sandhopper is the most ingenious creature of them
all. It's just like a mini-shrimp, about a centimetre long, with
a flattened curving body and several pairs of legs: five pairs
for crawling, three for paddling, and three back pairs for
springing. It lurks under flotsam and jetsam on the beach,
and when its cover is disturbed, a trigger mechanism acti-
vates its abdominal musculature and catapults it a foot or
more into the air.

A dainty dish? When you've got to eat your own body-
weight every day to stay alive, as godwits do, you can't afford
to be too choosy.

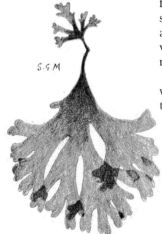

S.G.M

20

Scotland below the central belt, with a line of forts patrolling the frontier strung between the Firth of Clyde and the Firth of Forth.

The Scottish Highlands, and Ireland, were now the only areas of the British Isles beyond the Roman pale. Agricola certainly toyed with the idea of invading Ireland, but the requisite troops could not be made available. Instead he concentrated on a final surge northwards into the unwelcoming mountainous territory of the Caledonian tribes under their leader, Calgacus. Advancing north-eastwards from the Forth in 83 AD, with his fleet in close coastal support, Agricola defeated Calgacus and a huge army somewhere in Perthshire, and consolidated his victory by building a massive (but short-lived) legionary fortress at Inchtuthill in the Tayside Region.

In the following year he resumed his relentless progress northwards, with three legions and his fleet still in support. The Caledonians retreated before him, reluctant to give battle after their mauling the year before. Eventually, with the approach of autumn, Agricola managed to bring Calgacus to pitched battle at an unidentified site known only as Mons Graupius. Here, Tacitus is at his best as a historical essayist more interested in chaps than maps, as the celebrated clerihew has it ('The art of Biography/Is different from Geography...'); his account of the battle in his monograph on *Agricola* makes compelling reading. The ringing denunciation of the Romans that he puts into the mouth of Calgacus in his pre-battle speech is the classic utterance of the freedom-fighter:

> Former battles in which Rome was resisted left behind them hopes of help in us, because we, the noblest souls in all Britain, the dwellers in its inmost shrine, had never seen the shores of slavery and had preserved our very eyes from the desecration and the contamination of tyranny: here at the world's end, on its last inch of liberty, we have lived unmolested to this day, in this sequestered nook of story; for the unknown is ever magnified.
>
> But today the uttermost parts of Britain are laid bare; there are no other tribes to come; nothing but sea and cliffs and these more deadly Romans, whose arrogance you shun in vain by obedience and self-restraint. Harriers of the world, now that earth fails their all-devastating hands, they probe even the sea; if their enemy have wealth, they have greed; if he be poor, they are ambitious; neither East nor West has glutted them; alone of mankind they behold with the same passion of concupiscence waste alike and want.
>
> To plunder, butcher, steal — these things they misname 'empire': they make a desolation, and they call it peace.

But even such noble rhetoric failed to save the Caledonians; despite overwhelming superiority in numbers, they were utterly destroyed by the remorseless Roman war-machine, losing no fewer than 10,000 dead, against a mere 360 on the Roman side:

> The morrow revealed more widely the features of the victory: a grim silence on every side, the hills deserted, homes smoking to heaven, not a soul to be seen by scouting parties.

Tacitus's geography and topography are so scanty as to admit of no indisputable identification of the battle-site; but it is tempting to speculate that it could well have been on Culloden Moor where, more than 1600 years later, in 1746, another Caledonian army was to be shattered by the superior fire-power and discipline of a military machine from the south. Then as now it was the last strategic point where a native leader could hold an army of Highland tribesmen together before they melted away to their winter straths and glens; then as now the suppression of the Jacobite Rising by the Hanoverians left only a grim silence in the deserted hills.

And so, after forty years, the all-conquering march of the Romans had reached its farthest point. But the north of Scotland would never be tamed as thoroughly as the Jacobite clans were subdued by the Duke of Cumberland. Rome's resources were now stretched almost to breaking point; from then on, as far as the Romans in Scotland were concerned, it was downhill and backwards all the way.

First of all, the legionary fortress of Inchtuthill on the north bank of the River Tay was abandoned and systematically dismantled after only three years, as the Romans pulled back. Then the turf-built Antonine Wall, constructed by the emperor Antoninus Pius from the Firth of Forth to the Firth of Clyde to consolidate the northern frontiers of Rome in 142 AD, was abandoned after only twenty years. That left Hadrian's Wall, that formidable stone rampart strung between Newcastle-upon-Tyne and Solway Firth, as the ultimate frontier — and the most impressive and enduring legacy of Roman rule in Britain. Scotland and its restless tribes were left to their own devices, held in check only by their own domestic preoccupations and the Roman soldiery who garrisoned the fortlets of Hadrian's Wall.

In south Britain, more or less secure in the lee of the Wall and cushioned from internecine strife by the *pax Romana*, the 'Roman peace', the native British population was rapidly becoming 'civilised' and assimilating Roman ways. Roman-built towns sprang up — real towns, systematic and stone-built, with elegant houses and busy shops, with temples and theatres, arcades and offices, baths and banqueting-halls, hot water and hygiene, bread and circuses. There were large country estates and handsome villas for the wealthy, opportunities for the entrepreneurs, new techniques for the technocrats, creature comforts for the middle-classes, blood-sweat-and-toil for the manual labourers and slaves.

The Romans brought both discipline and luxury, both bureaucracy and taxation, both local self-government and a centralised administration buttressed by the imperial army. For the first time, Britain had an organised national infrastructure, with good roads and waterways to speed communications and facilitate the flow of exports and imports. Trade prospered, industry boomed, literacy was widespread, native craftsmen never had it so good. High-born Celtic ladies took eagerly to Roman high fashion, Celtic girls fraternised freely with handsome young Roman conscripts. Apart from the high and hilly expanses of the north and west, where native tribesmen clung stubbornly to their older life-styles, southern Britain became thoroughly Romanised, thoroughly cosmopolitan.

It might seem remarkable, on the face of it, considering the gulf between Northern Celt and Southern Roman, that the two cultures should have come to terms with one another so readily. But upper-class Celts had had close contact with the Roman world, either in Gaul or through trade, for more than a century before the Conquest. And besides, the Romans were always remarkably tolerant of the local styles and customs, and especially the religious practices, of the peoples they subjugated. There always seemed to be room for a new god or two, some new goddess or other, in the overcrowded Graeco-Roman pantheon of assorted deities.

Pukka Romans of patrician birth paid official homage to the Big Three of the classical gods, of course — Jupiter, Juno and Minerva. But the auxiliary troops recruited from every corner of the Empire brought with them their own tutelary gods to add variety and spice to the pagan mélange: Astarte, the Phoenician goddess of love, notorious in the Old Testament as Ashtoreth, the 'mother of abominations'; Sol Invictus, the Invincible Sun god from Syria, whose official birthday (December 25) and solar aureole (halo) would later be borrowed by Christianity; Serapis, the sacred bull-god of fertility from Egypt, animal incarnation of Osiris; Mithras, the god of light and truth from Persia, immensely popular with the army as 'protector of the Empire', a potent bull-slayer whose followers underwent secret initiation rites and celebrated his sacrificial meal of bull's-meat with a symbolic ritual of bread and wine

— an outrage to Christian eyes.

In Britain, the native Celtic gods in their turn became identified with, even hyphenated with, corresponding classical gods: Sulis-Minerva at Bath, for instance, joint goddesses of wisdom and healing; Apollo-Cunomaglus, both of them sun-gods, at Nettleton in Wiltshire; a host of local deities associated with war — Mars-Toutalis, Mars-Alator, Mars-Lenus, Mars-Corotiacus; Silvanus the woodland god, hitched to his Celtic equivalent, Callirius; and the ultimate pagan apotheosis of the concept of universal light before the rise of Christianity — Mithras-Sol.

Christianity itself, which would eclipse and outlive all other cults, both native and imported, had a hard time of it to start with. The early Christians were politically suspect in Roman eyes; they were considered a potential danger to state security because they refused to acknowledge the emperor as a god, albeit only one among many other gods; they even refused to accept the emperor's worldly authority. Their own One God, Jesus Christ, was king supreme of heaven and earth alike, Alpha and Omega, the beginning and the ending. It was this refusal to accept the emperor's divinity that was the only official reason for their being persecuted.

They were also rather uncomfortable people to have around, these early Christians, disconcertingly impervious to persecution and even martyrdom for their faith. They were therefore 'fanatics'. They were anti-social, and kept themselves to themselves. And they were usually extremely poor, and carried no political clout — except, perhaps, in an inverted way, as social scapegoats. That was certainly their role in the first great persecution under Nero in 64 AD: Nero needed scapegoats for starting the Great Fire of Rome, for which he himself was being blamed. Tacitus again:

> To suppress this rumour, Nero fastened the guilt on the notoriously depraved Christians, as they were popularly called, and punished them with every refinement . . . Their deaths were made a mockery. Dressed in wild animals' skins, they were torn to pieces by dogs, or were crucified, or were made into torches to be ignited after dark as substitutes for daylight. Nero provided his Gardens for the spectacle, and put on displays in the Circus . . . Despite their guilt as Christians, and the ruthless punishment it deserved, the victims were pitied. *(Annals)*

We know almost nothing about the earliest stirrings of Christianity in Roman Britain, or how the sporadic waves of persecution affected British Christians. By tradition, the first Christian to be venerated as a martyr in Britain was a man called Alban; but his identity and date are decidedly obscure. The earliest references to him occur in a fifth century *Life of St Germanus of Auxerre*, a Gallo-Roman bishop who visited Britain around 430 AD, and in the sixth century historical writings of the British cleric, Gildas (*On the Ruin and Conquest of Britain*, c.550). They suggest that Alban was a Romano-Briton from Verulamium (afterwards re-named St Albans in his honoured memory), and that he was martyred during one of the sporadic Christian persecutions that punctuated the history of Rome — but it's not clear which one; it could either have been in 209 AD, during the reign of the emperor Severus, or a century later under Diocletian — or neither. Anyway, Alban was apparently charged with the offence of harbouring a fugitive Christian priest; and although a pagan at the time, Alban was so impressed by the priest's demeanour and devotion that he gave himself up in the hunted man's place, and at his trial he loudly proclaimed his own conversion to Christianity. His subsequent public execution on a hill above the River Ver was accompanied by a positive plethora of elaborate miracles — the river ran dry to allow the multitude of would-be spectators to cross dry-shod, a spring burst out of the bare rock of the hillside to quench Alban's thirst, the executioner's eyes dropped out of his head as he brought the sword down, and so on. St Albans Cathedral is built on the presumed site of the execution.

Throughout those early years, Christianity had to be something of an underground cult. Its adherents had to behave like conspirators, exchanging arcane passwords and secret signs. One such secret symbol was a fish, because the Greek word for fish was *ichthys*, whose letters formed an acronym of *Iesous Christos Theou Yios Soter* — 'Jesus Christ, Son of God, Saviour'. The fish, or the *Chi-Rho* monogram (the first two letters of the Greek word for Christ), and the *Alpha-Omega* symbol (the first and last letters of the Greek alphabet, Beginning and Ending), were widely used all over the Christian world as recognition signals.

All this hole-and-corner stuff changed overnight after the Edict of Milan in 313 AD. This was the turning-point for the fledgeling Christian church. In that celebrated Edict, the emperor Constantine — Constantine the Great — gave civil rights and freedom of worship to Christians throughout the empire; eleven years later, in 324 AD, he promulgated Christianity as the official state religion of the Roman Empire.

It was a dramatic turn-about in the fortunes of the church, and it had been brought about by a dramatic turn-about in Constantine's own fortunes. He had had to fight his way to the throne against many rivals; on the eve of one of his most important battles, at the Milvian Bridge near Rome in 312, he saw a sign superimposed on the sun — the Chi-Rho monogram, and the words *In hoc signo vinces* ('In this sign thou shalt conquer'). For Christendom, it was the most significant instant conversion since that of Saul/Paul on the road to Damascus.

There is a degree of circumstantial evidence that some sort of organised church existed in Britain even before the Edict of Milan, because, only a year later, no fewer than four British bishops attended the Council of the Church at Arles. No completely indisputable traces of early church buildings have yet come to light; but an excavated villa at Lullingstone in Kent was found to have had a private chapel in it, adorned with the Chi-Rho monogram and the Alpha-Omega symbol. Another excavated villa, at Hinton St Mary in Dorset, had as the centre-piece of a mosaic floor a portrait of a clean-shaven Roman backed by the Chi-Rho symbol; this has been interpreted as an extremely rare early attempt to portray Christ.

Archaeological sites from all over Britain, but mainly in the south, have yielded ordinary household utensils with the Chi-Rho and Alpha-Omega symbols scratched on them. Similarly inscribed lead tanks have been found, which have been identified as baptismal baths for converts. The cult of Christianity clearly spanned all social classes, and equally clearly it was well-rooted and widespread by the end of the fourth century.

But it's just as certain that Christianity wasn't nearly as well-rooted or widespread in the west and north of Britannia as it was in the fatter lands of the south. Throughout the Roman occupation, there had always been a distinct North/South dichotomy. North Britain (*Britannia Inferior*) and South Britain (*Britannia Superior*) were under different authority; the south was a civilian area, but the north was a military frontier zone based on York. The north continued to be 'occupied'; the *pax Romana* brought some economic advantages — the exploitation of minerals, improved agriculture and an expansion of trade — but on nothing like the scale that the south enjoyed. As far as Christianity was concerned, there were doubtless churches or cult-centres in Romanised towns like York itself. But overall there was much less Romanisation than in the south; the old tribal patterns remained, encouraged by the Romans who imposed defined boundaries between tribes and fixed their meeting-places. There seems little doubt that these 'country Celts' adhered stubbornly to their older faiths, and continued to propitiate the ancient elemental spirits of groves and rivers, springs and wells, as their forefathers had always done.

Indeed, the first recorded glimmer of Christianity in the north appears on the far, 'barbarian' side of Hadrian's Wall early in the 5th century, through the agency of St Ninian. Tradition has it that Ninian was a British missionary who was born around 360 AD in the south-west of Scotland. He made a pilgrimage to Rome, where he was consecrated bishop by the Pope in 394; on his return journey he visited the ageing St Martin of Tours, the 'father of monasticism' in Gaul, at his little monastery at Marmoutier. Fired by bishop Martin's example, Ninian is said to have spent the rest of his life evangelising among the people who lived in the Borders and Lowlands of Scotland. He made his centre in Galloway at a place called Candida Casa, the 'White House', near his home at Whithorn, so called because it was built of light-coloured stone and not of timber. There has been much learned speculation and disagreement about Ninian and the real significance of his missionary activity; but his memory, and the memory of his pioneering 'White House', seems to have had a lasting influence on later generations of Celtic-speaking Christians in north Britain; his name was associated with innumerable springs and wells whose waters were believed to have healing properties, and a number of churches can still be found that were dedicated to him.

Down south, however, at the very time that Ninian was trying to kindle a spark in the north, an ominous threat to the security of British Christianity was looming large: after nearly four centuries of peace and prosperity under the authority of Rome, the *pax Romana*, such as it was, was coming to an end. In the early years of the fifth century, the Romans, increasingly beset by problems nearer home, pulled all their garrison troops out of the province of Britannia, leaving the native inhabitants to fend for themselves as best they could.

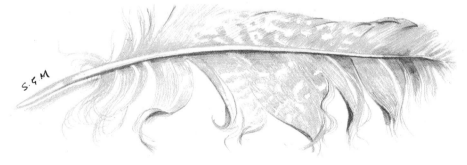

4 The Dark Ages

'The Dark Ages' is a blanket term that has been commonly — and indiscriminately — used to cover, or cover up, the period of European history between the 5th and the 11th centuries. It implies that between the departure of the Roman legions and the arrival of William the Conqueror, Britain was plunged into darkness by a sort of cultural power-failure, a spiritual black-out that affected the whole land for half a millennium.

As an overall picture, it is manifestly inaccurate. For one thing, it ignores the splendours of the 7th century, when the torch of Celtic Christianity burned so brightly and illuminated the north of England and much farther afield — the century in which Lindisfarne became the Cradle Island. It ignores the magnificent achievements of Anglo-Saxon and, later, Viking arts and crafts. The darkness has been in the eye of the beholder, not the beheld.

True, the withdrawal of Roman administration brought dislocation in its train, and profound change; but the dislocation was neither so abrupt nor so violent as the conventional image of a guttering candle, cruelly snuffed out, suggests. The break-down of Roman law and order, the 300-year-long *pax Romana*, was a lengthy and not always violent process.

Throughout the 4th century, the *pax Romana* in Britain had been more apparent than real. In Rome, there were imperial plots and counter-coups. There were rebellions in Britain itself, reflecting a general discontent with the imperial government. Troops were removed at whim to support pretenders to the imperial throne, defences were stripped of their garrisons. Scenting weakness, the 'barbarian' tribes began closing in, culminating in the so-called *barbarica conspiratio*, the Barbarian Conspiracy, of 367 when the province was attacked simultaneously and almost over-run by Scots from Ireland, Caledonians from Scotland, Saxons from the Low Countries and Franks from across the Channel.

In an attempt to re-impose authority, the Romans themselves encouraged the first Anglo-Saxon invasions of Britain by recruiting large numbers of German (Saxon) warriors to shore up Britain's defences. Distinctive German settlements and cemeteries have been found near several Roman towns and forts, which would become breeding-grounds for a 'Fifth column' within Britain after the Roman withdrawal.

The power-vacuum created by the departure of the Romans was filled by native chieftains and aristocrats who, although Romanised, were reasserting ancient tribal patterns. Some of them, notably the Kentish ruler Vortigern, continued the policy of recruiting German warriors to ward off attacks by German raiders; and although the archaeological record suggests that early relations between the British and the immigrant Saxons were friendly, it seems that the Anglo-Saxon newcomers — the English, we should call them now — rejected British rule after a time and asserted their own independence to the extent of starting to enlarge their territory by conquest.

This process was described in lurid terms in the middle of the 6th century by a Welsh cleric called Gildas, whose book *De Excidio et Conquestu Britanniae* ('The Ruin and Conquest of Britain') is the earliest surviving history of the British. He drew a graphic picture of the dreadful consequences of Vortigern's invitation: the guests turned into cuckoos in the nest, arrogantly demanding more and more supplies from their hard-pressed hosts and threatening to break all treaties unless their escalating demands were met. Soon the threats were carried out, in a devastating Saxon mutiny that 'burnt nearly the whole surface of the island, and licked the western ocean with its red and savage tongue'. Some of the British took up arms and fought the invaders off for a time under the leadership of a Roman aristocrat called Ambrosius Aurelianus, apparently a Roman of noble birth, who may have been the prototype of the legendary King Arthur.

Sad to relate, as far as romantics the world over are concerned, there is absolutely no evidence, no proof positive, that Arthur ever existed as a historical character. There is no mention of him in Gildas, the earliest of our sources; it is not until late in the 8th century, in the pages of *Historia Britonum*, written or adapted by the Welsh cleric Nennius, that Arthur appears as a *dux bellorum* who rallies the Britons of the south-west of England against the Saxons — 'that rascally crew', as Gildas called them. Nennius, and in greater detail the subsequent Welsh chronicler of *Annales Cambriae*, enumerate a series of twelve battles from Mount Baden in 518 AD (a British victory that is also mentioned by Gildas) to the final battle of Camlan (539 AD).

Certainly, there is abundant archaeological evidence of spirited British resistance until the middle of the 6th century, at least in the south-west. Ancient pre-Roman hill-forts like Castle Dore in Cornwall, Congresbury in Somerset, and above all, South Cadbury in Somerset, were re-occupied and refurbished by Romanised Britons, with massive wooden fortifications and handsome timber buildings. It is around South Cadbury in particular, exhaustively excavated by Professor Leslie Alcock in the 1960s and '70s, that later legends of Camelot and the Round Table accrued.

Like Robin Hood and other great figures of legend, Arthur was the kind of character who, if he had never existed, would have had to be invented. He comes to the surface in the sorrowing Welsh elegies of ancient bards mourning a golden past. The Britons had failed to stem the tide of Saxon conquest. They had been driven into the mountains of Wales or the fastnesses of Cornwall or across the Channel, in their thousands, to Brittany. And in the bitterness of defeat and exile, the Britons turned nostalgically to the glowing folk-memory of their hero, their Arthur. He became a symbol of national pride and nationalistic hope; and thus accoutred, he rode into the invincible realm of legend and romance, there to be enthroned, in the title of T. H. White's fine novel of 1958, as 'The Once and Future King'. In the *Black Book of Carmarthen* there is an early poem called 'The Stanzas of the Graves', in which the Celtic bards keen over their dead heroes and enumerate their graves; but they can find no grave for Arthur . . .

In this infectious miasma of nostalgia, in the shrill denunciations of priests like Gildas, and above all in the lack of secure historical records, we tend to lose sight of what the Anglo-Saxons brought, rather than what they took away. They changed the patterns of village life, with sturdy and spacious new timber houses, with new skills and crafts, with improved agricultural techniques. We tend instead to wallow in images of neglect, of grass growing in once immaculate Roman city streets — powerful images of delapidation and desolation as conjured up by the anonymous author of the Anglo-Saxon poem, *The Ruin* (itself now only a sad fragment):

> How wondrous this wall-stone, shattered by Fate;
> Burg-places broken, the work of giants crumbled.
> Ruined are the roofs, tumbled the towers,
> Broken the barred gate: frost in the plaster,
> Ceilings a-gaping, torn away, fallen,
> Eaten by age . . .
> Bright were the halls, lofty-gabled,

THEY CATCH OYSTERS, DON'T THEY?

Well, no, they don't actually. If there is one thing you can say with absolutely certainty about Oystercatchers (*Haematopus ostralegus*), it is that they don't catch oysters. Anything else that creeps or crawls or cowers on the foreshore, but not oysters — because oysters live below the low-tide mark, which is beyond the oystercatcher's feeding range.

It's a splendidly handsome, noisy bird, the óystercatcher, strutting along in its bold plumage of black and white, its courtier legs encased in orange stockings, its long sharp bill a brilliant red. At the first sign of danger it goes streaking away, yelling *klee-eee klee-eee* at the top of its voice — 'patrolling the shore with indignant whistle' as the late Eric Linklater, most rumbustious of Scottish novelists, once described it with his customary felicity of phrase.

Cockles and mussels, periwinkles and shrimps, crabs and lugworms — nothing is safe from the oystercatcher's probing, imperious bill. But the bill is seen at its best when the oystercatcher is tackling its favourite delicacies: limpets and mussels.

For limpets, the bill is used as a crowbar to prise these clinging little snails off the rocks to which they attach themselves so tenaciously with their sucker-like foot: lever-power against suction-power. But its method of dealing with mussels is particularly ingenious. When the mussel is lying under water, feeding, with its shell open, the oystercatcher severs the hinge-muscle with a stab of its powerful bill, leaving the creature helpless to protect itself. When the shell is closed the oystercatcher uses its bill as a piledriver, hammering away at the weak spot on the lower shell near the hinge until it breaks.

It's a skill that has to be learned by the young. Oystercatcher chicks are dependent on their parents for food for a comparatively long time and follow them closely, watching intently in order to learn the skills of the oystercatcher's highly specialised trade.

No, they don't catch oysters, it's true. But I'll bet they could, if they put their minds and bills to it.

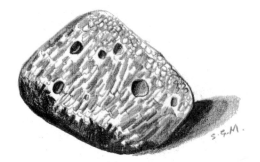

Many the bath-house; cheerful the clamour
In many a mead-hall, revelry rampant —
Until mighty Fate put paid to all that . . .

This gloomy picture can now be tempered by an accumulation of evidence that reveals that, although some towns and cities declined or were even abandoned, major centres like London, Canterbury and York continued to be occupied and to thrive.

It is sometimes assumed that since the Anglo-Saxon incomers were pagans, they must have been intent on extirpating Christianity wherever they went. But there is no evidence of this. Latin, the language of the Church and of written literature, survived as the common denominator of scholarship throughout Europe. Although secular literacy may have declined somewhat, it should be remarked that 150 years after the Roman withdrawal, a British cleric like Gildas could be writing in a correct, vigorous and elegant Latin that displayed a very considerable familiarity with the libraries of Christian learning.

The comparative paucity of written records meant that even such a meticulous scholar as the Venerable Bede, writing in the early 8th century — 'the father of English history', as he has been called — knew very little about the first decades of the Saxon incursion, and was forced to resort to dubious oral traditions. Thus, he declares that the leaders of the Saxon invaders of Kent were said to have been two brothers, Hengest and Horsa, who claimed descent through four generations from the pagan god Woden (*Odin* in Old Norse mythology) who had been the progenitor of many of the royal dynasties which took power in England. To a Christian scholar like Bede, Woden/Odin was obviously a mythical figure; and Bede must also have been aware of the suspiciously 'pat' nature of Hengest and Horsa (the names mean 'Gelding' and 'Horse') — brothers with alliterating names, like Romulus and Remus, play a stock part in the origin legends of many peoples. It is clear from Bede's major historical work, *Historia Ecclesiastica Gentis Anglorum* ('Ecclesiastical History of the English People', completed in 731), that his verifiable historical horizon was around the 550s at the earliest — the time of Gildas.

The years around 550 were the real watershed for Britain, and particularly North Britain. About the year 547 there was a devastating outbreak of Yellow Plague that swept through the British Isles. The Britons seem to have suffered from its effects more severely than the English; it created a new power-vacuum which the Saxons in the south, and the Angles in the north, were not slow to fill. It provided the impetus for another surge against the weakened natives, in the course of which many libraries may have been destroyed, and the shape of England's political and dynastic landscape for centuries to come was formed.

It was in 547, according to Bede, that the Anglian King Ida thrust his way northward across the River Tees and established the kingdom of Bernicia; he sited his royal headquarters on the formidable crag of Bamburgh, which dominates the north-eastern coastline just south of Lindisfarne itself. It had been a Celtic stronghold called Dinguaroy; but according to a late addition to the *Anglo-Saxon Chronicle*, King Ida fortified the massive rock with a stockade, which was later replaced by stone ramparts. But the Anglian hold on their territorial gains in Northumbria may have been tenuous to begin with. In the first extant historical reference to Lindisfarne, which the British called Medcaut, Nennius claims that in the time of Ida's son, Theodric — sometime in the 570s — the English were besieged on Lindisfarne for three days and nights by a Celtic king called Urbgen (Urien map Rheged). This written reference, coming as late as it does, has to be treated with caution — it is difficult to image a 'siege' of a tidal island which is relatively easy of access at low tide: perhaps 'blockade' would be a better term. But there is nothing in Bede to suggest a particularly secure Anglian hold on Northumbria until the beginning of the 7th century.

Meanwhile the second half of the 6th century saw a powerful resurgence of Christian evangelism in Britain — but not by the British, whose priests seem to have made no attempt to convert the English invaders. Bede is magisterially censorious about this backsliding on the part of the British:

> Among other unspeakable crimes, recorded with sorrow by their own historian Gildas, they added this — that they never preached the Faith to the Saxons and Angles who dwelt among them. But God in his goodness did not utterly abandon the people whom he had chosen, for he remembered them, and sent this nation more worthy preachers of truth to bring them to the Faith.

In Ireland, an Irish priest of royal blood, St Columba (521–597), who founded there the monasteries of Derry and of Durrow, was excommunicated and exiled in 561 after a particularly bloody battle in which he was directly involved. Accompanied by twelve faithful disciples he left his native country and two years later, in 563, he founded a monastery on the tiny Hebridean island of Iona — the original 'Holy Isle'. From there, he and his followers launched a series

PEREGRINES — Feathered Exocets!

Imagine a typically busy autumn day in Sandham Bay — feeding time for the thousands of migrant waders which congregate on Lindisfarne from the Arctic regions: huge flocks of tiny scurrying Dunlins, wind-blown like chaff; rippling grey carpets of Knots, those Canutes of the tide-lines (their Latin binomial, somewhat fancifully, is *Calidris canutus*); Turnstones diligently forking beneath the seaweed for hidden invertebrates in between brief twinkles of flight; all-action Sanderlings continually on the move, heads down, totally intent on the next mouthful; tall, long-beaked Bar-tailed Godwits pretending to be Curlews; Oystercatchers elegant in black-and-white plumage, orange legs and bright red beaks; red-legged Redshanks, the sentinels of the shore, up and away with clamorous alarm at the slightest hint of danger, flying fast and low.

Suddenly a slate-grey blur comes streaking past at terrific speed, and the beach explodes into panic. Peregrine! A Peregrine (*Falco peregrinus*) attack can be as devastating to a fleet of birds as an Exocet missile to a ship. The hunting Peregrine with its distinctive black moustaches is one of the fastest birds alive, reaching 50 mph in level flight with rapid shallow beats of its long pointed wings, and sometimes turning upside down to seize its prey from below with its wicked talons; or it may soar and glide until it has picked out its quarry, and then 'stoop' down on it at speeds of up to 180 mph. So ferocious is the dive that the head of the prey (even of a much larger bird, like a Wigeon) can be knocked clean off.

The Warden, David O'Connor, told me that during the autumn, Sandham Bay is sometimes used as a kind of practice range by a young Peregrine from the mainland (he wouldn't tell me where the nesting-site was — Peregrines have always been prized by falconers for their rapacity, and their numbers have been decimated by collectors and pesticides). According to David O'Connor, this young Peregrine seems less interested in making a kill than in practising its flight-skills — going out on manoeuvres, in effect.

Tell that to the waders — and the Marines!

36

of missions to the mainland and Western and Northern Isles of Scotland, where they had considerable success in converting the native Picts. Iona became a notable centre of Celtic Christianity and monastic learning, and the mother church of other monasteries all over the north.

And in the very year that St Columba died — 597 — there was another Christian 'invasion' from across the sea: the Roman mission inspired by Pope Gregory the Great and led by St Augustine. Letters written by Pope Gregory reveal that he had received reports that 'the English nation by the will of God wishes to come Christian, but the priests who are in the neighbourhood [*in Kent*] are negligent and fail to inflame their desire by encouragement'. So Augustine was despatched as 'Bishop of the English' with a retinue of 40 monks to Thanet in Kent; there they were given a warm welcome and a grant of land at Canterbury by King Æthelberht, the powerful ruler of Kent, who was married to a Christian Frankish princess, Bertha: Bede records that the marriage had only been agreed on condition 'that she be allowed to hold and practise her faith unhindered, with a bishop named Liudhard whom they had provided to be her chaplain'.

So Augustine's mission landed on fertile soil. According to Bede, there was already a church in Canterbury, dating back to Roman times, where the Queen was wont to pray; and in no time at all, King Æthelberht himself saw the error of his ways and submitted to baptism, which was the signal for all his subjects to be baptised as well, in their droves — the king 'showed greater favour to believers', as Bede delicately put it. The Roman mission prospered hugely at first, and by the time of Augustine's death in 604 there were bishoprics at Canterbury, Rochester and London; but he had failed to extend his archiepiscopal authority over the indigenous British church, and on Æthelberht's death in 616 there was a strong pagan reaction that caused the bishops of London and Rochester to take temporary refuge in Gaul.

By the start of the 7th century, we can put the misnamed 'Dark Ages' firmly behind us. Bede's magnificent narrative history is into its stride now, based on sound historical sources — papal letters and other correspondence, saints' *Lives* and other learned works, and the 'faithful testimony of innumerable witnesses, who either knew or remembered these things'.

To north and south, the Christian church — Celtic and Roman respectively — was poised, however tentatively and precariously, to make its inroads into the many warring Anglo-Saxon kingdoms of which England was composed at the time. The 7th century was to prove a crucial one for the history of Britain and the history of Christendom in the north.

At this time, 'Northumbria' was a vast reach of land north of the Humber, stretching from Yorkshire to the Lothians of Scotland. But it was not a single united kingdom; it consisted of two kingdoms — Deira, from the Humber to the Tees, and Bernicia, from the Tees to the Forth. Always there was tension or open warfare with neighbouring kingdoms — Mercia in the Midlands, East Anglia and Kent to the south, Wessex to the south-west, or the Scottish tribes north and west of the Firth of Forth. They were ruled by kings who, for the most part, were uncomprisingly committed to the pagan religion of their Germanic ancestors.

In Northumbria, the first major leader to arise among the northern English and achieve national status was an agressive and expansionist king of Bernicia called Æthelfrith. In 603 he hammered a huge Irish army that was trying to consolidate a kingdom in Argyll, in Scotland, at Bernicia's expense. Ten years later, after a long and bloody campaign to the south-west against the native British, he subdued them with a culminating victory at Chester (616). With this battle, Æthelfrith had extended his kingdom westwards over Cumberland and Lancashire right to the shores of the Irish Sea. Before the battle, too, he displayed his attitude to Christianity with ruthless simplicity; a host of monks from the monastery of Bangor in Wales were marshalled to pray for a British victory, and on the expressed principle that 'if they pray to their God against me, they are fighting against us even if they do not bear arms', Æthelfrid attacked them first, slaughtering some 1200 of them, before turning his attention on the enemy forces. As Stalin once sneeringly asked, 'How many divisions has the Pope?'

While Æthelfrith was extending Bernician territory and prestige almost at will, his southern neighbour, Deira, trembled. The heir to the Deiran throne, Edwin, son of Ælle, prudently took refuge in the court of King Rædwald of East Anglia. Æthelfrith demanded that Edwin be extradited or, preferably, killed; but Rædwald was persuaded by his wife, on a point of honour, to do neither. The stage was thus set for a massive trial of strength between the two super-powers of north and south. In the early autumn of 616 the two great armies met on the east bank of the River Idle, a tributary of the Trent, at the southern boundary of Deira; and in the ensuing encounter, Æthelfrith of

Bernicia was overwhelmed and killed by Edwin.

As was the custom, Æthelfrith's three sons — Eanfrith, Oswald and Oswiu — fled for their lives, in order to be able to fight another day if opportunity ever arose, as it most assuredly did. They took refuge with the Celts of Argyll, who were now on good terms with Bernicia again, and were sent to be educated at the monastery on Iona, where they were all converted to Christianity. In due course, all three would become kings of Northumbria in their turn. Their sister, princess Æbbe, would take the veil and become founder and abbess of a monastery on St Abb's Head, near Coldingham, just inside the Scottish border.

Edwin was now cock of the north, as ruler by conquest of both Deira and Bernicia, thereby creating a united Northumbria for the first time. He extended his authority even farther by annexing the islands of Anglesey and Man, according to Bede, and a few years later, when his former protector, King Rædwald of East Anglia, died, Edwin inherited his mantle as overlord of the English south of the Humber. Edwin was now the head of the greatest confederation of kingdoms that England had yet seen.

King Edwin of Northumbria was a thorough pagan, a prototype of the Heroic Age of Scandinavia and Anglo-Saxon England, when personal allegiance to one's lord, to the giver of gold, the ring-scatterer, was paramount. Bede recounts the justly celebrated story of the self-sacrificing devotion of one of Edwin's thanes, Lilla by name, who intercepted with his own body a poisoned dagger-thrust aimed at his lord by an assassin sent by the King of Wessex. The story also illustrates the alarmed apprehension of the West Saxons over Edwin's growing power in the south.

There was another king in the south who was never prepared to give Edwin his allegiance — King Æthelberht of Kent, patron of the Augustinian foundation at Canterbury. But sometime after Æthelberht's death in 616, Edwin sent an embassy to ask for the hand of his daughter, Æthelburh, no doubt hoping thereby to add Kent to his sphere of influence. He was given a somewhat dusty answer, according to Bede, to the effect that it was not permissible for a Christian maiden to be given in marriage to a pagan husband, lest the Christian faith and sacraments be profaned by the association. Edwin replied that he would place no obstacles in the way of the Christian faith, and that he would afford complete freedom to Æthelburh and her attendants, both men and women, priests and servants, to live and worship in accordance with Christian belief and practice — just as her father had once promised to her mother. Edwin also declared that he himself would be willing to accept the religion of Christ if, upon examination, his counsellors decided that it appeared more holy and acceptable to God than their own.

On these terms the marriage was agreed, and took place in 625; and it is not too fanciful to see this event as the moment of conception for Christianity in the north. Princess Æthelburh brought with her as her chaplain a newly consecrated bishop called Paulinus, who had been sent from Rome as a monk in 601 to assist St Augustine in Canterbury. He is described by Bede as a tall man, slightly stooping, with black hair, an ascetic face, and a venerable and majestic presence. He immediately 'began to toil unceasingly with God's help not only to maintain the faith of his companions unimpaired, but if possible to bring some of the heathen to grace and faith by his teaching'. But though he laboured long, the people of Northumbria remained impervious to his message.

On Easter Day, 626, Queen Æthelburh was delivered of a daughter, Eanflæd. It was the very day on which Edwin had escaped the assassin's dagger. Such was Edwin's delight that he gave his infant daughter to Paulinus to be consecrated to Christ; and accordingly, on the Feast of Pentecost, the little princess Eanflæd, together with 12 others of her family, became the first of the Northumbrians to receive baptism.

Edwin now had his own position to consider, as promised. From Rome, Pope Boniface sent him a long letter, quoted in full by Bede, urging him to accept the faith, and sent another to his Queen urging her to exert her influence on her husband. Edwin himself summoned a council of his advisers; and it was during that debate that Bede puts into the mouth of one of the king's men the immortal parable of the sparrow and the hall:

> Your Majesty, when we compare the present life of man on earth with that time of which we have no knowledge, it seems to me like the swift flight of a sparrow through the banqueting-hall where you sit feasting on a winter's day with your thanes and counsellors. Inside, there is a comforting fire to warm the hall; outside, the wintry storms of snow and rain are raging.
> This sparrow flies swiftly in through one door of the hall and out through another. While it is inside, it is safe from the winter tempest; but after a few moments of comfort, it vanishes from sight into the darkness whence it came.
> Similarly, man appears on earth for but a moment; of what went

LISTENING FOR BREAKFAST

The Carrion Crow (*Corvus corone corone*), better known in the north as the Corbie, is one of the brightest and wiliest of birds, as are all members of the crow family — as cunning and guileful as that other great predator, the Fox.

During the winter round Lindisfarne, the corbie feeds mainly on carrion, as its name suggests, but also on shellfish, which it sometimes smashes open by dropping them from a great height. But it is during the breeding season that the corbie comes into its own as one of the most notorious egg-thieves of the avian world. Its chief prey are the ground-nesting birds — Lapwings, Oystercatchers, Red-shanks, and the tiny Ringed Plovers which nest in the shingle at the high-water mark.

It stands there, the corbie, still and aloof as a black statue, studying the movements of parent birds to try to locate the nests for a quick snack at elevenses. If it fails to spot a nest which it knows must be somewhere in the vicinity, it can wait patiently until the eggs are about to hatch. Then it walks up and down the shore with its head on one side, *listening* — listening for the tell-tale cheep-cheep of the hatchling inside the egg, or for the tap-tap of the chick breaking the shell open. A much more nourishing meal it makes, too, at that stage.

Many birds put on an elaborate decoy display, running away and trailing a wing as if it's broken, and uttering distress cries to distract the predator's attention from the eggs or the chicks. It often works; but sometimes there's the wise old crow who has seen it all before, and just sits there in the front stalls and applauds the performance — before strolling down to listen for its breakfast.

Carrion Crows are unmitigated pests on a Nature Reserve. Quite a large number of them over-winter on the island, and there are always three or four pairs (they pair for life, by the way) trying to breed, while the wardens and the farm-hands try to discourage them. But shooting them merely creates space for more to come in, apparently.

Dead crafty, these corbies.

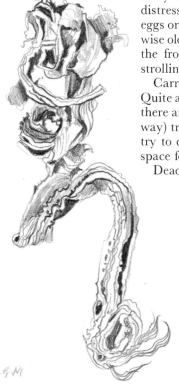

42

before this life, or of what follows, we know nothing. Therefore, if this new doctrine can bring us any more certain knowledge, it seems only right that we should accept it.

And so, on Easter Day, 627, King Edwin and all his nobles, along with many humbler folk, were baptised at York in a little timber oratory specially built for the occasion. Soon afterwards he gave orders to build an imposing stone basilica, which was to enclose that first small chapel, where Bishop Paulinus would have his episcopal see. With such royal protection, the fledgeling church would flourish, and the people of Northumbria would be quick to follow their king's example. The next few years, indeed, were spent in a positive orgy of wholesale baptising. On one occasion, according to Bede, Bishop Paulinus spent 36 days at the royal manor of Yeavering in Glendale, near Wooller:

> From dawn to dusk he did nothing else but proclaim Christ's saving message to the crowds who flocked to him from all the surrounding villages and countryside; and when he had instructed them he washed them in the cleansing waters of baptism in the River Glen, which was nearby.

These Anglian royals halls were extremely substantial places. The *villa regia* of Yeavering was excavated by Professor Philip Rahtz of the University of York in the 1970s, and revealed a most elaborate complex of buildings, including a Great Hall more than 80 feet long — a good sparrow-flight, indeed.

The foundations of Christianity in the north now seemed well and truly laid. The stone basilica in York was rising apace, although Edwin himself would not live to see it completed. Edwin's reign in Northumbria ushered in a brief Golden Age of peace and prosperity and security; Bede claims that in those parts of Britain where Edwin's writ ran, it was said that a woman with a new-born child in her arms could walk from sea to sea, and come to no harm.

And then, suddenly, everything fell apart. In October 633, two powerful rival kings, Cadwallon of Gwynned in north Wales, and Penda of Mercia, formed an unholy alliance against Edwin and invaded Northumbria. The opposing armies met at Hatfield Chase near Doncaster, not far from the site of Edwin's defeat of King Æthelfrith of Bernicia, sixteen years earlier. This time it was Edwin's turn to be defeated and killed in battle, along with his eldest son.

The hard-won unity of Northumbria was shattered, although the church was not — at first. Edwin's cousin, Osric, who had been baptised by Paulinus, inherited the throne of Deira, while Æthelfrith's eldest son Eanfrith returned from exile in Iona to claim his father's kingdom of Bernicia. But, according to Bede, both Osric and Eanfrith soon 'apostatised from the faith of the kingdom of heaven which they had accepted, and reverted to the corruption and damnation of their former idolatry'. Within a year, however, both had met their deaths at the hands of 'the godless Cadwallon, king of the Britons', who then occupied both the Northumbrian kingdoms for a whole year, 'ruling them not like a victorious king but as a savage tyrant, ravaging them with ghastly slaughter'.

Edwin's queen, Æthelburh, had managed to escape by boat with her children back to Kent, accompanied by Bishop Paulinus, who was soon appointed to the vacant bishopric at Rochester.

Bereft of Edwin's benign protection, and Paulinus' presence, the Roman mission to Northumbria disintegrated. The missionary structure that Bishop Paulinus had built up — too hastily, perhaps, with all those mass baptisms — collapsed utterly. Northumbria was sundered, the church destroyed; the Christian conception was stillborn.

But retribution was at hand, in the person of Æthelfrith's second son, Oswald, who came hurrying from his exile in Iona after his brother Eanfrith's death at Cadwallon's hands. He gathered a small army, and in 634 he faced up to Cadwallon's reputedly invincible forces at Rowley Burn, near Hexham, not far from Hadrian's Wall. The name of the battle-site, according to Bede, was *Hefenfelth*, meaning 'Heavenfield' — a sure omen of events to come, as he put it. Before battle was joined, Oswald with his own hands rammed a large wooden Cross into the ground in front of his troops, and, thus encouraged, his army, 'small in numbers but strong in the faith of Christ', hurled themselves at the enemy and won an overwhelming victory. The dastardly Cadwallon was killed, and Oswald, the deliverer of Northumbria, was immediately accepted as king of both Deira and Bernicia.

Northumbria was physically whole again. Cadwallon was out of the way, Penda was lying low in Mercia. A charismatic young Christian king was on the throne of Northumbria; the stage was now set for it to be made spiritually whole again.

5 St Aidan

It all really began — or began again for real, anyway — with an Irish-born monk called Aidan, a priest in the Columban monastery on that other Holy Isle — the island of Iona, off the west coast of Scotland:

> He cultivated peace and love, purity and humility; he was above anger and greed, and despised pride and conceit; he set himself to keep and teach the laws of God, and was diligent in study and prayer. He used his priestly authority to check the proud and the powerful; he tenderly comforted the sick; he relieved and protected the poor.

Thus wrote that great Northumbrian scholar-priest, the Venerable Bede, in his monumental *Ecclesiastical History of the English People*; such was his epitaph, his encomium, for St Aidan, the first bishop of Lindisfarne, the kindly monk who kindled the lamp of Christianity in the north of England. It was a lamp whose rays would illumine the civilisation of Western Europe, and give Lindisfarne a Golden Age whose afterglow confers upon this little island still an aura, an ambience, of remembered grace.

After King Oswald's stunning victory over Cadwallon at the Battle of Heavenfield in 634 — a victory that was perceived to have been attended by manifest divine approval — it was only natural that the new king should wish to restore in Northumbria the Christian faith that had been so zealously fostered by King Edwin and Bishop Paulinus. It was only natural, too, that he should turn for help not to the south, not to the Roman mission at Canterbury, but to the west, to the Celtic mother-church on Iona where he had spent his long exile and been received into the Christian faith. So Oswald sent messengers to Scotland to the abbot of Iona, who was called Segenius, asking him to send someone to help convert the Northumbrians back to Christianity.

Segenius sent a monk called Corman, a man of 'austere disposition', according to Bede, who had no success at all in his preachings — the English simply refused to listen to him. Corman went back to Iona, and complained to his superiors that he had been unsuccessful with the English 'because they were an uncivilised people of an obstinate and barbarous temperament'. Dismayed by this failure, Segenius held a conference to decide what to do next; and it was now for the first time that Aidan steps onto the stage of history. Aidan was present at the conference, and suddenly his voice was heard, directly addressing the monk whose mission had failed:

> It seems to me, brother, that you were too severe on your ignorant hearers. You should have followed the practice of the Apostles, and begun by giving them the milk of simpler teaching, until little by little, as they were nourished on the Word of God, they grew capable of a greater understanding of perfection and able to carry out the sublimest precepts of Christ.

Bede put these words into Aidan's mouth a hundred years after the event; but he was a conscientious historian, careful with his sources — 'In accordance with the principles of true history, I have laboured honestly to commit to writing whatever I could ascertain from common report, for the instruction of posterity'. It was this 'common report', and his own commonsense, that told him that simple people needed simple stories, miracle stories, to help them understand the deeper mysteries of faith. What he has Aidan say chimed in perfectly with his own perceptions:

> All who were at the conference paid close attention to all he said, and realised that he was indeed worthy to be made a bishop and sent to instruct ignorant unbelievers, since he had proved himself pre-eminently endowed with the grace of discretion, which is the mother of all virtues. They therefore consecrated him bishop, and sent him to preach. Time was to show that Aidan was remarkable not only for discretion, but for many other virtues as well.

In Northumbria, Aidan was received with open arms by King Oswald, who must have known him at Iona and now offered him any site in the realm he wished to choose to be his see; and Aidan chose the semi-island of Lindisfarne. There were all sorts of good reasons for his choice. It was conveniently close to the royal citadel of Bamburgh, and the royal villa of Yeavering. It was intimately connected to the mainland, but sufficiently apart from it to encourage a sense of willing withdrawal — it was of the world, but not worldly; insular, but not isolated. And, of course, it must have reminded him of Iona.

We cannot be absolutely certain of the precise place where Aidan built his monastery on Lindisfarne, nor of the precise nature of its buildings. Today's visitors are irresistibly drawn to the sombre dark-red ruins of the magnificent Priory Church, tucked in between the village and the steeply rearing ridge of the Heugh; but these are many

ST AIDAN — A WAY WITH HORSES

According to The Venerable Bede, St Aidan never sought nor cared for worldly possessions, and gave away to the poor whatever he received from kings or wealthy noblemen — especially horses.

It wasn't that he had anything against horses; it was simply that this intensely ascetic and humble bishop preferred Shanks's ponies. Bede wrote:

> Whether in town or country, he always travelled on foot unless compelled by necessity to ride, and whenever he met anyone, whether high or low, he stopped and spoke to them.

Since King Oswald himself frequently accompanied him on these journeys to act as his interpreter (for Aidan spoke no English), it must have been a real eye-opener for the local peasantry.

But Bede's favourite horse-story concerns Aidan's dear friend, King Oswine, who succeeded King Oswald as ruler of Deira:

> He had given Bishop Aidan a very fine horse, in order that he could ride whenever he had to cross a river or if any other urgent necessity compelled him, although the bishop ordinarily travelled on foot. Not long afterwards, when a poor man met the bishop and asked for alms, the bishop immediately dismounted and gave the beggar the horse with all its royal trappings; for he was most compassionate, a protector of the poor and a father to the wretched.
>
> When this action came to the king's ears, he asked the bishop as they were going in to dine:
>
> 'My lord bishop, why did you give away the royal horse which was necessary for your own use? Have we not many less valuable horses or other things which would have been good enough to give to the poor, without giving away a horse that I had specially selected for your personal use?'
>
> The bishop answered at once: 'What are you saying, your Majesty? Surely this son of a mare is not dearer to you than that Son of God?'

As Kipling was later to write in his poem *If-*:

> Or walk with Kings — nor lose the common touch . . .

centuries later than the original foundation (*cf* ch 12).

Celtic monasteries of this period were for the most part rather simple affairs, consisting of a few beehive-shaped huts or cells made of wattle-and-daub or timber or occasionally stone, surrounded by a low earthern enclosure wall. Within this enclosure there would also be a small thatched church (also made of wood, or stone), a communal refectory and kitchen, a dormitory for novices, an infirmary, a small *hospitium* (guest-house), and a library and *scriptorium* (writing-room) for the copying of sacred texts. Outside, there would be farm-buildings and work-shops, and perhaps a kiln for baking bread. Nothing in Bede suggests that Aidan's monastery was anything but simple, even primitive, in the extreme.

Until quite recently it had been commonly assumed that the Priory Church must have been built directly over the foundations of the early monastic buildings; but this assumption has now been called into question by a test archaeological excavation undertaken in 1962 by Dr Brian Hope-Taylor on the flat-topped length of the Heugh. Superficial traces of some sort of early occupation-sites had long been visible there; and it was the tempting possibility that they might represent the remains of Aidan's monastery that prompted Dr Hope-Taylor's trial dig. The full results of his investigation have not been published yet; but I understand that the excavation confirmed the existence of structures that closely resembled early Irish monastic cells. There was no associated material by which they could be directly dated; but it is certain that they were abandoned long before 1200, and therefore there is no known historical context for them except in the 7th and 8th centuries.

Dr Hope-Taylor also detected the foundations of a larger rectangular building of dressed stone, lying east-west along the Heugh, which he has tentatively identified as a church; it, too, was found to have been abandoned before 1200, and its stones robbed for other building purposes. Once again, it is tempting to associate this structure with a stone church built by later incumbents of the see during its two centuries of active occupation.

The Priory, on the other hand, seems to have been built over an early cemetery, because the bulk of the material unearthed from underneath the present ruins during restoration by the old Ministry of Works several decades ago was a series of gravestones and grave-markers. Could this have been the graveyard associated with the original monastery? It seems very likely. Certainly, the site on top of the Heugh

49

is consistent with the kind of exposed sites deliberately chosen for other such monastic centres in 7th-century Northumbria, like Wearmouth (founded in 673) and Jarrow (founded in 681); these were the twin monasteries where the Venerable Bede himself spent all his working life from the age of seven.

Whatever the precise location of that first monastery on Lindisfarne, it quickly became a power-house of spiritual and educational activity, according to Bede:

> Henceforward many Scots arrived daily in Britain, and proclaimed the word of God with great devotion in all the provinces under Oswald's rule, while those of them who were in priest's orders ministered the grace of baptism to those who believed. Churches were built in several places, and the people flocked gladly to hear the word of God, while the king of his bounty gave money and lands to establish monasteries, and the English, both noble and simple, were instructed by their Scots teachers to observe a regular and disciplined life.

We are told that Aidan started a school at the monastery, for which he selected twelve young Anglo-Saxon boys for training for the priesthood (as bishop, he had the authority to ordain priests and consecrate other bishops), several of whom were later to make their own mark on the early history of the church: St Eata, who became the fifth bishop of Lindisfarne; St Cedd, who evangelised the East Saxons of Essex and founded an abbey at Lastingham in Yorkshire; and St Chad, Cedd's younger brother, who became bishop of Mercia with his see at Lichfield, and consecrated the first cathedral there in 700.

The outstanding feature of Oswald's reign was the warm and close relationship between the king and his bishop, which Bede reported with unqualified approval:

> The king always listened humbly and readily to Aidan's advice, and diligently set himself to establish and extend the Church of Christ throughout his kingdom. And while the bishop, who was not yet fluent in the English language, preached the Gospel, it was most delightful to see the king himself interpreting the word of God to his thanes and leaders; for he himself had obtained perfect command of the Scottish tongue during his long exile.

A church was founded at Bamburgh, for the use of the king and bishop alike. The monasteries that were founded directly through Aidan or by one of his followers from Lindisfarne included those at Melrose, Hexham and Coldingham; and Aidan also did much to encourage the establishment of convents and 'unisex' or double monasteries. In 646 a house was created at Hartlepool (*Hereteu*) by a lady called Heiu, described by Bede as 'a devout servant of Christ who is said to have been the first woman in the province of Northumbria to take vows and be clothed as a nun, which she did under the supervision of Bishop Aidan'. She was succeeded as abbess there by St Hilda, a lady of the royal house of Edwin, who had originally been converted to Christianity by Bishop Paulinus. Hilda 'quickly set herself to establish a regular observance, as she had been instructed by learned men; for Bishop Aidan and other devout men, who knew her and admired her innate wisdom and love of God, often used to visit and advise her'. After Aidan's death, Hilda went on to even greater things, and in 657 she founded a double monastery at Whitby (*Streanæshealh*); it was a foundation specifically associated with the Northumbrian royal house, and is notable for the tremendous wealth of finds unearthed by workmen employed by the old Ministry of Works in the 1920s. A re-examination in 1968 by Professor Philip Rahtz confirmed that it had been an unusually large and densely occupied site from its foundation until its eventual abandonment in the 9th century, with evidence of considerable cultural and trade contacts with the Continent.

Aidan's monastery on Lindisfarne was a much simpler and less elaborate foundation than Whitby. Bede more than once stresses the frugality and austerity with which Aidan and his successors lived:

> They had no property except cattle, and whenever they received any money from rich folk, they immediately gave it to the poor; for they had no need to acquire money or provide lodging for important people, since such only visited the church in order to pray or hear the word of God. Whenever opportunity offered, the king himself used to come with only five or six attendants, and when he had visited the church to pray, he used to leave. But if they happened to remain for a meal, they were content with the plain daily food of the brothers, and asked nothing more, for the sole concern of these teachers was to serve God, not the world: to satisfy the soul, not the belly.

It was the same when Aidan went visiting:

> And if, as sometimes happened, he was summoned to dine with the king, he went with one or two of his clergy, and when he had eaten sparingly he would hurry away either to read with his people or to pray . . .
>
> He would never keep silence about the sins of the rich, out of respect for their position or fear, but he would correct them sternly and outspokenly. He would never give money to powerful men of the world, but only food on such occasions as he entertained them;

on the contrary, if he ever received gifts of money from the rich he would distribute them for the use of the poor or for the redemption of those who had been unjustly sold into slavery. Many of those whom he had ransomed in this way later became his disciples, and when they had been instructed and trained, he ordained them into the priesthood.

This obstinate refusal to conform to the accepted standards of English high society had a profound effect on the perceptions of the populace towards these holy Irishmen:

Accordingly the religious habit was held in high esteem, and whenever any priest or monk paid a visit, he was joyfully welcomed by all as the servant of God. And if anyone met him on the road, they ran to him and bowed, eager to be signed by his hand or receive a blessing from his lips. Whenever he spoke, he was given an attentive hearing, and on Sundays the people flocked to the churches and monasteries, not to obtain food but to hear the word of God taught. When a priest visited a village, the people were quick to gather in some cottage to hear the word of life, for priests and clerics always came to a village solely to preach, baptise, visit the sick and, in short, to care for the souls of its people.

What an evocative picture of pastoral serenity these words conjure up! After the frenetic and short-lived mass baptisms of Bishop Paulinus, St Aidan's mission achieved its effect by example, by self-sacrifice, by joy, by compassion, by devotion to principle, by dedication to humanity. On Lindisfarne today, nothing is easier than to see in the mind's eye the scenes of busy tranquillity, of tranquil busy-ness, which characterised those far-off days: monks tending their fields and animals, monks studying and copying out the Scriptures, monks in meditation or prayer, a life imbued with a profound harmony between body and spirit, between nature and the supernatural, superintended by the gentle pervasive presence of St Aidan himself.

It was a marvellous decade of peace and profound heart's-ease in the troubled early years of Northumbria; but all too soon it was to come to a devastating end, politically at least. King Penda of Mercia, the destroyer of Edwin, had long been nursing his bitter hostility towards Northumbria, and in August, 642, he launched a full-scale invasion; Oswald was defeated and killed in battle at a place which Bede calls *Maserfelth*, and which is now generally identified as Old Oswestry — 'Oswald's Tree' in the sense of 'Oswald's Cross', no doubt named after Oswald's planting of the Cross before battle, as at Heavenfield. His body was hacked to pieces, but almost immediately he was canonised by popular acclamation, and miracles were soon recorded from the place where he had fallen, or associated with his bodily relics. As C. F. Battiscombe comments in his authoritative volume on *The Relics of St Cuthbert* (1956): 'It is not for nothing that the Northumbrian people, whose heroic poetry had idealised the conception of the warrior king, should have chosen just such a warrior king as their earliest saint, a Christian Beowulf, who died defending his people against the dragon of heathenism.'

Northumbria was sundered again. But King Penda did not pursue his victory to the extent of making himself overlord of the kingdom. Instead, the throne of Bernicia was taken over by Oswald's younger brother Oswiu, last of the three sons of Æthelfrith, while Deira reverted to a king called Oswine, the son of that King Osric of Deira whom Cadwallon had killed in 633.

These political changes made no apparent difference to Aidan's mission, which continued its steady work in both Bernicia and Deira. Of the two kings, it was Oswine of Deira with whom Aidan seemed to have most in common, rather than with Oswald's brother Oswiu. Bede described Oswine as a man of great holiness and piety, deeply loved by all, courteous and generous to high and low alike, and above all a man of deep humility. It was Oswine who gave Aidan a valuable horse which Aidan promptly gave away to a beggar. Aidan seems to have realised, according to Bede, that King Oswine with his special endowments of virtue and moderation would not last long in the rough regalities of Northumbrian politics; after the incident with the horse, Bede tells us that Aidan wept:

> I know that the king will not live for very long, for I have never seen so humble a king as he. I feel that he will soon be taken from this life, for this nation is not worthy of such a king.

His presentiment soon came true. The latent rivalry between Deira and Bernicia for the overlordship of Northumbria, never far below the surface, erupted into open conflict in 651. But the issue was not resolved by battle, but by assassination: Oswine was betrayed into his enemy's hands by a thane he had considered his most trusted friend, and King Oswiu of Bernicia had him put to death. This crime took place at Gilling, near Catterick, and later Oswiu built a monastery there in expiation of his sin.

But that was of no comfort to Aidan. Only twelve days after the murder of his beloved friend, Oswine, Aidan himself fell ill at Bamburgh, where he died on August 31, 651.

When he fell ill, we are told by Bede, a tent or lean-to was erected for him against the west wall of the church he had built at Bamburgh in happier days. As he drew his last breath, he was reclining against one of the posts that strengthened the outer wall of the church. This particular timber post was miraculously preserved when the church was later destroyed, on two occasions, by fire. Today, inside the church tower in the sacristy of Bamburgh Church, there is an old, blackened beam quite markedly different from the others; and visitors are invited to draw the conclusion that this was the very baulk of timber against which St Aidan breathed his last on earth.

The monks of Lindisfarne came to fetch his body home, and he was buried in the island cemetery, perhaps underneath the present ruins of the Priory. Later, when his successor, Finan, replaced Aidan's original church with a rather more substantial structure of hewn oak thatched with reeds, his body was translated to a place of honour at the right-hand side of the altar. He did not rest there undisturbed for long, however; when Colman, the third bishop of Lindisfarne, left Lindisfarne for Iona in 664, he took some of Aidan's relics with him. Others are said to have found their way to the famous abbey at Glastonbury in Somerset. The remainder, according to the 12th century chronicler, Simeon of Durham, were placed in the coffin-reliquary of St Cuthbert when the monks eventually abandoned their monastery, to end up, after many years of vicissitude and wanderings, in Durham Cathedral.

Thus ended the earthly reign of Aidan over Lindisfarne. Bede recounts, with an historian's discreet scepticism, one or two miracles with which Aidan was associated — he supplied some holy oil with which a storm at sea was assuaged, and he prayed successfully for a wind to blow away the flames and smoke when Bamburgh Castle was fired by Penda of Mercia during the reign of King Oswiu. But miracles apart, what shines through Bede's account of Aidan's ministry is his profound respect, his love, indeed, for the kindly, considerate man from Iona who first made Lindisfarne the Cradle Island of the north. The Venerable Bede never knew Aidan in person, for Aidan died twenty years before Bede was born; but through Bede's words, the saint lives on, not just in the pages of the *Ecclesiastical History of the English People*, but in all the lovely, lonely places of the little island he hallowed for ever with his presence.

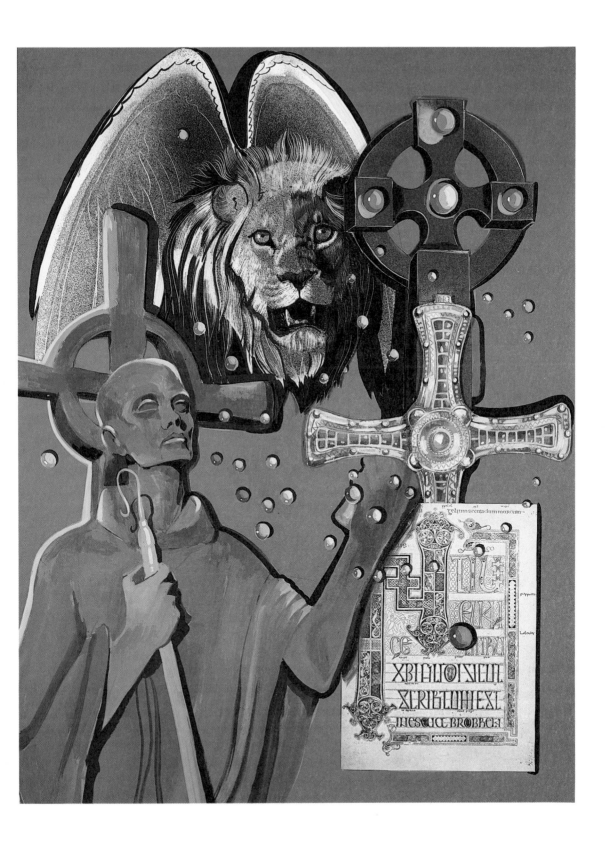

ST AIDAN — CONCRETE AND CANVAS

In the churchyard of the medieval parish church of St Mary the Virgin, overlooking the ruins of the Norman Priory, there stands a tall, gaunt figure. It is a more than life-size sculpture of St Aidan, 11 ft high, ascetic of face and figure, bearing aloft in his left hand a torch that symbolises the light of the Gospel, with his bishop's crozier in his right. His head is framed against a Celtic cross that seems to adumbrate a halo of sanctity. The statue was unveiled in the presence of her Majesty the Queen in 1958.

It was fashioned by a noted local sculptress, Miss Kathleen Parbury, who is now in her eighties. She visited the island for thirty years, resided there for ten years, but now lives on the mainland at Beadnell due to ill-health. She built up the figure of St Aidan in clay, then took moulds from the clay and cast them, all by her self, in concrete — heavy work indeed! She used red sandstone as an aggregate to tone in with the red colouring of the Priory Church ruins.

Miss Parbury also designed the magnificent carpet that adorns the sanctuary before the altar in St Mary's Church. It is an exact scaled-up copy of an illuminated cross-carpet page from the Lindisfarne Gospels introducing the Gospel according to St Mark — Mark of the Lion. It is a superb creation, richly decorated with fret and interlace and shield-like peltas, every nook and cranny of the pattern crammed with dynamic activity interwoven into a coherent whole.

The design was transferred onto canvas with the help of four students at Alnwick College of Education; thereafter it was painstakingly embroidered in tent-stitch, under Miss Parbury's supervision, by a group of 18 Lindisfarne seamstresses. It took them two whole years to complete, and the sumptuous carpet was dedicated in 1970.

S.G.M.

6 Whitby —664 And All That

There is a litany of classroom dates that lingers on in the memory of everybody's schooldays — high-points of history, once learned, never forgotten: dates like 1066 (Hastings), 1215 (Magna Carta), 1314 (Bannockburn), 1492 (Christopher Columbus), 1603 (Union of the Crowns), 1815 (Waterloo), and so on and so on. But one more date should be added to everyone's formulary of simple facts: 664, the year of the Synod of Whitby; for that Synod, or conference, that year in particular, marked a highly significant watershed in the history of the Celtic church in Britain, and the story of Lindisfarne itself. It was the year in which the Celtic church of the north and west was forced to bend the ecclesiastical knee to the Roman 'catholic' (meaning 'universal') church of the south — and all because of the cut of a monk's tonsure, and the proper date of Easter.

Ever since the withdrawal of the Roman legions from Britain, communications between the continental church and the Celtic/British church had been growing increasingly difficult. As a result, the Celtic church had gone its own way on several points of church practice, and church government. By the time of St Columba in the late 6th century the divergence was sufficiently marked to occasion outright mutual hostility where the two met and clashed. In 585, an Irish monk called St Columbanus went with twelve followers to Gaul where he founded three monastic centres at Annegray, Luxeuil and Fontaine on strictly Celtic lines — so strict, indeed, that he fell foul of the Roman establishment, including Pope Gregory the Great himself, and was eventually sentenced to be deported in 610. Although he was at least 70 years old by then, Columbanus eluded his would-be captors and crossed the Alps to Italy, where he founded, amidst further bitter controversy, the Celtic monastery and abbey of Bobbio in the Apennines. One of his followers, St Gall, made his way to Switzerland, where he settled in a cave near Lake Constance, on the site of the later cathedral and town named after him — Sankt Gallen.

Austere establishments of this kind, deep in the heartlands of Roman Catholicism, sharpened the conflict between the two churches over the manner of Christian rites and observances to be followed. They worshipped the same God, of course, with no real difference in doctrine; but they worshipped Him in distinctly different ways. Both churches had strong monastic traditions; but whereas Roman monasteries were adjuncts of the church, Celtic monasteries *were* the church. The Irish system was essentially tribal, whereas the Roman system was essentially territorial. Irish monasteries were ruled with a rod of iron by the abbot, who had total authority over all the monks and priests and even the bishop, whose functions were relatively minor. The abbot could be as eccentric and autocratic as he pleased, and could impose whatever system of penitential discipline he fancied — and some of the rules adopted by Celtic houses sound ludicrously masochistic to modern ears. The abbot could prescribe severe beatings and lengthy bread-and-water 'stretches' for all or any offences against asceticism, such as gluttony leading to vomiting, indolence, lustful thoughts, bestiality, sleeping in church, drunkenness, unpunctuality, and so on. The only excess allowed was in the punishments meted out for real or imagined sins; and the monks apparently loved it.

In comparison, the Benedictine regime of the Roman monasteries sounds positively luxurious — comfortable bedding, soothing morning calls, a choice of two cooked dishes at the daily meal, a pint of wine a day. Celtic monks lived in conspicuous poverty; Roman monks lived well. Celtic monks were unworldly, Roman monks were worldly. Celtic bishops practised humility, Roman bishops paraded pomp. Celtic bishops were ministers of their flocks, Roman bishops were monarchs of their dioceses. Celtic clergymen said, 'Do as I do', and hoped to be followed; Roman clergymen said 'Do as I say', and expected to be obeyed. Like the Roman Empire that they were wanting to re-establish throughout Europe, the mandarins of the Roman hierarchy were basically authoritarian and imperialist in their outlook; the Celtic clergy knew it, and didn't like it.

There were minor variations of liturgy between the two churches, which were of little concern, and slight differences in the form of the blessing. There was a significant difference in the method of consecration of bishops: in the Celtic church it took only one bishop to consecrate another — a practice which led continental clergy to question the very validity of Celtic episcopal consecration. There was a conspicuous difference in the style of tonsure, although we don't know precisely what it was; the Romans shaved the familiar round patch on the crown of the head, leaving a fringe like a Crown of Thorns, while the

UNDERTAKER ON THE SHORE

They look like storks dressed as undertakers — somewhat dishevelled undertakers, to be sure — with their dark bluey-grey plumage and wispy black crest and those spindly Ronald-Searle shanks, and that patiently wary stance: professional mourners with a veiled eye to the main chance.

Herons (*Ardea cinerea*) are regular winter residents on Lindisfarne; and occasionally a heron in Scandinavia will launch itself across the North Sea with a following wind, and flap its ungainly way to winter quarters on Black Law, the shingle sanctuary for Terns across the water from Lindisfarne harbour. They fly with their long legs trailing straight out behind them and their heads drawn back, folding their necks into an S between their shoulders; once they are airborne they make stately galleon progress, but getting off the ground in the first place is a cumbersome business accompanied by much flailing of their great tented wings.

On land the heron is transformed from a clumsy hang-glider into a murderously effective killer. It stands in the shallows as still as a sentry, often on one leg, looking thoughtful and preoccupied, its head hunched into its shoulders or tilted to one side and its eyes half-closed. But there is nothing somnolent about the speed of its reflexes when anything edible stirs within range of that lethal yellow beak: down it comes with the force of a pick-axe, skewering its prey with unerring aim. A contented gulp, a couple of deliberate stalking steps, and the sentinel position is resumed.

Other birds hate the heron, and fear it. In the air it is frequently set upon by hoodlum Rooks, on the ground it is often raucously mobbed by Gulls. Now that killer beak seems inadequate against these practised muggers of the seashore, and the heron cowers beneath the attack, screeching hoarsely in fear and anger, its tufted crest standing on end with alarm. For a moment all poise is abandoned, and the undertaker looks like any other frightened victim. Then, the onslaught over, it shakes its ruffled dignity and assumes once again that professionally unobtrusive look of the mourner-in-waiting.

60

Celtic tonsure may have meant shaving the front of the scalp from ear to ear, or may even have looked like a Mohican plume-cut with the sides of the skull shaved.

But the fundamental disagreement was over the method of calculating the date of Easter. The Celtic missionaries were still using tables based on a system that had been agreed centuries earlier, while the Romans had refined the system in a series of Papal pronouncements that had never reached the Celtic church. As a result, the two churches now celebrated Easter on different days. Apart from the social awkwardness involved, it might seem to us a fairly trivial dispute; but it was only a symptom of a much more basic argument, about church government and, ultimately, power: which church would dominate the other?

The Venerable Bede had no doubts about the matter: he was solidly pro-Roman/English, solidly anti-Celtic/British. Despite his declared admiration for Aidan as a man of God, Bede made no bones about his disapproval of Aidan's 'inadequate knowledge of the proper observance of Easter . . . I cannot approve or commend his failure to observe Easter at the proper time, whether he did it through ignorance of the canonical times, or in deference to the customs of his own nation . . . The true facts are evident to any scholar.'

During Aidan's lifetime, his shortcomings in this respect had been tolerated, according to Bede:

> . . .for it was realised that although he was in loyalty bound to retain the customs of those who had sent him, he nevertheless laboured diligently to cultivate the faith, piety and love that marks out God's saints. He was therefore rightly loved by all, even by those who differed from his opinion on Easter.

But there was to be no such condescension from Bede for Aidan's successor as bishop of Lindisfarne, another Iona-trained Irish monk, whose name was St Finan. In Bede's eyes, Finan was 'a hot-tempered man whom reproof made more obstinate, and openly hostile to the Truth'.

One reason why the Easter controversy had remained dormant during Aidan's rule at Lindisfarne had been the continuing threat posed by the pagan Penda, king of Mercia and implacable enemy of Northumbria. Penda had kept Northumbria's political aspirations in check, so far as any expansion southward might be concerned. It was Penda's pagan Mercia that had effectively separated the Celtic mission in Northumbria from the Roman mission in Kent; it had stood between the stream of Christianity wanting to press south from Lindisfarne and the stream pressing north from Canterbury, thus preventing or at least postponing a crisis of confrontation. But towards the end of Penda's lifetime, that barrier was beginning to crumble through ties of marriage and friendship between younger members of the two rival dynasties of Northumbria and Mercia. King Oswiu's eldest son, Alhfrith (who leaned towards the Roman camp), the sub-King of Deira, married one of Penda's daughters, Cyneburh; while his close friend, Penda's son, Peada (who was a pagan), the sub-king of the Middle Angles in the Wash, married Oswiu's daughter Alhflæd in 653.

This marriage gave Oswiu and Finan an opportunity they were not slow to exploit. Oswiu refused to allow his daughter to marry a pagan, so Peada obligingly accepted baptism from Finan; and to make assurance doubly sure, Finan sent a mission of four Lindisfarne priests — the first graduates of the school that Aidan had founded — to accompany the bride back to Middle Anglia and consolidate the conversion.

Despite these family entanglements, Oswiu and Penda squared up to each other in a final armed showdown in the year 654. Penda gathered a large confederacy of allies against Northumbria, and had humiliated Oswiu into buying him off with huge payments of treasure. Eventually, in November, 654, Oswiu offered Penda pitched battle at an unidentified stream called the *Winwæd*, somewhere near Leeds. Despite being outnumbered by three to one, Oswiu's dedicated army won a famous victory over the Mercian host. Penda himself was killed, along with the king of the East Angles; and with Penda's death, the last bastion of English paganism fell. Oswiu thus became Christian overlord not only of Northumbria but also of Mercia and all the southern English peoples.

Oswiu promptly made his son-in-law Peada a vassal king of southern Mercia, and bishop Finan equally promptly consecrated one of the Lindisfarne Four, St Chad, as bishop of Mercia, with his diocese owing allegiance to Lindisfarne. (Soon afterwards, Peada was 'foully assassinated through the treachery, it is said, of his own wife' — Oswiu's daughter, Alhflæd). Meanwhile bishop Finan, using Mercia as a springboard, despatched two of the Lindisfarne Four even farther south, to Essex, where King Sigeberht of the East Saxons was baptised and Chad's brother, St Cedd, was consecrated bishop of a diocese that included London itself. No wonder Bede felt such animosity for bishop Finan and his aggressive missionary tactics!

From the Roman point of view, the enemy was now at the very gates of Canterbury, and a spirited counter-attack was launched. There were now several clerics in Northumbria who, although their training had been Iona-orientated, had developed a more cosmopolitan outlook through travels in the south. One of these, an Irish monk called Ronan, who had studied theology and law in Italy and Gaul, now engaged Finan in bitter disputation over the question of Easter; according to Bede, Ronan 'convinced many, or at least persuaded them to make a more careful inquiry into the truth. But he entirely failed to move Finan . . .'

In the event, the only thing that moved Finan was his death in the year 661. He was succeeded by another Celtic-trained monk sent from Iona, called Colman. He was a kindly old man — even Bede acknowledged, however grudgingly, his goodness, and the Christian frugality and austerity which governed the life of the monastery on Lindisfarne. It was during Colman's brief tenure of the episcopacy that the Easter controversy came to a head and was settled, once and for all, at the Synod of Whitby in 664.

With a less aggressive bishop in the see of Lindisfarne, the cradle of Christianity in the north, it was doubtless inevitable that the Easter dispute should be forced to the surface for resolution. But it also seems that it may have been King Oswiu's own domestic problems that brought matters to a head. Oswiu had always been of the Celtic persuasion, ever since he had been educated from childhood at Iona during his years of political exile; his second wife, however, adhered to the Roman practice. Her name was Eanflæd; she was that baby Northumbrian princess, daughter of King Edwin, who had been born on Easter Day in 626 (*cf* ch 4), and had then been smuggled by boat to safety in Kent after her father was killed by Cadwallon and Penda in 633. Soon after Oswiu had succeeded his brother Oswald in 642 (*cf* ch 5), Oswiu had married this princess of the House of Edwin to consolidate his dynastic control of Deira; but by then, Eanflæd had been 'converted' to Roman catholicism at the royal court of Kent, the seat of Augustine's original mission.

This led to some confusion in the royal household at Bamburgh, in that Easter had to be kept twice: 'When the King had ended Lent and was keeping Easter, the queen and her attendants were still fasting and keeping Palm Sunday,' says Bede. But it also led to confusion amongst the people: 'This dispute began to trouble the minds and consciences of many, who feared that they might have received the name of Christian in vain'. There was another factor that may have influenced the king to grasp the nettle at last: in 665 the two tables which regulated the respective dates of the Celtic and Roman Easter were due to diverge to an exceptionally embarrassing extent.

Whatever the reason, King Oswiu summoned a synod to convene at Whitby, the royal Northumbrian monastery ruled by St Hilda, in order to hear the pros and cons from both parties and come to a decision that would be binding on them both.

Bishop Colman led for the Celtic case:

> The Easter customs which I observe were taught me by my superiors, who sent me here as a bishop; and all our forefathers, men beloved of God, are known to have observed these customs. And lest anyone condemns or rejects them as wrong, it is recorded that they owe their origin to the blessed evangelist St John, the disciple especially loved by our Lord, and all the churches over which he presided.

Leading for the opposition was a career cleric called Wilfrid — St Wilfrid to posterity — who had been trained at Lindisfarne under Aidan but had switched sides after spending five years studying the religious customs of Italy and Gaul, and was now a protégé of Queen Eanflæd. The simple-hearted, elderly bishop Colman was no match for this subtle and sophisticated young cosmopolitan scholar, who proceeded to dazzle and bemuse the Synod with a wealth of erudition. He was also extremely offensive to his opponents:

> The only people who are stupid enough to disagree with the whole world are these and their obstinate adherents the Picts and Britons, who inhabit only a portion of these two islands in the remote ocean.'

Colman's attempts to defend the good name of St John were contemptuously brushed aside by Wilfrid on the ground that St John had known no better at the time. Colman fell back on a justification of his position through St Columba:

> Are we to believe that our most revered Father Columba and his successors, men so dear to God, thought or acted contrary to Holy Scripture when they followed this custom? The holiness of many of them is confirmed by heavenly signs, and their virtues by miracles; and having no doubt that they are Saints, I shall never cease to emulate their lives, customs and discipline.

It was all too easy for Wilfrid as he swooped in for the kill (he reminds me irresistibly of the sort of smooth young hatchet-man sent in by some multi-national company to take over a local business and sort out the natives). St Columba and the other Celtic saints he disparaged with the faintest of praise — 'I do not deny that they were true servants of God and dear to Him, and that they loved Him in primitive simplicity'; but if they had been lucky enough to have had a Catholic adviser, they would have seen the error of their ways and accepted his guidance:

> For although your Fathers were holy men, do you imagine that they, a few men in a corner of a remote island, are to be preferred before the universal Church of Christ throughout the world? And even if your Columba — or, may I say, ours also, if he was the servant of Christ — was a Saint of potent virtues, can he take precedence before the most blessed Prince of the Apostles, to whom our Lord said: *'Thou art Peter, and upon this rock I will build my Church, and the gates of hell shall not prevail against it, and to thee I will give the keys of the kingdom of heaven'?*

One cannot help feeling that King Oswiu, as chairman of the Synod, had known the score beforehand. He intervened now, to press Colman to acknowledge that these had, in fact, been Christ's words to Peter. The poor bishop could only agree. Whereupon (*with a smile*, according to Wilfrid's biographer, Eddius Stephanus, though not according to Bede) the king delivered his judgement — the judgement that would establish unity in the church and, no doubt, peace in his own household:

> Then, let me tell you, since Peter is guardian of the gates of heaven, I shall not contradict him. I shall obey his commands in everything to the best of my knowledge and ability; otherwise, when I come to the gates of heaven, he who holds the keys may not be willing to open them.

Bitterly disappointed at the decision, St Colman resigned from his episcopacy at Lindisfarne and went back to Iona, taking with him some of Aidan's relics and many of his Iona-trained diehards, both Irishmen and Englishmen. From Iona he went to Ireland, where he founded a monastery of his own on the island of Inisbofin, off the west coast. His last request to King Oswiu before he left Lindisfarne was that the abbot of Aidan's foundation monastery at Melrose, St Eata, one of Aidan's original twelve pupils, should be appointed abbot of Lindisfarne as well (previously, bishops of Lindisfarne had acted as abbots, too); Colman knew that although Eata was prepared to accept the new Roman order, he would ensure that the Celtic traditions fostered at Lindisfarne would not be entirely lost. Eata was duly appointed abbot of Lindisfarne, only to become bishop soon afterwards when Colman's immediate successor, a royal appointee called Tuda, died in the great epidemic of the Yellow Plague which devastated Britain in 664 and carried off innumerable churchmen.

Of the other main *dramatis personae* in the Whitby spectacular, King Oswiu reigned on in peace and prosperity until his death in 670; despite his murder of King Oswine, his 28 years on the throne of Northumbria established his reputation as a wise and steadfast prince of Christendom.

St Cedd, one of Aidan's first pupils, whom bishop Finan had appointed bishop of Mercia and who acted as interpreter at the Synod, was swept away in the Yellow Plague of 664. His brother, St Chad, switched his allegiance to Rome and was appointed bishop of York, only to be deposed in favour of the high-flying Wilfrid and translated to the bishopric of Mercia at Lichfield.

And what of Wilfrid himself, the victor of Whitby? He already had his own monastery at Ripon, and now he was consecrated bishop there. But he wasn't satisfied with a minor consecration in England; instead he went to Compiègne in Gaul, to be consecrated in style — carried on a golden throne by a squad of bishops and escorted by 120 armed men. He became bishop of York in place of St Chad, then archbishop, and became extremely wealthy. But he never quite made it to the top; ten years later, in 678, he fell from grace, and despite a successful appeal to the Pope against wrongful dismissal, his power and influence were shorn, and he ended up almost where he had started, as bishop of Hexham and Ripon.

He had been the catalyst that brought the pure strain of Celtic monasticism in the north of England to an end, thirty years after Aidan had founded his monastery on Lindisfarne. It was the end of an age, the start of a new order. Iona was now eclipsed, Canterbury in the ascendant. Romantic nostalgia for more simple times might tempt us to mourn the passing of that age; but 664 did not spell the end of Lindisfarne, or its influence, by any means. Quite the contrary. The foundations laid by Aidan provided a sure base for future growth. Under the new dispensation, the Celtic and the Roman strains cross-fertilised one another; simplicity and grandeur came together in a new harmony. It was St Wilfrid who added the sonorous beauty of Gregorian chant to the spare pieties of the Celtic service. From the new order emerged other giants of the missionary church, like Benedict Biscop (founder of the joint monasteries of Wearmouth and Jarrow), and St Willibrord, trained at Ripon by Wilfrid, future archbishop of Utrecht and founder of the great monastery of Echternach in

HEDGEHOGS IN THE TOILS

S.G.M.

The year 1982 was, you might say, the Year of the Hedgehog (*Erinaceus europaeus*). It was in February of that year that a certain Major Adrian Coles, of Knowbury in Shropshire, founded the British Hedgehog Preservation Society and persuaded Shropshire County Council to instal a ramp underneath a cattle-grid on the A411 near Ludlow, to provide an escape-route for hedgehogs unfortunate enough to fall through the bars into the pit below.

It sounded like just another absurdity of the English; but people flocked in their hundreds to join this new Society to protect this hapless, unassuming, flea-ridden little creature: a creature, what's more, that is daft enough to think that an adequate defence against an onrushing motor-car is to roll itself into a ball and erect its tough yellow-tipped spines.

Yet there is something oddly endearing about the hedgehog, and on Lindisfarne *every* year is the Year of the Hedgehog. That great naturalist, Richard Perry (*A Naturalist on Lindisfarne*, 1946), waxed almost lyrical about it:

> . . . the hedgehog strolling in the evening sunshine over a sandy link in the dunes. At every encounter his resemblance to a small bear becomes more pronounced: with his slow, deliberate, rambling walk, and the manner in which his ankles and the soles of his feet are stuck out gingerly and turned right up at every jointed step. Even at a distance of a few feet he is short-sighted: his hearing is more acute: his sense of smell most; for when I am about three or four yards from him, and can see his beady black eye, he turns about, wrinkling his shiny black pointed nose in my direction — the breeze is blowing across our axis — and, when I speak to him, rolls up with a bang. (p76).

The island fishermen care about hedgehogs, too. So inquisitive are the creatures that they frequently get themselves enmeshed in the salmon-nets during their perambulations along the shore by the harbour. With infinite care, the fishermen disentangle the spines from the mesh to set the animal free; or if it's only a small piece of used net, they cut the net away to let the wee beast escape.

Yes, Holy Island is a sanctuary for hedgehogs, too.

Luxembourg. Thus did the light of Lindisfarne shine with an added brilliance even farther afield than before.

The monasteries of England, now all united under the one universal authority, were to blossom as never before as centres of illumination, of learning and literacy and magnificent works of art.

Saintliness did not die at Whitby; it was given a new dimension. And no one symbolised this transition, this cross-fertilisation, this interweaving of the strands of Celtic and continental churchmanship, better than the most renowned of the nine saints associated with Lindisfarne: St Cuthbert.

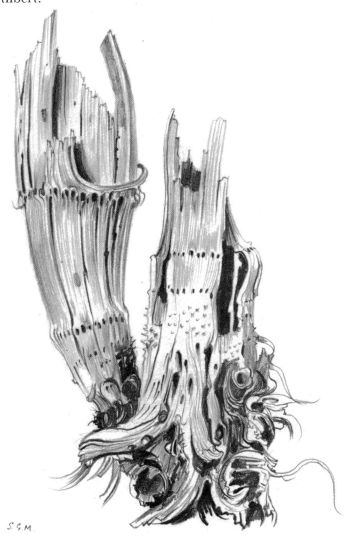

S.G.M.

7 St Cuthbert

On the night of August 31, 651 — the night that St Aidan died in his lean-to shelter at Bamburgh — a sturdy, fair-haired youth called Cuthbert was out in the Lammermuir hills keeping watch over some sheep in the valley of the river Leader, near Melrose in the Scottish Border country. His fellow shepherds were all asleep, and he himself was holding vigil and saying his prayers when, suddenly, he saw a vision:

> For through the opened heaven — not by a parting of the natural elements but by the sight of his spiritual eyes — like blessed Jacob the patriarch in ... Bethel, he had seen angels ascending and descending, and in their hands was borne to heaven a holy soul, as if in a globe of fire.
>
> Then immediately awaking the shepherds, he described the wonderful vision just as he had seen it, prophesying further to them that it was the soul of a most holy bishop or some other great person.
>
> And so events proved; for a few days afterwards, they heard that the death of our holy bishop Aidan, at that same hour of the night as he had seen the vision, had been announced far and wide.

That was how an unnamed monk at the monastery on Lindisfarne described, in the so-called *Anonymous Life of St Cuthbert* (written around 700, only a few years after the saint's death), the precise moment which decided the young Cuthbert to dedicate his own life to the service of God. This concise, sparely-written *Life* was later expanded by the Venerable Bede, first in a metrical version around 705, and then in a more diffuse prose *Life of St Cuthbert* around 720. Bede could not resist embellishing the plain account of that vision:

> On a certain night while his companions were sleeping, he himself was keeping watch and praying according to his custom, when he suddenly saw a stream of light from the sky breaking in upon the darkness of the long night. In the midst of this, the choir of the heavenly host descended to the earth, and taking with them, without delay, a soul of exceeding brightness, returned to their heavenly home.
>
> The youth beloved of God was strongly moved by this vision to

70

subject himself to the grace of spiritual discipline and of earning everlasting life and happiness amid God's mighty men, and immediately he gave praise and thanks to God and also called upon his companions with brotherly exhortation to praise the Lord . . .

And in the morning, learning that Aidan, bishop of the church at Lindisfarne, a man of specially great virtue, had entered the Kingdom of Heaven at the very time when he had seen him taken from the body, Cuthbert forthwith delivered to their owners the sheep which he was tending, and decided to seek a monastery.

These two *Lives* are the main sources for our knowledge of the man who was destined to become the most renowned and best-remembered of all the northern saints. Countless churches were to be dedicated to him, the length and breadth of Britain; in Scotland, the Ayrshire town of Kirkcudbright ('Cuthbert's Church') was to be named after him. His cult, fuelled by stories of his body remaining uncorrupted after death, spread like wild-fire throughout Britain and Western Europe. There are no fewer than thirty-eight surviving manuscript copies of Bede's *Life*, fourteen of them in continental libraries, while eight copies of Bede's *Metrical Life* also remain on the continent, and the seven extant copies of the *Anonymous Life* were also written on the continent.

But we know very little for certain about his origins or early upbringing. He seems to have been born around the year 634 — that time of mixed disaster and triumph for Northumbria, when Cadwallon and Penda ravaged it after the death of Edwin, before Oswald fought his way to the throne at the Battle of Heavenfield; but his place of birth and social standing are matter for surmise. His name, Cuthbert, strongly suggests that he was of Anglo-Saxon stock, rather than British; but a later legendary source, the so-called *Irish Life of St Cuthbert*, which may have been composed at Melrose late in the 12th century, claims that he was of Irish descent, the son of an Irish princess called Sabina.

All we know from the two English *Lives* is that when he was eight years old he was handed over into the care of a Christian foster-mother called Kenswith in an unidentified village called *Hruringaham*; this lady, who was still alive when the *Anonymous Life* was penned, always meant a great deal to Cuthbert; he called her 'mother' and would visit her often in later life — on one occasion, indeed, when the village caught fire, Cuthbert lay down in front of her door and prayed, until a wind sprang up that drove the flames away from the threatened houses.

The mere fact of having been fostered might suggest noble birth, for it was not unusual for well-born children to be placed in fosterage in those days. Cuthbert also seems to have owned a horse, which would have been beyond the means of a peasant; and there is a passing reference in the *Anonymous Life* to a period of military service (his meagre rations in camp were miraculously supplemented by divine intervention). But all this is inference; saints' *Lives* tended to be hagiographies, not biographies.

It is the personality rather than the parentage of the youthful Cuthbert that comes across. He was a cheerful, good-natured boy, well-built and athletic, fond of games and good at them, a conspicuous left-hander, courteous to strangers and kind to animals. He was 'affable and pleasant in his manners', according to Bede; 'happy and joyful at all hours', according to the *Anonymous Life*. But he was also a rather earnest and pious boy, with a marked predilection for prayers and good works, and an engagingly naive faith in angels and their efficacy at ministering to his needs. A few ingenuous 'miracles' are recounted concerning his early years: a child reproves him for indulging in boisterous horseplay, saying that such behaviour ill became a future bishop; an 'angel' mounted on horseback tells him how to heal his inflamed knee by (very sensibly) suggesting a poultice. On another occasion, when he was stormbound without food in a deserted summer shieling one winter's day in the wilds near Chester-le-Street, his horse pulled down part of the thatch to reveal a warm loaf and some meat carefully wrapped up in a linen cloth; Cuthbert had no hesitation in ascribing this to a literal godsend, and Bede delicately paints the lily by adding that he gave half of the loaf to the horse — of course!

He had the courage of his convictions, too. Bede alone tells of an incident on the banks of the Tyne when Cuthbert was still only a boy. A party of monks was fetching timber for their monastery on some rafts, when a terrible storm blew up and started sweeping them out to sea. Their brethen in the monastery launched boats to rescue them, but could not reach them; there was nothing they could do but kneel in desperate prayer. On the opposite bank of the river, a crowd of hostile peasants gathered, jeering at the monks in their mortal danger and taunting them to save their skins with the help of their God — Christianity had clearly not taken very deep root in those parts at the time. Cuthbert was there, too. He tried to shame the crowd into silence, but they only scoffed at him and cursed the monks for having robbed them of their old pagan gods. Nevertheless, Cuthbert knelt in prayer in their midst, his head bent to the ground; and immediately the wind

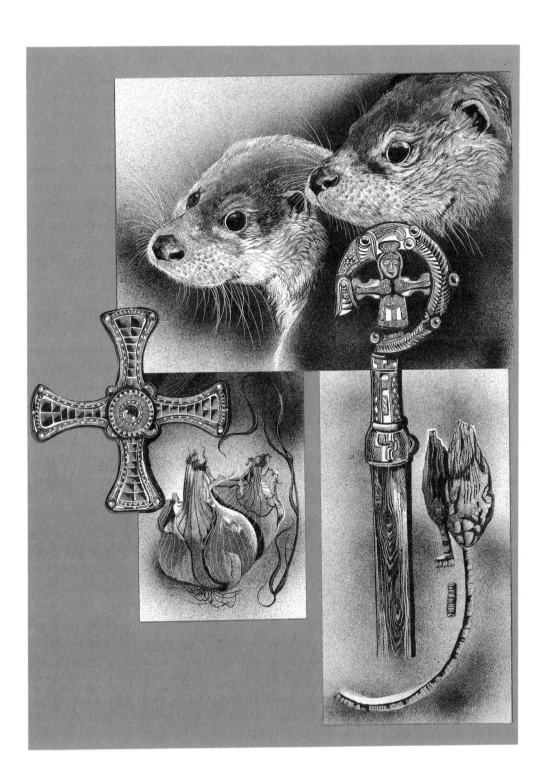

ST CUTHBERT, WITH OTTERS

Tales about St Cuthbert's love for all creatures, furred or feathered, great or small, are legion. One gets the impression from the *Lives* that he virtually declared Lindisfarne a Nature Reserve, 1300 years before the Nature Conservancy Council!

On one occasion, when he was prior of Melrose, Cuthbert made a pastoral visit to a mixed monastery at Coldingham, built high on a windswept cliff (now known as St Abb's Head) two miles north of Eyemouth. It was governed by an abbess of royal birth, St Æbbe, daughter of King Æthelfrith of Northumbria and sister of King Oswald and King Oswiu. Although neither of the *Lives* mentions the fact, we might conjecture from Bede's *Ecclesiastical History* that Cuthbert's visit, at St Æbbe's urgent request, was connected with problems of unseemly conduct and lax discipline; for when the monastery later burned down, in the 680s, Bede claimed it as a divine judgement on the wicked licentiousness of its inmates, both nuns and monks alike.

During his stay at Coldingham, Cuthbert would steal out of doors alone at night, as was his custom, to keep vigil and pray. An inquisitive brother monk followed him one night. He watched the saint go down the steep path to the sandy beach at the foot of the cliffs, and then walk into the sea up to his arm-pits, where he spent the night praying and singing hymns with only the tumultuous waves for accompaniment.

At daybreak, Cuthbert came out of the sea and knelt on the sand to pray. As the *Anonymous Life* puts it:

> And immediately there followed in his footsteps two little sea-animals [*four-footed creatures, which are called otters* — Bede], humbly prostrating themselves on the earth; and licking his feet, they rolled upon them, wiping them with their skins [*fur* — Bede] and warming them with their breath. After this service and ministry had been fulfilled and his blessing had been received, they departed to their haunts in the waves of the sea.

The watching monk was so awed and frightened that he fell ill. Next day he confessed his espionage to Cuthbert, who pardoned him on condition that he told no one what he had seen — until after the saint's death. The penitent monk kept his promise, according to Bede — 'but after the saint's death he took care to tell it to many'.

74

turned and shepherded the five rafts safe and sound to shore.

Yes, that took courage for a teenage boy.

Such was the youth, aged about 16 or 17, who set out to enter a monastery soon after seeing the vision of St Aidan's soul being carried to heaven. He didn't have very far to go. Only a few miles away was the monastery of Melrose, the first and most celebrated of the religious houses established by Aidan as satellites of Lindisfarne. It stood in a thickly-wooded place, now called Old Melrose, about three miles from the magnificent ruin of the present medieval abbey by the River Tweed, in the heart of the Walter Scott country. According to Bede, whose account of Cuthbert's arrival at Melrose is based on eyewitness evidence from an aged monk at Jarrow, Cuthbert was drawn to Melrose rather than to Lindisfarne because of 'the fame and sublime virtues of the monk and priest Boisil'; Boisil, after whom the Roxburghshire town of St Boswells got its name, was prior of Melrose at the time, while the abbot was one of Aidan's original pupils at Lindisfarne, St Eata.

It so happened that prior Boisil was standing at the gates of the monastery when Cuthbert arrived, riding a horse and carrying a spear. The sight of Cuthbert approaching seems to have triggered a flash of prescience in the kindly old prior's mind, for he exclaimed to those standing by: *'Ecce servus Dei!'* ('Behold the servant of the Lord!'). Boisil made the boy welcome, and when the abbot, Eata, returned from his travels a few days later, Cuthbert was accepted into the monastery as one of the brethren and received the tonsure.

Curiously enough, the author of the *Anonymous Life* makes no mention at all of Boisil, and only the most perfunctory reference to Cuthbert's stay at Melrose (professional jealousy of a rival daughter community, perhaps?). It is from Bede alone that we learn anything of Cuthbert's early Melrose years, and the training he received at the hands of Boisil. Cuthbert's competitive spirit showed immediately:

> He sought at once to observe the rules of the regular life equally with the other brethren, or even to excel them in zeal for a stricter discipline, being more diligent in fact in reading and working, in watching and praying. Moreover . . . he sedulously abstained from all intoxicants; but he could not submit to such abstinence in food, lest he should become unfitted for necessary labour.

Boisil was Cuthbert's godfather, in the sense of being his 'father-in-God'; in his latter years, Cuthbert referred to Boisil as 'the venerable servant of Christ, Boisil, a man to be named with all honour, who formerly in his old age, when I was but a youth, brought me up in the monastery of Melrose', and as one of the many who 'both in purity of heart and in loftiness of prophetic grace, far exceed me in my weakness'.

Promotion came to Cuthbert when Alhfrith, son of King Oswiu, was appointed sub-king of Deira after his father's ultimate victory over Penda of Mercia at the Battle of Winwæd in 654. 'For the redemption of his soul', Alhfrith established a monastery at Ripon and invited Eata, the abbot of Melrose, to take charge of it. Among the Melrose monks chosen to get the Ripon community started was Cuthbert, who was appointed guest-master there — a highly responsible post, for one never knew when the guests might be angels in disguise. And so, indeed, it came to pass for Cuthbert, with the arrival on a snowy winter's day of a mysterious young traveller who refused all food but who left behind him, as a reward for his good welcome, three marvellously fragrant new-baked loaves of unusual whiteness and excellence — and no footprints in the snow:

> From that time he was very often held worthy to see and talk
> with angels and, when hungry, to be refreshed by food prepared for
> him by the Lord as a special gift.

The sojourn at Ripon did not last long — only a couple of years or so — for now church politics became a serious factor in the person of that up-and-coming young cleric, Wilfrid, the future 'victor' of Whitby. Although he had been educated at Lindisfarne (*cf* ch 6), Wilfrid had fallen under the spell of Rome while still a student; at the age of 18, in 652, with the active encouragement of Queen Eanflæd (Oswiu's consort), he had travelled to Rome with another young high-flier, Benedict Biscop, who would later achieve lasting fame as the founder of the joint monasteries of Wearmouth and Jarrow. When Wilfrid returned home in 658, a fully professed monk of the Roman order, he found a ready convert to Romanism in Eanflæd's step-son, King Alhfrith, who gave him an estate at *Stanforda* (probably Stamford in Lincolnshire). No doubt prompted by Wilfrid, King Alhfrith tried to persuade Eata and his Celtic clergy at Ripon to accept the Roman Easter and other rites. This was probably in the year 660. Eata refused to change his ways and was dismissed by the king; Wilfrid was appointed abbot of Ripon in his stead, and Eata and Cuthbert and the others returned to Melrose.

A few months after their return, probably early in 662, England was ravaged by an outbreak of the Yellow Plague that devastated Europe on several occasions in the 7th century. Both Cuthbert and the prior, Boisil, caught the disease, which seems to have been a form of bubonic plague with jaundice as one of its symptoms; Bede, quoting a priest called Herefrith, a former abbot of Lindisfarne who had been a monk at Melrose at the time, gives an affecting account of this episode in his *Life*. When Cuthbert's fever reached its crisis, the brethren spent the whole night in vigil and prayer for his recovery:

> When one of them told him about this in the morning — for they had done it without his knowledge — he replied forthwith: 'Then why do I lie here? — for doubtless God has not despised the prayers of so many good men. Bring me my staff and my sandals'.
>
> And immediately he arose and began to try to walk, leaning upon his staff; and as his strength grew from day to day, he recovered his health; but as the swelling which appeared in his thigh gradually left the surface of his body, it sank into the inward parts and, throughout almost the whole of his life, he continued to feel some inward pains . . .

Prior Boisil was to be less fortunate, however. No sooner was Cuthbert recovered than he hastened to see his old friend and mentor. Boisil knew that his own end was near, and that he had only seven days left in which to continue his teaching. It did not occur to Cuthbert to question the prophetic words:

> Cuthbert, never doubting the truth of his words, answered, 'And what is it best for me to read, which I can finish in one week?'
>
> 'The apostle John,' replied Boisil. 'I have a book consisting of seven quires, of which we can get through one every day, with the Lord's help, reading it and discussing it between ourselves so far as is necessary.'
>
> They did as he said. They were able to finish the reading in time because they dealt only with the simple things of 'the faith which worketh by love' and not deep matters of dispute. So when the reading had been completed in seven days, Boisil the man of the Lord, having been attacked by this disease, reached his last day and, having spent it in great gladness, he entered into the joy of perpetual light.

It has a serene and unforced sweetness, that scene: the saintly old man and his loving disciple quietly reading aloud and meditating the inspiring simplicities of the Gospel of St John, while Boisil's life ebbed gently to its end. Cuthbert himself was never to forget it; and, years later, he would tell his friends that Boisil had then prophesied that he would be a bishop one day — a prediction that caused him much heart-searching and sorrow, and may well explain his later self-imposed exile in a hermit's cell on the Inner Farne:

Even if I could possibly hide myself in a tiny dwelling on a rock, where the waves of the swelling ocean surrounded me on all sides, and shut me in equally from the sight and knowledge of men — not even thus should I consider myself to be free from the snares of a deceptive world; even there I should fear lest the love of wealth should tempt me and somehow or other should snatch me away.

After Boisil's death, Cuthbert was appointed prior of Melrose in his place, and immediately plunged into a rigorous schedule of missionary journeys into the remoter parts of the Border country and the Northumbrian hills. There was much work to be done, for the devastations of the plague had shaken the faith of many of the newly converted:

For many of them profaned the faith they held by wicked deeds, and some of them also at the time of the plague, forgetting the sacred mystery of the faith into which they had been initiated, took to the delusive cures of idolatry, as though by incantations or amulets or any other mysteries of devilish art, they could ward off a blow sent by God the creator. So he frequently went forth from the monastery to correct the errors of both kinds of sinners, sometimes riding on a horse but more often going on foot . . .

He was wont to penetrate those parts especially and to preach in those villages that were far away on steep and rugged mountains, which others dreaded to visit and whose poverty as well as ignorance prevented teachers from approaching them. And giving himself up gladly to this pious labour, he attended to their instruction with such industry that, leaving the monastery, he would often not return home for a whole week, sometimes even for two or three weeks, and even occasionally for a full month; but he would tarry in the mountains, summoning the rustics to heavenly things by the words of his preaching as well as by the example of his virtue.

It was during this period of intensive evangelistic safaris into darkest Northumbria that both the Anonymous Author and Bede record a crop of undemanding miracles — undemanding on our credulity, that's to say. He cast out devils, he healed the sick; a sea-eagle supplied him with fish for dinner when it was robbed of its catch by Cuthbert's young companion (and was rewarded by the good man by being allowed to keep half of it); three slices of dolphin flesh, found by lucky chance, succoured him and his crew when they were driven ashore in a snowstorm; and so on and so on.

In 664, the celebrated Synod of Whitby was held, as a result of which the Celtic church in Northumbria was obliged to acknowledge the supremacy of Rome as the mother church of England. It was the start of a new era for everyone — not least Cuthbert himself. Bishop Colman of Lindisfarne refused to accept the Roman dispensation and went back home to Ireland; at his instigation, however, Eata, the abbot of Melrose, was appointed abbot of Lindisfarne as well, to serve under the new bishop, Tuda. With two monasteries to look after now, Eata appointed Cuthbert as prior of Lindisfarne; and thus it was that Cuthbert migrated to the Cradle Island with which his name has ever since been most closely associated.

It might seem odd that Cuthbert and Eata, who only four years earlier had been peremptorily dismissed from Ripon for refusing to implement the Roman ritual there, should now be placed in charge of such a sensitive centre as Lindisfarne, the mother monastery of Northumbria. The sources say nothing about their change of heart. Had King Alhfrith been too high-handed with them previously? Had they seen what Bede would undoubtedly have called the error of their ways? Or did they simply act out of obedience and/or practical realism?

We shall never know for certain; but there is a fleeting hint in the *Anonymous Life* that Cuthbert, at least, may have suffered inner turmoil — we are told that he had 'fled from worldly glory and sailed away privately and secretly', before he was 'invited and constrained' by Eata to take up the call to Lindisfarne. But once the decision had been made, Cuthbert remained as unswerving in his loyalty to the Roman order as he had previously been committed heart and soul to the Celtic rule.

It cannot have been easy for Cuthbert at first, for not unnaturally there were 'certain brethren in the monastery who preferred to conform to their older usage rather than to the monastic rule', as Bede puts it. Every day the brethren would meet to discuss a chapter of the rule — hence the name Chapter House for the meeting-place; and Cuthbert had to win over the recalcitrants to a new, modified rule which adhered to the Roman letter while still observing the Celtic spirit. It called for the most skilful and diplomatic exercise of his authority, both as prior and a man of acknowledged virtue:

> Nevertheless he overcame them by his modest virtue and his patience, and by daily effort he gradually converted them to a better frame of mind. In fact, very often during Chapter debates of the Rule, when he wearied of the bitter contentions of his opponents, he would suddenly get to his feet and depart, with placid appearance and demeanour, thus adjourning the Chapter meeting; but nevertheless on the following day, as if he had suffered no opposition the previous day, he would give the same instruction as before to the same company, until, as we have said,

he gradually converted them to his own way of thinking.

It must have tried the patience of a saint, indeed!

Bede draws for us a sympathetic portrait of the prior as man of God going about his workaday chores inside and outside the monastery, disciplined and devoted. His clothes were of the plainest cut, made of wholesome natural wool, neither costly nor coloured, 'neither ostentatious nor dirty'. He kept up his missionary work on the mainland, and his fame as a miracle-worker spread, to such an extent that he could apparently heal the sick and exorcise devils by remote control, as it were — simply by the power of his prayers. His zeal for keeping prayerful vigils became a byword; he would spend three or four nights at a stretch without sleep, and during the day he would ward off drowsiness by manual work or by walking round the island on tours of inspection, singing psalms the while to keep himself awake. And always, in everything he did, this blazing intensity:

> He was so full of penitence, so aflame with heavenly yearnings, that when celebrating Mass he could never finish the service without shedding tears. But, as was indeed fitting while he celebrated the mysteries of the Lord's passion, he would himself imitate the rite he was performing, that is to say, he would sacrifice himself to God in contrition of heart.
>
> Moreover he would urge those present to lift up their hearts and to give thanks to our Lord God, himself lifting up the heart rather than the voice, sighing rather than singing.
>
> In his zeal for righteousness he was fervid to reprove sinners, yet he was kind-hearted and forbearing in pardoning the penitent, so that sometimes when wrong-doers were confessing their sins to him, in his pity for their weakness he would be the first to burst into tears and thus, though himself righteous, by his own example would show the sinner what he ought to do.

But while Cuthbert was quietly and patiently setting his own house in order on Lindisfarne, matters were not going so well in the wider world in the aftermath of the Synod of Whitby. Bishop Tuda, Colman's successor at Lindisfarne, was carried away by yet another virulent outbreak of the Yellow Plague. So was Bishop Cedd of the East Saxons. And so, even more significantly, was Archbishop Deusdedit of Canterbury. His appointed successor also fell victim to disease before he could take up office. As a result, the see of Canterbury, the headquarters of the new united church of England, was left vacant and rudderless at this critical period for the future of the church. It was not until 669 that a new archbishop took up the reins at Canterbury — the great scholar and career churchman, Theodore of Tarsus.

During this interregnum it was individual kings who called the ecclesiastical tunes. After Tuda's death in 664, the vast Northumbrian diocese was carved up, and Lindisfarne ceased for a time to be the bishop's seat; King Oswiu, no doubt prompted again by his son, King Alhfrith of Deira, allotted to Wilfrid a bishopric based on Ripon, with what seems to have been a tacit agreement that, after consecration, he would become bishop of all Northumbria with his seat at York. But matters didn't work out that way: Wilfrid spent two long years in Gaul, stage-managing a spectacular consecration for himself in the presence of no fewer than 12 Gaulish bishops, and during his absence his patron, Alhfrith, seems to have fallen out with King Oswiu, because at this point Alhfrith simply disappears without explanation from the historical record. By the time Wilfrid returned in 666, he found that King Oswiu had appointed Cedd's brother, St Chad, as bishop of York — whereupon Wilfrid prudently retired to his monastery at Ripon to bide his time with as much patience as his energetic ambition would allow. He had to wait until 669. In the autumn of that year the new archbishop of Canterbury, Theodore of Tarsus, came north on an official visitation to try to impose some sort of order on the chaos which reigned in the English church.

Archbishop Theodore immediately took exception to Bishop Chad's Celtic-style consecration on the ground that it was irregular. Chad obligingly offered to resign his rank as bishop, but Theodore merely 'completed' his consecration in the Catholic manner and shifted him sideways to become bishop of the Mercians, based at Lichfield. This move created space for Wilfrid to be installed as bishop of York and the effective head of the Northumbrian church.

Wilfrid was now in his element. He started building a great church at Ripon, whose crypt is still in existence very much as he left it, and restoring the old Paulinus church at York. And in striking contrast to the humble circumstances chosen by Aidan and Cuthbert and other Celtic churchmen, he started living in ostentatious state; his biographer, Eddius, refers to his 'temporal glories and his riches, the number of his monasteries, the greatness of his buildings, his countless army of followers arrayed in royal vestments and arms'.

It would be hard to imagine two churchmen at this time with less in common than Wilfrid and Cuthbert; they were as far removed from one another as a peacock is from a mistle thrush. Although he conformed loyally to the Roman rule, Cuthbert still exemplified in his person and by his example all the traditions of penitential asceticism and devotional eccentricity of the old Celtic mission; and one can imagine that bishop Wilfrid must have kept a wary eye, at least, on the growing celebrity of his subordinate on Lindisfarne.

As Wilfrid tended more and more towards worldly pomp and pageantry, Cuthbert yearned with ever-increasing intensity for a less and less worldly life-style. He craved solitude, not to escape from the cares of the world but as a means of coming closer to God. Although he had always been a gregarious man by nature, a man who had thoroughly enjoyed the task of entertaining visitors as guest-master of the monastery of Ripon, at the core and centre of his being he felt a profound compulsion to become a recluse, a holy hermit. From his earliest days as prior of Lindisfarne he would steal away from time to time and retreat into prayer and meditation:

> Now indeed at the first beginning of his solitary life, he retired to a certain place in the outer precincts of the monastery which seemed to be more secluded.

This 'certain place in the outer precincts of the monastery', in Bede's words, was a formal place of retreat known as the hermitage. Such sanctuaries, especially island sanctuaries, were the most characteristic, and the most extreme, of all the institutions of the early Celtic church.

Lindisfarne had its own hermitage right from the earliest times of the monastic foundation — a tiny scrap of an island, only a quarter of an acre in extent, lying barely a hundred yards off the south-west corner, which had been used as a retreat by the good St Aidan himself. It was formerly called Thrush Island, or Hob Thrush; but because of its association with Cuthbert, it is now familiarly known as St Cuthbert's Isle, or even more familiarly as Cuddie's Isle.

Like Lindisfarne itself, it is only islanded at high tide; at low tide it offers relatively easy access to anyone prepared to scramble over a ridge of slippery rocks. From the beach on Lindisfarne it looks an unassuming sort of place, just a hump of land girt with a low rampart of black dolerite rock to keep the sea at bay, and capped with a covering of green. Today it is crowned by a simple but impressive wooden cross that was erected in the 1930s on the site of the altar of a small medieval chapel whose remains are still visible, if only just. At the time of the Dissolution of the Monasteries, this chapel was dedicated to St Cuthbert; it was about 25 ft long and 13 ft broad, and it lay within a rather curious curved enclosure wall, forming a kind of platform, that earlier antiquarians took to be some sort of breakwater.

St Cuthbert's Isle was excavated (after a fashion) in the 1880s by

MUSSEL-HUNTERS ALL

Man is not the only creature that fancies mussels for tea. The Common Mussel (*Mytilus edulis*) is an important part of the diet of many shore-birds, including the Eider duck, that aristocrat of the duck family with its noble Roman nose.

Eider ducks have long had the reputation of being 'tame', perhaps because the brave mother duck refuses to abandon her nest when closely approached by humans. By tradition they were St Cuthbert's favourite birds, which is why they are still called 'Cuddy's ducks' on Holy Island. In the 12th century a Durham monk called Reginald wrote:

> They are so tame that they nest inside dwelling-houses, where they come to the table, and construct their nests under your bed, yes, and even under bed-coverings . . .

A century later, another monk wrote:

> Such is the tameness they derive from the sanctity of the place, or rather from those who by their residence have sanctified it, that they will allow themselves to be seen and touched by man.

The tradition of tameness lives on to this day, even on the mussel-beds where man and eider are theoretically in competition. In Budle Bay, just north of Bamburgh, a team of three mussel-fishermen from Lindisfarne — George 'Steptoe' Kyle and his father George 'Dodo' Kyle, and George 'Bash' Moody — regularly husband and harvest the mussel-beds in the hand-numbing cold of winter. They have become a familiar presence to the resident eiders there, which now come and feed trustingly around their feet on broken or discarded mussels — just as they did in St Cuthbert's time. In fact, says Steptoe Kyle, they can be a bit of a nuisance, getting in the way of the work.

Three of the regulars are particularly tame: two ducks (one of them nicknamed Ringer because she was ringed as a fledgeling) and a lone drake, conspicuously handsome in his black and white plumage. The drake is so tame that he will take titbits from the hand. But it's noticeable that when the men throw a handful of mussels to the waiting eiders, it is always the mousey-brown ducks that get there first if, in soccer parlance, it's a fifty-fifty ball.

There's a moral for mankind there, somewhere . . .

S.G.M.

84

Major-General Sir William Crossman, the great-grandfather of the present Lord of the Manor and owner of Lindisfarne, Col Humphrey Crossman. The gallant General had been with the Royal Engineers during his army career, which may well have given him a taste for digging things up when he retired from the army and inherited Lindisfarne. On St Cuthbert's Isle he 'laid bare', in his own words, the remains of the walls, and found that the chapel had a door with a stone lintel on the south side, with a set of well-cut stone steps leading up to it that are still visible. Professor Rosemary Cramp of Durham University believes that these features could well be medieval.

As well as the chapel, Crossman detected the remains of another building in the south-east corner of the island, where the vegetation today is at its thickest. Crossman hazarded the guess that it was a two-roomed structure consisting of a bedroom and a kitchen with its own hearth. Close to these foundations he found the remains of some still earlier work, which 'he would venture to suggest' might 'fix the site of the cell to which St Cuthbert was wont to retire'.

That particular site is now so drowned in scurvy grass that it's impossible to make anything of it with the naked eye. General Crossman was doubtless right in associating it with the original hermitage, but it takes a considerable exercise of the imagination to do so now. It didn't inhibit Sir Walter Scott, however, in his lengthy romantic poem *Marmion*:

> But fain St Hilda's nuns would learn
> If on a rock by Lindisfarne
> St Cuthbert sits and toils to frame
> The sea-borne beads that bear his name.
> Such tales had Whitby's fishers told,
> And said they might his shape behold,
>   And hear his anvil sound:
> A deadened clang, — a huge dim form
> Seen but and heard when gathering storm
>   And night were closing round.
> But this, a tale of idle fame,
> The nuns of Lindisfarne disclaim.

No matter that there were never any nuns on Lindisfarne — it's a pretty legend, this evocation of the spectre of Cuthbert glimpsed in storm and gathering dark, busy at his anvil forging 'the sea-borne beads that bear his name'. St Cuthbert's beads, as they are called, or just Cuddie's beads, are in fact the fossil-fragments of small marine creatures, lily-shaped crinoids of the family Echinodermata (which also includes sea urchins and starfish), and are properly called *Crinoidea* or, more colourfully, Feather-stars. Today these crinoids swim about freely; but in their earliest form, back in Palaeozoic times, the animal itself was perched on a long stalk which anchored it to the sea bottom. This stalk was made up of a series of calcareous discs, like vertebrae, anything up to three feet long. The animal was shaped like the calyx of a sea-lily with five pairs of coloured, feathery arms gathering in any food that floated by. When the animal died, the stalk disintegrated, and it is these fossilised, lead-coloured discs which form the 'beads' associated with St Cuthbert. They can be found, albeit with difficulty, on the beach opposite the islet; and the fanciful can thread them into rosaries to reinforce the association . . .

Others, less romantically, take their fishing-rods across and sit it out at high tide, contentedly angling for their supper in the shape of small flounder-like sand-dabs. In the spring, most appropriately, they can enjoy the company of two or three nesting pairs of Eider ducks, Cuthbert's favourite birds — Cuddie's ducks, to give them their local name.

We do not know how often, or for how long at a time, Cuthbert would go into retreat on St Cuthbert's Isle. But he must soon have found it all too accessible — for others; paradoxically, the more a hermit sought solitude, the more his solitude would be invaded by pilgrims anxious to imbibe from him the wisdom and insight he was presumed to be gaining by his undistracted communings with God! At all events, St Cuthbert's Isle was to be only an apprenticeship for the ultimate eremitical fulfilment of his life:

> When he had fought there in solitude for some time with the invisible enemy, by prayer and fasting, he sought a place of combat farther and more remote from mankind, aiming at greater things.

Hull-down to the south he could always see the uninhabited Farne Islands beckoning to him, just as they had once beckoned to St Aidan as a place of retreat during Lent. And in 676, some twelve years after his appointment as prior of Lindisfarne, he sought permission from the abbot, Eata, to go and seek solitude on the Inner Farne. He was then about 42 years old:

> Now after he had completed many years in that same monastery, he joyfully entered into the remote solitudes which he had long desired, sought and prayed for, with the good will of that same abbot and also of the brethren. For he rejoiced because, after a long and blameless active life, he was now held worthy to rise to the repose of divine contemplation.

8 The Hermit of Farne

The Farne Islands are a group of about 25 lumps of black and uninviting rock thrusting out of the North Sea some two miles off the coast of Northumberland. They form the eastern terminal of a remarkable geological formation of igneous rock known as the Great Whin Sill; this came about many millions of years ago, when cracks in the earth's crust were filled under intense pressure with molten rock which, when it cooled, formed stretches of extrusive dykes that surface here and there like the tumbledown remains of ancient walls.

The largest of the group, and the nearest to the mainland, is Farne Island itself, which is usually known as the Inner Farne. At low tide it measures some 16 acres; most of it is bare rock, but there are about 5 acres of vegetation clinging to life on a thin covering of peaty soil — chiefly maritime grasses like Red Fescue (*Festuca Rubra*) and Sea Meadow-Grass (*Puccinellia fasciculata*) and Yorkshire Fog (*Holcus lanatus*), starred in season with the white flowers of Sea Campion (*Silene maritima*) and the delicate pink of Thrift (*Armeria maritima*). The west and south sides of the island are ramparted with precipitous basalt cliffs some 80 or 90 feet high, with a sentinel rock stack standing proud off the southern tip. At the western corner there is a large rock fissure called the Churn; when wind and tide conspire, the sea boils into the fissure and barges its way up to a blow-hole at the top, spouting through it up to a height of 50 or even 100 feet like a plumed geyser. To the east, the surface of the island tilts down to sea level to a tiny patch of sandy beach which affords a haven for small boats: St Cuthbert's Cove.

A forbidding, inhospitable place, you might think — bleak and sterile. But sterile it certainly is not. It fairly teems with life; for the Inner Farne is home and sanctuary for literally thousands of birds: Terns dancing and darting like swallows, colonies of Shags and Cormorants ungainly as people walking in frogman's flippers, Guillemots and Razorbills looking stiff and awkward as a male-voice choir in their penguin suits, Kittiwakes constantly calling out their name, Fulmars clucking hoarsely or spitting venomously at intruders, Eider ducks placidly incubating eggs in unlikely tufts of grass, clown-nosed Puffins squatting in incongruous solemnity.

Such is the Inner Farne now, and such it was more than 13 centuries ago when Cuthbert first set foot on the island to build himself, as Bede puts it, *'civitatem suo aptam imperio'* — 'a city fitted for his rule, and in it houses equally suited to the city'. But first of all he had to deal with the indigenous inhabitants:

> No one had been able to dwell alone undisturbed upon this island before Cuthbert, the servant of the Lord, on account of the phantoms of demons who dwelt there; but when the soldier of Christ entered, armed with the 'helmet of salvation, the shield of faith, and the sword of the spirit which is the Word of God, all the fiery darts of the wicked one' were quenched, and the wicked foe himself was driven far away together with the whole crowd of his satellites.

According to a later source, the demons were banished by Cuthbert to the nearest islands to the west, the twin Weduns or 'Wideopens'. There is a graphic description of them in the *Life of Bartholomew*, written early in the 13th century by Geoffrey of Coldingham (this Bartholomew, who died in 1193, was one of a succession of hermits who followed Cuthbert as inmates of Farne):

> The brethren, when enjoying their rest after labour, have seen them on a sudden, clad in cowls and riding upon goats, black in complexion, short in stature, their countenances most hideous, their heads long, the appearance of the whole troop horrible. Like soldiers they brandished in their hands lances, which they darted after the fashion of war.

The elements of the 'city' which Cuthbert built for his hermitage on Farne are only briefly sketched in the *Anonymous Life:*

> Digging down almost a cubit into the ground, through very hard and stony rock, he made a space to dwell in. He also built a marvellous wall another cubit above it by placing together and compacting with earth, stones of such great size as none would believe except those who knew that so much of the power of God was in him; therein he made some little dwelling-places from which he could see nothing except the heavens above.

There was one huge block of stone that defeated all the efforts of four monks to fetch in their cart from another part of the island; nevertheless, on their next visit, they found the monster stone snugly positioned in the wall where Cuthbert had wanted it placed — evidence to them of angelic aid.

The Venerable Bede, who elsewhere in his writings displays considerable interest in old construction techniques, such as the

89

ST CUTHBERT'S OTHER ISLAND

The teeming wildlife on the Inner Farne, both fauna and flora, is very much the same today as it was all those centuries ago when Cuthbert came here for his last retreat: all except for two alien incomers. One is a tiny yellow-flowering plant called *Amsinckia intermedia*, a rare import from California, which arrived in a sack of poultry-feed at the turn of the century. The other is the Rabbit — dozens of them, in an extraordinary range of colours from orange to white; they are the wild descendants of domesticated rabbits introduced by the lighthouse-keepers of old, for the table.

Of physical evidence of Cuthbert's sojourn nothing now remains, alas. It's thought that his oratory cell was on the site of the present island Tower, built in 1500 by Prior Thomas Castell of Durham after the Convent of Durham had established a small Benedictine monastery on Cuthbert's island hermitage in 1255; the seepage well in the ground floor is believed to be Cuthbert's original home well. Prior Castell's Tower, after serving as a fortlet and a beacon lighthouse, now provides accommodation for the National Trust wardens.

Nearby stands St Cuthbert's Chapel, originally built around 1370, which had become derelict by the 19th century, when it was completely renovated by Archdeacon Charles Thorp of Durham in 1848. Only a built-up window in the south wall survives from the original fabric. The interior contains some handsome 17th century woodwork that came from Durham Cathedral, as did the fine canopied oak stalls. Very occasionally, divine service is conducted there.

Down by the landing-stage there is a little stone building known as the 'Fishe House', which is believed to be the remains of a primitive guest-house built by the Benedictine monks for pilgrims; it is more than likely that it was built on the site of Cuthbert's original *hospitium*.

According to The Venerable Bede, Cuthbert erected a Cross at the south-east of the island, where the lighthouse now stands. It was probably of wood. But Professor Rosemary Cramp of Durham University believes that a fragment of a stone Cross, now in the Cathedral collection at Durham, belongs to an ancient Cross carved on Lindisfarne and erected on the Inner Farne in honour of the saint.

S.·9·M·

measurements of Hadrian's Wall, gives a more detailed account of Cuthbert's hermitage:

> It is a structure almost round in plan, measuring about four or five poles [*60-90 feet*] from wall to wall. The wall itself on the outside is higher than a man standing upright; but inside he made it higher still by cutting away the living rock of the floor, so that the pious inhabitant could see nothing except the sky from his dwelling, thus restraining both the lust of his eyes and of the thoughts, and lifting the whole bent of his mind to higher things. He made this same wall not of cut stone nor of bricks and mortar, but just of unworked stone and turf that he had removed from the excavation in the middle of the dwelling . . .
>
> He had two dwellings in his dwelling-place, namely an oratory and another habitation suitable for common uses. He finished the walls by digging and cutting away the natural soil both inside and outside, and he placed on them roofs of rough-hewn timber and straw.
>
> Away at the landing-place for the island there was a larger house in which the brethren who visited him could be received and rest, and not far away there was a well for their use.

There was another structure, however, which both sources refer to delicately as 'a certain small building' or 'a hut, very small but suited for his daily needs' — a latrine, to put it bluntly. For this he needed a 12-foot baulk of timber to place over a cleft in the rock which was flushed by the tides twice a day. The monks whom he asked to bring him the necessary timber on their next visit unaccountably forgot to do so; but no matter — 'the very sea', as Bede put it, 'was ready to do service to the servant of Christ when he needed it'. That same night, the tide providentially brought in a piece of driftwood of the exact length required, and deposited it precisely on the spot where it needed to be placed for the 'little house' . . .

There were other daily necessities to cope with, particularly the problem of water-supply. The guest-house (*hospitium*) he built down by the landing-stage had its own well, conveniently placed for the use of visitors, but Cuthbert himself had none. Yet this, too, was provided by miraculous aid: at Cuthbert's bidding, the monks dug down into the rock surface inside the enclosure wall of his hermitage, and presently, in response to Cuthbert' prayers, fresh water appeared in the hole. The *Anonymous Life*, no doubt on the analogy of Moses striking the rock, claims that it was 'a fountain of living water which broke out of the rocky ground and poured forth before him'; Bede, more circumspectly and more accurately, merely notes that it was simply 'water that came from within the rock . . . it never bubbled over and covered the floor, nor failed through exhaustion of its supply'. The Anonymous Author claimed to have tasted it, and enjoyed it:

> The great sweetness of its flavour we have proved and still thankfully prove by tasting it, even until the present day. And that servant of God and hermit declared, as I learned from the report of most trustworthy people, that he enjoyed in that God-given water the sweetness of every kind of drink.

Today there are two shallow wells on the island, which it is tempting to associate with St Cuthbert. As Bede said, they are not springs, nor are they artesian (self-pumping) wells; they are seepage or drainage wells, with an excellent recovery rate of about 20 gallons an hour. But as for 'the great sweetness of its flavour' — the water tastes not only brackish, but is highly polluted. Laboratory tests have shown that its contamination level is three times higher than samples taken from the outlet area of the local sewer; it is definitely not for drinking, and should only be used for washing after being thoroughly boiled. The pollution is caused by the covering of birds' droppings on the island — the rainwater leaches through it before seeping into the wells.

The other problem concerned provisions. At first, Cuthbert ate bread brought over by visitors from Lindisfarne; but he wanted to be self-sufficient, so he asked for tools and some wheat to sow. This proved somewhat optimistic, given the conditions on Farne Island; even though the wheat was sown in spring-time, not a blade of corn appeared. It was now midsummer, but despite the lateness of the season, Cuthbert decided to try barley instead — and this time an abundant crop sprang up. No sooner did this harvest begin to ripen, however, than it was attacked by flocks of birds which set to with a will, eagerly gobbling up the grain. According to Bede, it took only a gentle word of rebuke from Cuthbert to make them desist:

> 'Why', he said, 'do you touch the crops that you do not sow? Or is it, perchance, that you have greater need of them than I? If, however, you have received permission from God, do what He has allowed you; but if not, depart and do not injure any more the possessions of another.'
> Thus he spoke, and at the first sound of his commands, the whole multitude of birds departed and thenceforward refrained altogether from attacking his crops.

Perhaps exasperated farmers should try installing Cuthberts in their fields, instead of scarecrows!

On another occasion when he was working in his field, he saw a pair

SLUM-CLEARANCE FOR SEALS

They look so helpless and appealing, with those melting human eyes. How could anyone bear to kill a seal pup?

Yet that was the agonising decision the National Trust had to make over the Farne Islands, which are the breeding ground of one of Britain's largest colonies of Grey Seals (*Halichoerus grypus*). The trouble was gross overcrowding. After the last War, the seal population began to increase at an alarming rate, probably as a result of protective legislation, and the fragile ecology of the islands was becoming seriously threatened. The impact of thousands of Grey Seals hauling their massive bodies all over the ground every autumn to pup was causing severe erosion of the thin layer of soil. This in turn was affecting the ability of Puffins to excavate their nesting-burrows — and this at a time when their populations over much of Britain was declining.

From the seals' point of view, too, the overcrowding was taking its toll. Grey Seals are notoriously messy on their breeding grounds; but the Farne Islands were becoming a positive seal-slum, with rotting carcasses spreading infection and disease. The rate of infant mortality was relatively high, at 20%, partly because of the sheer density of animals. Wandering pups which had lost their mothers were attacked by other, normally placid, females; and fights between massive bulls also took their toll of the helpless youngsters.

And so, for the good of the seals themselves and for the sake of the islands' ecology, the National Trust reluctantly decided on a seal cull to reduce the population. The first attempts, early in the 1960s, were not entirely successful, and the problems continued. So in 1972 the Trust steeled its collective nerve again and embarked on a major operation designed eventually to reduce the population of about 8,000 seals by some 3,000 adults and pups. This time it seems to have been much more effective; since 1975 the production of pups has been falling. In addition, wardens are employed to frighten off seals trying to come ashore on particularly vulnerable areas — by shooting them, if necessary, as a last resort.

Seal-watchers are now keeping their fingers crossed that the position has been stabilised. But seals are unpredictable animals. Just like humans, really . . .

94

of ravens, which had been on the island for a long time, tearing straw from the thatch of the guest-house to make nesting-material. With a gesture of his right hand, Cuthbert bade them refrain, but the ravens ignored him. That got Cuthbert's dander up (or, as the Anonymous Author puts it, 'at last his spirit was moved'):

> Sternly bidding them in the name of Christ to depart from the island, he banished them. Without any pause or delay, they deserted their home according to his command. But after three days, one of the two returned to the feet of the man of God as he was digging the soil, and settling above the furrow with outspread wings and drooping head, began to croak loudly, with humble cries asking his pardon and indulgence. And the servant of Christ, recognising their penitence, gave them pardon and permission to return.
>
> And those ravens at the same hour having won peace, both returned to the island with a little gift; for each held in its beak about half of a piece of hog's lard, which it placed before his feet. He pardoned their sin, and they remain there until today.
>
> Trustworthy witnesses who visited him told me that for the space of a whole year they greased their skin-boots with the lard.

Mention of boots raises a rather unsavoury aspect of Cuthbert's sojourn on the Inner Farne. It seems that he had a marked reluctance to take off his skin-boots more than once a year, for the ritual annual feet-washing on Maundy Thursday (the 'mandatory' Thursday before Easter). It sounds almost too revolting to contemplate; but Bede justifies this conspicuous disregard for hygiene on the ground that 'he had so far withdrawn his mind from the care of his body and fixed it on the care of his soul alone that, having once been shod with the boots of skin that he was accustomed to use, he would wear them for whole months together.'

In his first years as a hermit on Farne, Cuthbert's seclusion was by no means total. He had frequent visits from the monks of Lindisfarne (it was they, for instance, who persuaded him to take off his boots on Maunday Thursdays so that they could wash his feet), and Cuthbert would emerge from his hermitage to receive and entertain them at the guest-house. Later he tended to remain immured in his cell, according to Bede:

> Then, when his zeal for perfection grew, he shut himself up in his hermitage, and, remote from the gaze of men, he learned to live a solitary life of fasting, prayers and vigils, rarely having conversations from within his cell with visitors, and that only through the window. At first he opened this and rejoiced to see and

be seen by the brethren with whom he spoke; but, as time went on, he shut even that, and opened it only for the sake of giving his blessing or for some other definite necessity.

Despite his increasing withdrawal from worldly matters, streams of visitors, not only from the neighbourhood of Lindisfarne but also from what Bede calls 'the remoter parts of Britain', made their way across the water to Cuthbert's tiny 'city', bringing to him their sins, their fears, their ailments, their troubles, in the hope of receiving consolation from a man of such obvious sanctity:

> Nor did their hope deceive them. For no one went away from him without enjoying his consolation, and no one returned accompanied by that sorrow of mind which he had brought thither.

The Anonymous Author ends his account of this distinct and memorable period of Cuthbert's life and career (Book III) with a pithy paragraph of lingering tenderness:

> And so for several years he continued to live a solitary life, cut off from the sight of men; but in all conditions he bore himself with unshakeable balance, for he always kept the same appearance and the same spirit. At all hours he was happy and joyful, neither looking sorrowful at the remembrance of sins nor elated by the loud praises of those who marvelled at his way of life. His conversation, seasoned with salt, consoled the sad, instructed the ignorant, and appeased the angry, for he persuaded them all to put nothing before the love of Christ. And he placed before the eyes of all the greatness of future benefits and the mercy of God, and revealed the favours already bestowed: namely, that God spared not His own Son, but delivered Him up for the salvation of us all.

But there was one matter that *did* cause Cuthbert much perturbation of mind and spirit: the deathbed prophecy by his old friend and godfather, prior Boisil of Melrose, that he was destined to become a bishop. It was the very last thing that Cuthbert wanted; but in his heart he knew that one day the prophecy would come true — and he quailed at the prospect.

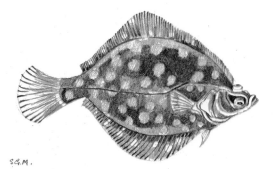

S.G.M.

9 Bishop Cuthbert

In the year 684, Cuthbert broke his self-imposed seclusion in his hermitage on Farne to make a rare, if not indeed unique, visit 'abroad', at the request of the abbess Ælfflæd of Whitby. Ælfflæd, who had succeeded St Hilda at Whitby in 680, was the daughter of King Oswiu of Northumbria and had long been formally pledged to a life of service: on the eve of the fateful Battle of Winwæd in 655 between Oswiu and King Penda of Mercia, her father had vowed, if victorious, to dedicate his infant daughter's life to God.

Cuthbert had already been of help to her, at long distance. She had been afflicted with a disease that crippled her so severely that she could neither walk nor even stand upright; one day she had thought about Cuthbert, and had inwardly wished that she had something that belonged to him, for she was sure that thereby she would be healed. Soon afterwards, a messenger arrived from Farne, bringing with him a gift from Cuthbert. It was a linen girdle, which she put on at once; within three days, she was fully restored to health. (Bede relates that he was told this story by a former abbot of Lindisfarne, Herefrith, who had heard it from the lips of Ælfflæd herself).

And now, in 684, she sent an urgent message to Cuthbert, saying that she wanted to talk over 'matters of importance'. It was agreed that they should meet on Coquet Island, at the mouth of the River Coquet, as a convenient staging-post between Whitby and Farne, for there was a celebrated community of monks there, apparently. It transpired that what Ælfflæd wanted to talk about was politics; she knew that her brother, King Ecgfrith of Northumbria, was planning to appoint Cuthbert as bishop, and she wanted to find out from Cuthbert, with his prophetic powers, what fate lay in store for Ecgfrith and the throne of Northumbria.

To understand the significance of this meeting we have to go back in history a few years. King Oswiu had died in 670 after a long reign in which he had done much to consolidate the position of the church in Northumbria and reconcile the conflict between the Celtic and Roman orders. He was succeeded by his second son, Ecgfrith (the eldest son,

Alhfrith, sub-king of Deira, had disappeared from the scene by then, *cf* ch 7). Ecgfrith was a Christian, of course; but he was also a warrior-king in the pagan Germanic tradition, a man of robust likes and dislikes, autocratic and overbearing by nature. At first he seems to have been on friendly terms with bishop Wilfrid of York, who then ruled the ecclesiastical roost in Northumbria with all but royal pomp and power; but Wilfrid overreached himself when he persuaded Ecgfrith's virgin wife, Queen Æthelthryth (St Audrey), to take the veil rather than consummate the marriage — having persuaded her to give him a site at Hexham on which to found a monastery. Æthelthryth abandoned the chilly marriage bed to become the founder and abbess of Ely, leaving Ecgfrith with a smouldering resentment of Wilfrid that would seize the first opportunity for revenge. This resentment was fanned by Ecgfrith's second wife, Iurminburg, who played cunningly on her husband's latent jealousy of Wilfrid's wealth and magnificence.

Ecgfrith's chance of revenge came in 677, when Archbishop Theodore of Canterbury was persuaded to divide Wilfrid's diocese into three. When Wilfrid objected too strenuously he was deposed without ceremony, and retired to Rome to lodge an appeal with the Pope himself. Meanwhile Eata, the abbot of Lindisfarne and Melrose, was appointed bishop of Bernicia (one of the three new divisions of Northumbria), with the choice of a seat either at Lindisfarne or Wilfrid's new monastery of Hexham.

In 680, Wilfrid came back from Rome with a written document from the papal synod upholding his complaint, confirming him in his possession of his monasteries at Hexham and Ripon, and restoring him to the see of York with powers to appoint new bishops of his own choice. But King Ecgfrith would have none of it. Not only did he refuse to accept the papal judgement — he had Wilfrid thrown into prison for nearly a year and then expelled from Northumbria. Archbishop Theodore made no overt move to protect Wilfrid; indeed, he took the opportunity of confirming Eata as bishop of Lindisfarne and appointed another bishop to Hexham.

The new bishop of Hexham did not last long before being deposed for some unexplained reason, and by 684 the see was vacant. The church was in disarray. In addition, war-clouds were gathering to the north, where Ecgfrith's aggressive policy towards the Picts in Scotland was leading him into open conflict with his Scots kinsman, King Brudei mac Bili.

Such were the circumstances in which the abbess Ælfflæd sought her urgent meeting with Cuthbert on Coquet Island:

> Suddenly, in the midst of their talk, she fell at his feet and adjured him by the terrible awe-inspiring name of the King of Heaven and of His angels to tell her how long her brother Ecgfrith would live and rule over the kingdom of the English.

Cuthbert tried to avoid giving a direct answer, but eventually let her know obliquely that Ecgfrith would perish within a year. The woman wept bitter tears; but then, drying her eyes, she adjured him to tell her who would succeed to the throne, since Ecgfrith had no sons or brothers. This was not strictly true, however; Ecgfrith had an illegitimate half-brother, Aldfrith (not to be confused with his disgraced brother, Alhfrith!), the son of King Oswiu and an Irish princess called Fina. This Aldfrith was a man of deep scholarly interests, who was at that time living in exile on the island of Iona.

Faced with Ælfflæd's straight question about the succession to the throne, Cuthbert gave a riddling reply:

> 'Ecgfrith will have a successor whom you will embrace with as much sisterly affection as if he were Ecgfrith himself.'
> 'I beseech you,' she said, 'tell me where he is.'
> Cuthbert replied: 'You see how this great and spacious sea abounds in islands? It is easy for God to provide from any of these a man to place over the kingdom of the English.'

Ælfflæd understood the reply to mean Aldfrith, and was satisfied — as well she might be; for Aldfrith was destined to reign for two brilliant decades (685–705) of what has been called the Golden Age of Northumbria, when scholarship and the arts flourished — the period which saw the creation of the magnificent Lindisfarne Gospels (*cf* ch 10). But she was still curious to know how Cuthbert would react if he were appointed to the vacant bishopric of Hexham. Once again, Cuthbert replied in prophetic vein:

> 'I know that I am not worthy of such a rank; nevertheless I cannot escape anywhere from the decree of the Ruler of Heaven. Yet if He has determined to subject me to so great a burden, I believe that after a short time He will set me free, and perhaps, after not more than two years, He will send me back to my accustomed rest and solitude.'

That same autumn, at a place called 'Twyford' near the River Aln (probably Alnmouth), Archbishop Theodore held a synod, which was also attended by King Ecgfrith. At this assembly, Cuthbert was unanimously appointed bishop of Hexham. Letters and messengers were sent to Farne Island, but nothing would induce Cuthbert to leave his hermitage. Eventually King Ecgfrith himself, accompanied by bishop Trumwine of Abercorn in West Lothian in Scotland, sailed to the island with a retinue of distinguished churchmen:

> They all knelt down and adjured him in the name of the Lord, with tears and prayers, until at last they drew him, also shedding many tears, from his sweet retirement and led him to the synod. When he had come, in spite of his reluctance he was overcome by the unanimous will of them all and compelled to submit his neck to the yoke of the bishopric.

By a happy arrangement with his former abbot, Eata, now the bishop of Lindisfarne, he was allowed to exchange sees: Eata took Hexham, and Cuthbert was appointed to the bishopric on his beloved Lindisfarne. He was consecrated by Archbishop Theodore at York on Easter Day, March 26, 685.

Meanwhile, King Ecgfrith was on the war-path again. In 684 he had sent an army to Ireland which wrought considerable havoc; and now, in the spring of 685, he launched an invasion of the province of the Picts, against all the advice of his counsellors and his new bishop, Cuthbert. Headstrong as ever, Ecgfrith paid no heed; he swept through the Lothians and into Fife, across the River Tay and into Angus. But here King Brudei lured Ecgfrith and his army into the narrow mountain passes of Strathmore; and at the ensuing battle of Nechtansmere (Dunnichen Moss, near Forfar) on Saturday, May 20, 685, his forces were annihilated and he himself killed. His personal bodyguard (*comitatus*) fell to a man, defending their stricken lord in true heroic tradition.

It so happened that Cuthbert was in Carlisle on his first episcopal visitation during the weekend of the battle. Queen Iurminburg was also there, staying at her sister's convent nearby to await news of the outcome of Ecgfrith's expedition. On the Saturday afternoon, while he was being taken on a tour of the impressive Roman ruins in the city, he became troubled in spirit, according to the *Anonymous Life*:

> The bishop meanwhile stood leaning on his supporting staff, with his head inclined towards the ground, and then he lifted up his eyes heavenwards again with a sigh and said, "Oh!oh!oh! I think that the war is over and that judgement has been given against our people in the battle.'
>
> Then when they urgently asked him what had happened and desired to know, he said evasively, 'Oh my sons, look at the sky, consider how wonderful it is, and think how inscrutable are the judgements of God', and so forth.

MIGRANT VIKINGS

I should declare an interest here; to me, the most eagerly awaited winter visitors to the Nature Reserve — to Fenham Flats in particular — are the Whooper Swans (*Cygnus cygnus*). The reason is quite simple: they come from my own homeland, Iceland.

They are big, solid, confident creatures, their necks proud and straight, their yellow, black-tipped bills so bright that even their cheeks seem yellow, too. They carry their Icelandic passports, in a way: the plumage of their heads and upper necks is stained a rusty red from constant summer feeding in Icelandic lakes and pools that are rich in iron compounds.

On Lindisfarne they congregate in a herd of up to, sometimes over, 400 birds — the largest wintering herd in England. Not every Whooper Swan in Iceland takes the high road to Holy Island of an autumn. Many of them stay at home all winter, if they are lucky enough to have been born and brought up in areas warmed by the natural hotsprings that seethe and simmer just below the surface — a sort of geothermal central heating of the marshlands. On Lindisfarne, the main attraction seems to be the underwater flowering Eel grass (*Zostera angustifolia*), which is the principal ingredient in the Whooper Swan's diet — as well as that of Wigeon and the rare and welcome Pale-bellied Brent Goose.

They are aggressive, noisy fellows, Whooper Swans, trumpeting their presence to all who care to hear — hence their name. I think of them as migrant Vikings still, born with a certain swagger to their step, quick to anger and pugnacity if they suspect their territorial rights are being threatened.

In his *A Naturalist on Lindisfarne* (1946), Richard Perry described then with exquisite skill:

> As I approached closer they began to walk over the mud towards the Lough, trumpeting more urgently, cob and pen sounding their respective *gwuk* and *gwoog* antiphonally, as pairs of the larger Gulls will do. Once in the water of the Goat they moved together in straight-necked groups and, with a continual dipping of high-carriaged heads, began to utter a kind of twittering trumpeting of divers musical notes — a beautiful medley of sound, as like a bugle-call as anything I had heard in Nature — before eventually taking wing in *silent* flight . . . until their bugling died away into an intermittent *whoomper, whoomper* . . .

102

> But after a few days they learned that it had been announced far and wide that a wretched and mournful battle had taken place at the very day and hour in which it had been revealed to him.

The Battle of Nechtansmere was of crucial historical importance. It was vitally important to the history of Scotland, for if Ecgfrith had won, Scotland might well have become a permanent province of the Anglian kingdom of Northumbria and become a mere extension of England. It was of tremendous importance to the cultural life of the north of England, because it brought to the throne of Northumbria the scholarly Aldfrith under whose patronage the arts would flourish as never before. And it was of considerable personal importance to Wilfrid, because the death of his implacable enemy, Ecgfrith, allowed a reconciliation with Archbishop Theodore and a restoration of much of his previous power; he was put in temporary charge of the bishopric of Hexham when bishop Eata died, and later was given York and Ripon as well, thus making him once more bishop over the whole of Northumbria with the exception of Cuthbert's diocese of Lindisfarne. Although it is nowhere stated in so many words, it was not a situation that Cuthbert could have found particularly comfortable or congenial.

Curiously enough, the accounts of Cuthbert's brief episcopate, both in Bede and the *Anonymous Life*, are disconcertingly perfunctory — what Sir Frank Stenton in his monumental *Anglo-Saxon England* called 'a mere tissue of miracles'. The Anonymous Author in particular seems at a loss for words:

> Though it is not in our power to narrate how he distinguished himself, yet it is nevertheless better to describe some part than to omit the whole. He continued with the utmost constancy to be what he had been before; he showed the same humility of heart, the same poverty of dress, and, being full of authority and grace, he maintained the dignity of a bishop without abandoning the ideal of the monk or the virtue of the hermit.

He is shown carrying out his episcopal and pastoral duties, faithfully and energetically: ordaining priests, administering confirmation, visiting remote villages afflicted by the plague, comforting the bereaved and healing the sick, often by seemingly miraculous means. He made the rounds of the monasteries in his diocese; he visited the abbess Ælfflæd at one of the daughter houses of Whitby, and dropped his knife at dinner in a state of shock when he saw a prophetic vision of the death of a pious shepherd on the estate; he visited the abbess Verca at South Shields, where the water he was drinking took on the taste of wine (it was Verca who sent him the linen cloth in which his body would be wrapped after his death); and he had a meeting with an old hermit friend, Herbert, who lived on an island in Derwentwater, to whom he confided his belief that he did not have much longer to live.

Although he was still only in his early fifties, his health was obviously beginning to fail him; the years of relentless austerities had taken their toll of even his strength and robust constitution:

> So, having spent two years in episcopal rule, Cuthbert the man of God, knowing in his spirit that the day of his departure was at hand, threw aside the burden of his pastoral care and determined to return to the strife of a hermit's life which he loved so well, and that as soon as possible, so that the flame of his old contrition might consume more easily the implanted thorns of worldly cares.

Right at the end of the year 686, Cuthbert retired again to his hermitage on Farne Island. He resigned his see, no doubt knowing that he did not have long to live. He kept the Christmas feast with the brethren on Lindisfarne, and then took boat for Farne:

> And when a crowd of brethren stood around him as he was about to go aboard his ship, one of them, an aged monk of venerable life, strong in the faith but now weakened in body by dysentery, said:
> 'Tell us, Lord Bishop, when we may hope for your return'.
> And the bishop, who knew the truth, gave a plain answer to this plain question, saying:
> 'When you bring my body back here.'

For nearly two months, Cuthbert was able to enjoy his new-found quiet and solitude again, until the onset of his final sickness. Here, Bede's account of the saint's death far surpasses the token mention in the *Anonymous Life*, for Bede had the advantage of a personal eye-witness account given to him by the then abbot of Lindisfarne, Herefrith, who ministered to Cuthbert during his dying days.

Cuthbert fell ill on a Wednesday, and remained very ill for three weeks. Herefrith had been on the island with some other monks for three days, and on the Wednesday morning he had approached the window of Cuthbert's cell for the usual benediction. Cuthbert came to the window, and Herefrith realised at once that he must have had an attack during the night. The monks had been planning to return to Lindisfarne that day, but Herefrith now begged Cuthbert to allow some of them to stay to look after him. Cuthbert, however, refused:

> 'Go on board your vessel and return home safe and sound. And when God has taken my spirit, bury me here on the south side of my oratory, to the east of the Holy Cross I have erected there."

He gave instructions that his body was to be wrapped in the cloth which had been given to him by the abbess Verca of South Shields, and buried in a stone sarcophagus they would find hidden under a pile of turf near the oratory.

Despite further entreaties, Cuthbert was adamant that they should leave, and return only 'at the proper time — when God wills and when He himself shall direct you'. Much against their will the monks departed, intending to return as soon as possible; but for five anxious days, storms at sea made the journey impossible. When they eventually managed to land on the island, they found Cuthbert lying in the guest-house he had built for visitors many years earlier. It was as if he had been waiting for their return, for the comfort of human company in his distress; but he said he had only left his cell in order that those who came to minister to him would not have to enter it.

The monks who had sailed the boat over had to return at once, leaving Herefrith to look after the sick man. Herefrith warmed some water and bathed a suppurating ulcer on his foot, and gave him some warmed wine to drink. It turned out that Cuthbert had been lying there helplessly for five days and nights. He had had no food except for five onions which he had kept under the covers of his bed — and even then, he had only nibbled at one of them to allay his feverish thirst.

Cuthbert was now extremely weak and wasted, and when the monks returned with the boat and the abbot Herefrith had to return to Lindisfarne, Cuthbert allowed two of the brethren to stay behind to minister to him — a priest called Beda, who had been accustomed to serve him personally, and an old monk called Walhstod who suffered from an apparently incurable dysentery.

Back on Lindisfarne, the monks were unhappy to hear of Cuthbert's desire to be buried on Farne Island, and several of them returned with Herefrith to try to persuade him to change his mind and allow his body to be interred on Lindisfarne. Cuthbert demurred at first: he had wanted to be buried on Farne Island because that was where he had fought his battle for the Lord, and also because he knew that after his death there would be an influx of 'criminals and fugitives' seeking sanctuary at his tomb, which would cause the monastery great inconvenience.

It was an inconvenience that the monks were eager to accept, however, and in the end he acceded to their pleas. He counselled them to bury him in the interior of the church on Lindisfarne so that the monks could visit his sepulchre when they wished, but could also exercise some control over others who might wish to do so.

As his end drew near, Cuthbert asked to be carried back to his little cell and oratory. It was nine o'clock on the morning of Tuesday, March 19, 687. No one had been allowed to enter the cell for years, but now the monks asked that one of them should be allowed to go inside with him. Cuthbert chose Walhstod, the monk who suffered from dysentery. At three o'clock in the afternoon, brother Walhstod emerged, miraculously cured of his illness, and bade the others enter. Cuthbert was lying in a corner of the oratory, opposite the altar; he was too weak to say much, but he struggled to deliver his farewell instructions and exhortations. He adjured them always to keep peace and charity among themselves, to be unanimous in their counsels, and to show hospitality and kindness to others. He also, rather surprisingly, commanded them to 'have no communion with those who depart from the unity of the Catholic peace, either in not celebrating Easter at the proper time or in evil living' — a backward reference to the Celtic-Roman clash over Easter which sounds rather more like Bede himself than Cuthbert. He gave a final injunction which hindsight might interpret as having been prophetic, in the light of what happened to his relics in later years:

> 'And if necessity compels you to choose between two evils, I would much rather that you take my bones from their tomb and carry them away with you to whatever place of rest God may decree, rather than consent to iniquity and put your necks under the yokes of schismatics.'

The dying saint passed the rest of the day and night in quiet prayer; and then, when it came time for the night office of Lauds and Matins, he received communion from Herefrith:

> And, raising his eyes to heaven and stretching out his hands aloft, he sent forth his spirit in the very act of praising God to the joys of the Heavenly Kingdom.

And so Cuthbert died, early in the morning of March 20, 687, just as his brethren on Farne Island were singing the Lauds and had reached the 59th Psalm (Psalm 60 in the Authorised Version), which begins: 'O God, thou hast cast us off and hast broken us down; thou hast been angry and hast had compassion on us'. One of the monks ran to higher ground and lit two torches as a signal to the monk manning the watch-tower on Lindisfarne, seven miles away. The watchman ran to the church where the assembled brethren also happened to be singing the same psalm. It seemed to them that this coincidence was a prophetic warning of trials and troubles which would afflict Lindisfarne in the year following the saint's death.

They washed the saint's body, wrapped his head in a head cloth, and placed the unconsecrated Host on his breast. He was then robed in his episcopal vestments, 'wearing his shoes in readiness to meet Christ', and then the body was wrapped in a shroud of waxed cloth. The cortege sailed for Lindisfarne, where the body was received by a great company and choirs of singers, and then placed in its stone sarcophagus and buried under the floor of the church to the right of the altar.

The monks had clearly expected miracles to happen at Cuthbert's tomb, and a few miracles duly occurred and were duly recorded: a demented boy was healed by means of some soil which had been moistened by the water in which the saint's body had been washed, and so on. But these in themselves were not sufficient to establish, or to explain, the potent and widespread cult that was to spring up round the name and relics of St Cuthbert; for that, we have to look to an event that occurred eleven years after Cuthbert's death — the exhumation of the saint's body for elevation, and the revelation that it was still incorrupt.

Exactly eleven years to the day after Cuthbert's death and entombment, on March 20, 698, the stone sarcophagus in which his body had been laid under the floor beside the altar was ceremonially opened, in order that the bones could be 'elevated' into a coffin-reliquary in the same place but above the floor, for greater ease of veneration — the equivalent of the formal canonisation of later times. The bishop of Lindisfarne, a learned monk called Eadberht, had given his permission, but was not present at the ceremony — he had retired to the hermitage on St Cuthbert's Isle for prayer and meditation during Lent. His retreat was rudely interrupted when a group of monks came bursting in on him in a state of intense agitation and excitement. They said that they had found the body of St Cuthbert completely undecayed after eleven years in the grave, as intact and whole as if it were still alive, the joints of the limbs still flexible, much more like a sleeping than a dead man, as Bede puts it. The *Anonymous Life* is even more graphic:

> The skin had not decayed nor grown old, nor the sinews become dry, making the body tautly stretched and stiff; but the limbs lay at rest with all the appearance of life and were still moveable at the joints. For his neck and knees were like those of a living man; and when they lifted him from the tomb they could·bend him as they wished. Moreover, none of his vestments and footwear which touched the flesh of his body was worn away.

Not only were all his garments undefiled, according to Bede; they seemed to be perfectly new and wondrously bright.

In their terror and amazement, the monks did not dare to touch the clothing that was nearest the skin; but they removed the 'outer garments' to show to the bishop, 'to show the miracle of his incorruption':

> He joyfully received these gifts and gladly listened to the story of the miracles, kissing the garments with great affection, as though they were still wrapped around the father's body.

The bishop ordered that the body should be wrapped in a new garment and enshrined in the light wooden chest which had been prepared for it as a reliquary; and the coffin was then placed on the pavement of the sanctuary, beside the altar. The *Anonymous Life* adds that the head-cloth in which his head had been wrapped was removed and that the new sandals which had been put on the body in 687 were replaced. There is no mention of the waxed linen winding-sheet that the abbess Verca had provided; but in addition to the sandals and the chasuble (the 'outer garments'), the monks put aside some bodily relics of the saint for future use, including some of his hair (according to Bede's *Ecclesiastical History*, this was used to cure a tumour on the eyelid of a young man at the monastery of Dacre, near Ripon, and was kept in a special reliquary at the Lindisfarne monastery). And although there is no specific documentary evidence to go by, it now seems safe to assume (Battiscombe, *The Relics of St Cuthbert*, p 25) that when St Cuthbert's body was elevated in 698, the coffin also contained the jewelled pectoral cross, the double-sided ivory comb and the portable silver-cased altar which are now on display, along with other Cuthbert relics, in the Treasury of Durham Cathedral.

And so Lindisfarne acquired a *bona fide* saint, complete with associated relics, elevated and canonised by general consent and the approval of the bishop; and the Cuthbert cult began.

Many people nowadays jib at the idea of 'sanctity' and 'miracles' — and most especially, the alleged miracle of physical incorruptibility. But the story told by the monks can easily be reconciled with commonsense explanations. It was not unusual for bodies, in early Christian times, to be superficially embalmed with a compound of myrrh and aloes, or bedded in the coffin in sand and salt. A body thus treated, particularly when wrapped in a waxed linen winding-sheet and interred in a stone sarcophagus in the dry, sandy soil of a place like Lindisfarne, could well have become mummified — at least sufficiently to make the monks *think* that the body was completely fresh and undecayed after eleven years. Normal folk-tale exaggeration would account for the rest.

The concept of 'sanctity', too, was differently regarded in medieval times than it is today. I sometimes think of it as a kind of posthumous honorary degree, conferred on people who had shown outstanding ability or conspicuous courage of their convictions; the Venerable Bede, for instance, was surely canonised for his literary achievements as much as for his piety. Politics came into it too: Cuthbert was probably no more saintly than someone like Aidan, for instance — but he was politically more acceptable as a 'figurehead saint' of the north than Aidan, because he represented both the old, passing Celtic tradition and the new dominant Roman ecclesiasticism. In his life and career, both as Celtic monk and Roman bishop, he symbolised and bridged the two cultures at a critical point in the history of the English church.

Nor must we overlook the sensational impact that the news of his uncorrupted body must have had at the time, on people who were conditioned to hope for miracles and expect miracles. Cuthbert was by no means unique in this respect. But it was this, above all, that established him as the greatest of all the Northumbrian saints and fired the extravagant cult associated with him for many centuries.

That cult, indeed, may have served to obscure the real person behind the accoutrements of legend. His burning asceticism and thirst for seclusion may be alien to contemporary ways of thinking, but in their own time they were considered the highest form of Christian endeavour. He was an endearing, likeable, kindly man, both human and humane, who carried his conviction to lengths that would be considered excessive, even absurd, today; some might even say that he loved his God not wisely but too well. But the passion and sincerity of that love can never be gainsaid. Let Bede have the last word on him, in his *Ecclesiastical History*:

> Above all else he was afire with heavenly love, unassumingly patient, devoted to unceasing prayer, and kindly to all who came to him for comfort. He regarded the labour of helping the weaker brethren with advice as equivalent to prayer, remembering that He who said 'Thou shalt love the Lord thy God' also said 'Love thy neighbour'.

10 The Lindisfarne Gospels

The year following Cuthbert's death in 687 was a time of great trial and tribulation for the little monastery on Lindisfarne, as Bede says:

> For after the man of God was buried, so great a blast of trial beat upon that church that many of the brethren chose to depart from the place rather than be in the midst of such dangers.

Although Bede mentions no names, it is difficult not to associate this period of trouble with the fact that Wilfrid took over the see of Lindisfarne, either on Cuthbert's death or, earlier, on his resignation from the bishopric. Wilfrid was now in charge of the whole Northumbrian diocese, just as he had been from 669 until its division in 678. Wilfrid had no cause to love Lindisfarne, even though he had received his early training there; Lindisfarne had been the heart and centre of the Celtic 'heresy' he had fought and defeated at the Synod of Whitby, Lindisfarne had provided three of the bishops who had usurped his diocese (Chad, Eata, and Cuthbert himself), Lindisfarne still seemed to have a potent hold on the affections and loyalties of the common people through the example of humble men like Aidan and Cuthbert. It would be no surprise if Wilfrid had taken the opportunity of paying off old scores — perhaps by trying to sweep away the last Celtic traditions of monastic observance and imposing an unadulterated Benedictine rule. To many of the brethren, devoted to Cuthbert's memory, such an imposition might well have been regarded as intolerable.

Be that as it may, the time of tribulation came to an end in 688 when a successor to Cuthbert was eventually appointed — Bishop Eadberht. Bede describes him thus in his *Ecclesiastical History:*

> . . . A man who was well known for his knowledge of the Scriptures, his obedience to God's commandments, and especially for his generosity. For each year, in accordance with the Law, he used to give a tenth of all beasts, grain, fruit and clothing to the poor.

No doubt Eadberht's unassuming piety, like that of Cuthbert, was much more to the liking of the Lindisfarne fraternity, and we hear of no

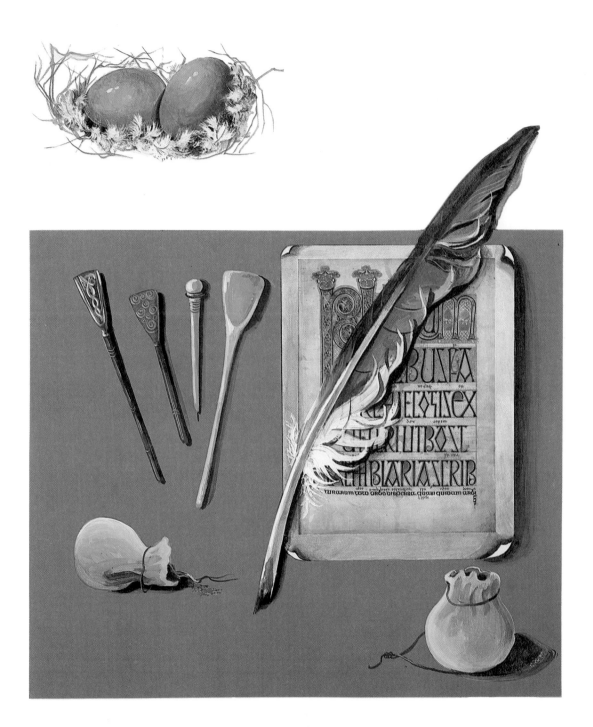

111

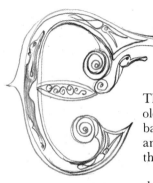

LINDISFARNE GOSPELS

The making of books and, even earlier, pages, is one of the oldest and most enduring technologies of mankind, dating back at least to the 4th century BC. And yet what a fragile and evanescent thing it is, a book, to which to commit man's thoughts and words for immortality!

In his little scriptorium in the monastery on Lindisfarne, the master-scribe Eadfrith had only the most elemental of materials with which to make the *Lindisfarne Gospels*. Vellum sheets of scraped and cured calfskin. Pens cut from goose-quills. Ink made from soot bound with nothing more elabo-rate than the whites of birds' eggs. A stylus or two of bronze or bone for sketching his designs on wax tablets and pricking their outlines onto the vellum. Sachets of colouring from plant or mineral pigments.

And, above all, consummate inspiration, skill, and time.

But after the completion of such a masterpiece, what then? Terentianus Maurus, a grammarian of the 3rd century AD living in Egypt, wrote: *Pro captu lectoris, habent sua fata libelli* ('Books have their fate, depending on the reader's capacity'). Books have always been at the mercy of the whims of history, of fire and storm and war and greed and fear and sheer human carelessness.

Simeon of Durham, the 13th century Northumbrian chronicler, tells a story, no doubt apocryphal, of the fate that very nearly overtook the precious *Lindisfarne Gospels* when the refugee Lindisfarne community tried to flee to Ireland in the 870s and their ship was overwhelmed by a storm:

> In this storm while the ship was lying over on her side, a copy of the Gospels, adorned with gold and precious stones, fell overboard and sank into the depths of the sea . . .
>
> Amidst their lamentations their pious patron came to their aid; for appearing in a vision to one of them, Hunred by name, he bade them seek at low-tide for the manuscript which had fallen from the ship into the midst of the waves . . .
>
> Accordingly they go to the sea and find that it had retired much further than it was accustomed; and after walking three miles or more they find the sacred man-uscript of the Gospels itself, exhibiting all its outer splendour of jewels and gold and all the beauty of its pages and writing within, as though it had never been touched by water . . .

further troubles there throughout the ten years of his episcopacy; and when he died, in May, 698, barely two months after the elevation of Cuthbert's body, he was accorded the signal honour of being buried in the saint's sarcophagus underneath Cuthbert's new coffin-reliquary.

For people like myself (and, I suspect, the Venerable Bede) who find Cuthbert much the more endearing of the two men, Wilfrid tends to come out of the Northumbrian saga with rather less lustre, despite the fact that he, too, was eventually canonised as a saint. Yet he was a man of outstanding ability in his own right, a shrewd administrator, an energetic ecclesiastical entrepreneur, and a man of considerable personal courage and character who seems to have borne the spectacular ups and downs of his chequered career with admirable fortitude. He was also a vigorous and successful evangelist; during his period of exile from Northumbria, he spent five years converting the pagan South Saxons in the 680s before his recall to the north after the death of King Ecgfrith at Nechtansmere in 685. He also did sterling work preaching the gospel in Frisia or Friesland (the Low Countries) on his way to Rome in 678-9 to appeal to the Pope against the division of his diocese of Northumbria.

Wilfrid was essentially a builder — a builder of churches, and a builder of empires. He created an empire of monasteries scattered all over England, which he governed through abbots responsible directly to himself. He rebuilt the tumbledown Paulinus church at York, importing stonemasons and glaziers from the continent. He built magnificent churches at Ripon and Hexham which were the glories of their age; although only the crypts of the originals now survive, they were long, soaring buildings of polished stone, the lead roofs supported by a forest of delicate columns, the windows glazed with multi-coloured glass, the walls covered with reliefs and paintings. He encouraged the making of magnificent books; his biographer, Ennius, records that he had a copy of the four Gospels (now lost, alas) made for his monastery at Ripon,

> . . . written out in letters of purest gold on purpled parchment, and illuminated. He also ordered jewellers to construct for the books a case all made of purest gold and set with most precious gems.

It was conspicuous aestheticism, compared with the conspicuous asceticism of the early days of Lindisfarne.

He filled his churches not only with fine books but with splendid music as well. His pupils who graduated from the monastery school at

Ripon carried the missionary torch of Northumbrian churchmanship far and wide — above all, his most celebrated pupil, Willibrord, who went to Frisia in 690 as a member of an English mission and became the principal evangelizer of the Low Countries, as Archbishop of Utrecht in Holland and the founder of a great monastery at Echternach in Luxembourg; there is a statue of him in the square in the town centre of Utrecht, and every year on Whit Tuesday there is a processional dance of pilgrims to his ornate tomb in the crypt of the basilica at Echternach.

But the chief credit for the brilliant flowering of learning and scholarship and book-production in Northumbria in the second half of the 7th century should go to Wilfrid's slightly older contemporary, Benedict Biscop, a Northumbrian nobleman and courtier of King Oswiu who renounced the worldly life at the age of 25 and established the great twin monasteries of Wearmouth (now Monkwearmouth) and Jarrow. He made no fewer than six journeys to Rome, spent two years at the famous monastery on the Mediterranean island of Lérins, off the coast of Cannes, and accompanied the newly consecrated Archbishop Theodore to England to take up his appointment at Canterbury in 669. But Benedict Biscop was no church careerist; his overwhelming passion was to build up an unparalleled collection of books, relics and religious ornaments for the two monasteries he founded — Wearmouth in 674, and its sister house five miles away and south of the River Tyne at Jarrow in 681.

These were the twin monasteries where the Venerable Bede spent all his working life. He entered Wearmouth as a child of seven in 680; a year or two later, when Benedict Biscop sent his prior, Ceolfrith, as founding abbot of Jarrow with 22 brethren (10 lay and 12 monks), young Bede went with them. For the rest of his long life (he died in 735), Bede was to stay at Jarrow, making journeys no farther afield than York and Lindisfarne. Benedict Biscop's great library became his world and his university, the source of all his erudition and inspiration.

From Bede, the torch of learning – and not just Northumbrian learning, but European learning — was handed on to his pupil, Egbert, who became archbishop of York and founded the celebrated School at York; and one of York's most notable scholars was Alcuin, who later became head of Charlemagne's palace school and his personal adviser on doctrinal issues. Alcuin played a crucial role in the revival of western learning in the Carolingian empire, as the outstanding missionary of Northumbrian learning and letters on the continent.

And thus the line of succession seeded in Lindisfarne stretched and branched luxuriantly from Northumbria to western Europe.

It could not have been achieved without enlightened royal patronage; and Northumbria was exceptionally fortunate in that respect in the second half of the 7th century. King Ecgfrith, however implacable his personal enmity towards Wilfrid, had no aversion to the Roman church as such — indeed, it was Ecgfrith who gave Benedict Biscop 50 hides (about ten square miles) of land at the mouth of the River Wear for his first monastery, and another grant of land at Jarrow in 681. But it was Ecgfrith's successor, his illegitimate half-brother, Aldfrith, who was the real catalyst of learning and the arts in all Britain.

Aldfrith was in all probability the first fully literate king that England had ever seen. As an illegitimate son of King Oswiu and an Irish princess, it must have seemed unlikely that he would ever inherit the throne, and so he was educated for the priesthood, probably at the monastery of Malmesbury in Wessex; from there he went to Ireland, where he studied for many years, and then on to Iona, where he was living at the time of his unexpected accession to the throne of Northumbria. He was long remembered in Ireland as a writer of Irish poetry. But in addition to his learning and artistic interests he showed consummate skill in the art of kingship. He inherited a kingdom almost in ruin, certainly in dire peril, as a result of Ecgfrith's disastrous expeditions against the Picts and the Irish; and throughout his 20-year reign he had to display considerable statecraft to keep his northern borders secure against the rampant Picts. Sir Frank Stenton summed him up well in his *Anglo-Saxon England*: 'He stands beside Alfred the Great of Wessex among the few Old English kings who combined skill in warfare with desire for knowledge'.

Within this new-found political security, King Aldfrith presided over what has been called the Golden Age of Northumbria, a period of astonishing brilliance in all the known arts and crafts of the time. Some of the most striking achievements were in sculpture, especially the tall, sculptured stone crosses of which the Ruthwell Cross in Dumfriesshire is such a supreme example. For the last hundred years, this magnificent Cross, soaring to a height of 18 ft, has stood in a specially-built apsidal extension to the village church. The art-work is clearly southern in inspiration, figure-carving of profound humanity and grandeur, elaborated with vine-scroll ornament intertwined with birds and beasts. The Christian themes expressed include John the Baptist, Christ in Glory, the hermit saints Paul and Anthony, the Flight into Egypt, the Visitation, Christ with Mary Magdalene washing His feet, and the Crucifixion. In the borders there are long runic extracts from *The Dream of the Rood*, most beautiful of Anglo-Saxon religious poems, in which the tragedy and triumph of the Crucifixion is told to a Dreamer poet by the timber Rood, the Cross itself. It seems to date from the first half of the eighth century, and as Professor Rosemary Cramp says in her Jarrow Lecture on *Early Northumbrian Sculpture* (1965): 'No other Cross illustrates so perfectly the intellectual background of Northumbrian Christianity'.

The Ruthwell Cross, and its headless contemporary in the village churchyard at Bewcastle, near Hadrian's Wall in Cumbria, show a marvellous fusion of Celtic, Anglian and continental motifs and skills. There are several hundreds of these sculptures still surviving, many of them fragmentary; and some are now to be seen in the little Priory Museum on Lindisfarne, having been excavated from the environs of the Norman Priory ruins there in the 1920s.

Carving on substances other than stone, being less durable, is less likely to have survived. But one or two masterpieces of Northumbrian art have survived, particularly the magnificent Franks Casket which is now in the British Museum. It's a box made of whalebone, decorated all over with narrative scenes taken, apparently at random, from classical, Anglo-Saxon and Biblical sources — the sack of Jerusalem by the emperor Titus in 70 AD, the suckling of Romulus and Remus by the wolf, the story of Weland the Smith, the archer 'Aegili' (Egil?) defending his house, the Adoration of the Magi, and so on. The scenes are bordered with inscriptions in Anglo-Saxon runes and occasional Latin captions. It's a remarkable piece of work, quite obviously Northumbrian in workmanship, and dating in all probability from the time of King Aldfrith.

Wood was even more perishable than stone or metal or whalebone; but one precious example of wood carving survives that can definitely be dated to Northumbria's Golden Age, and comes unquestionably from Lindisfarne itself — the oak coffin-reliquary made by the monks of Lindisfarne to receive the elevated body of St Cuthbert in 698. It was a roughly-carpentered casket, about 5 ft 6 ins long; the end panels were lightly incised with figures of a seated Virgin and Child, and of the Archangels Michael and Gabriel, while the long sides depicted rows of angels and the Twelve Apostles, and the lid was decorated with a figure of Christ surrounded by the symbols of the Four Evangelists. This coffin was found in a very fragmentary condition, the innermost of three coffins, when the tomb of St Cuthbert in Durham Cathedral was formally opened for inspection in May, 1827. The surviving fragments have been pieced together, and are on display in the Treasury of Durham Cathedral.

The carvings seem little more than graffiti at first glance: primitive, almost childish-looking scrawls, simple pen-and-ink drawings in comparison with the full-blooded oils of the Ruthwell Cross, as it were. Yet there is something profoundly appropriate and satisfying about these humbly-drawn figures; their sweet, moon-like, haloed heads, the starkness of their draperies, softly utter the transfigured piety and passion of all the saints of Lindisfarne.

But the crowning achievements of the artists of the Golden Age of Northumbria were undoubtedly the magnificent illuminated books they produced: superb masterpieces of manuscript writing and decoration. And of these, the most beautiful and the most treasured is the glorious copy of the four Gospels known as the *Lindisfarne Gospels*, 258 folio pages of fine script and magnificent coloured illustrations. It is now in the British Library in London; but it was made in the scriptorium, or writing-room, of the monastery on Lindisfarne, sometime in the 690s, and it was made with immense love and care in honour of the chief saint of Lindisfarne, Cuthbert himself.

Books and book-making were a vital part of the conversion of Britain and the continent to Christianity. We know that St Columba, the founder of Iona, was an expert scribe. We know that when St Augustine came to England on his evangelising mission in 597 (the year of St Columba's death), he brought a number of Italian-made books with him; indeed, what is believed to be one of them, an illuminated copy of the Four Gospels, is still in existence and is preserved in the library of Corpus Christi College, Cambridge. Books were essential for the proper conduct of the liturgy and for teaching in the monastic schools, and were in constant demand from missionaries on evangelizing journeys abroad. The Venerable Bede, no mean scribe himself, noted Cuthbert's prowess at reading during his training at the monastery of Melrose (*cf* ch 7). The giving of handsome books to other churches and monasteries for ceremonial usage was considered the height of distinction.

The making of books was an extremely skilled and laborious craft. The pages were made of vellum (the skin of calves or sheep), and had to be prepared with great care; they were then ruled between prick-marks to ensure that the lines were straight. The pens had to be cut, from reeds or goose-quills (there was certainly no shortage of geese over-wintering

117

on Lindisfarne, then or now). The dark brown, almost black, ink had to be made, with soot or lamp-black bound with white of egg. Then the great ornamental pages — the 'cross-carpet pages', as they are called — had to be prepared. The scribe would perhaps make trial patterns and designs on wax tablets, and then transfer them to the precious vellum in the form of intricate clusters of prick-marks, compass holes, rulings and grid-lines. These would then be lightly sketched in with ink, before the page was coloured in with a mass of glowing plant or mineral pigments — red and white lead, yellow ochre, orpiment (a bright yellow derived from arsenic trisulphide), green verdigris, bright-green malachite (hydrated copper carbonate), red kermes (obtained from the bodies of oak-eating insects), bright-blue from imported lapis lazuli, blue from indigo or woad, pinks and purples prepared from plants and alkalines. Then the completed book would be bound in leather, usually stamped or impressed, and sometimes richly encrusted with semi-precious stones.

One of the Anglo-Saxon Riddles in the tenth-century *Exeter Book* (now in the library of Exeter Cathedral) describes the whole process of book-making, from the calf's point of view (Riddle No 26, translated by Kevin Crossley-Holland):

> An enemy ended my life, deprived me
> of my physical strength; then he dipped me
> in water and drew me out again,
> and put me in the sun where I soon shed
> all my hair. ·
>   After that, the knife's sharp edge
> bit into me, and all my blemishes were scraped away.
> Fingers folded me, and the bird's feather
> often moved over my brown surface,
> sprinkling meaningful marks; it swallowed more wood-dye,
> and again travelled over me,
> leaving black tracks.
>   Then a man bound me,
> he stretched skin over me and adorned me
> with gold; thus I am enriched by the wondrous work
> of smiths, wound about with shining metal . . .
>   . . . Ask what I am called,
> of such use to men. My name is famous,
> of service to men and sacred in itself.

The answer to the Riddle is, of course, a book, because all manuscript books in those days were Christian in inspiration.

One of the earliest surviving masterpieces is the so-called *Book of*

Durrow (now in Trinity College, Dublin), named after the Irish monastery of Durrow in County Meath, which was originally founded by St Columba. This intricately-ornamented copy of the Gospels found its way to Durrow in the eleventh century; but it was made about 675, either on Iona or somewhere in Northumbria. Another is a badly-damaged and sadly incomplete copy of the *Durham Gospels* now in the library of Durham Cathedral, which was in all probability made by a scribe at Lindisfarne during the reign of King Aldfrith. The same scribe made the celebrated *Echternach Gospels* which is now in the National Library in Paris; it seems likely that it was a gift from Lindisfarne to St Willibrord to handsel his foundation of the monastery of Echternach in Luxembourg in 706 — a member of Willibrord's household was present at Lindisfarne shortly after the elevation of St Cuthbert's relics in 698 and was miraculously cured of a sudden crippling illness by a visit to his shrine.

Where the *Lindisfarne Gospels* book is concerned, we are in the happy position of being able to do without guesswork or surmise — because we know precisely who made it, who bound it, who decorated the binding, and who later inserted an Anglo-Saxon interlinear translation of the Latin text. All this information is contained in a colophon, or tailpiece, on the last page, which was added about 250 years later:

> Eadfrith, Bishop of Lindisfarne, originally wrote this book, for God and for St Cuthbert and, jointly, for all the saints whose relics are on the island.
>
> And Ethelwald, Bishop of Lindisfarne, impressed it on the outside and covered it, as he well knew how to do.
>
> And Billfrith the hermit forged the ornaments which are on it on the outside, and adorned it with gold and with gems and also with silver-gilt — pure metal.
>
> And Aldred, unworthy and most miserable priest, glossed it in English between the lines with the help of God and St Cuthbert . . .

We know enough about all these men to be able to place the book squarely in its proper context. Bishop Eadfrith succeeded Bishop Eadberht as bishop of Lindisfarne in 698, the year of Cuthbert's elevation. It was he who commissioned, or 'commanded', both the *Anonymous Life* of Cuthbert, and Bede's version; and he rewarded Bede by inscribing his name in the Lindisfarne *Liber Vitae*, so that he would be remembered in the prayers of the community. According to Bede, bishop Eadfrith also restored Cuthbert's oratory on Farne Island for a later incumbent, the hermit Felgild.

It would have been impossible for Eadfrith to have undertaken such a mammoth task as writing the *Lindisfarne Gospels* after his election as bishop; it must have taken him two years to complete, at the very least, because Eadfrith not only wrote out the text in a stately, formal script called 'insular majuscule' ('insular' because it derived from Ireland) — he also designed and drew and painted all the breath-taking pages of ornamentation. It seems obvious that he embarked on the project when he was still an ordinary, albeit senior, member of the brotherhood — head of the scriptorium, no doubt — in anticipation of the elevation of the relics in 698.

When Eadfrith died in 721, he was succeeded as bishop of Lindisfarne by Ethelwald, who had been a member of the Lindisfarne community sometime before 705, when he was transferred to Melrose. Again, it seems obvious that he must have carried out the binding of the manuscript as soon as it was completed. This original binding has long since disappeared, but it would doubtless have been of leather, like the exquisite little copy of the Gospel of St John, the so-called *Stoneyhurst Gospel*, which was found inside Cuthbert's coffin when it was opened at Durham in 1104; this book had been made at the twin monasteries of Wearmouth and Jarrow, perhaps as a gift to Lindisfarne in honour of the elevation (remembering Cuthbert's predilection for St John's Gospel at his friend Boisil's deathbed, *cf* ch 7), and its binding is of birchwood boards covered with red goatskin, with a raised decoration on the front cover moulded over cords.

We don't know precisely in what form the hermit Billfrith forged the ornamentation of the binding, nor what jewels he used. The present ornamental binding was made in 1852 by a London firm of silversmiths, decorated with silver and gems, using a design based upon motifs from Eadfrith's own illuminations in the *Gospels*. The British Museum's Keeper of Manuscripts at the time, Sir Frederic Madden, disliked it intensely: 'The binding is hideous, as it now stands, and the effect wretched enough to bring us into ridicule'. But I don't think that many people share that view today; it is now an antiquity in its own right, a rather splendid example of Victorian antiquarianism.

Of the fourth man mentioned in the colophon, the writer himself, the priest Aldred, not very much is known; but he advanced to be Provost of Chester-le-Street in County Durham in the second half of the 10th century — and it was at Chester-le-Street that Cuthbert's relics rested for more than a hundred years before being transferred to Durham in 995 (*cf* ch 11). It was at Chester-le-Street that Aldred added the priceless colophon which has made the *Lindisfarne Gospels* not just the

121

FISHERS OF THE SEA

The Cormorant (*Phalacrorax carbo*) — big, cumbersome, and oddly uncouth-looking — is a common resident on the Farne Islands. It also features in the decoration of the *Lindisfarne Gospels* — further proof, if such were needed, that the scribe and illustrator of the *Gospels* was a man with intimate knowledge of the wildlife of the places hallowed by St Cuthbert and St Aidan.

At first glance they're unlovely birds. In flight they have no grace, lumbering along like Second World War bombers, slow and plodding as they home in low over the sea. Landings are pure farce, skidding and lurching wildly, then taxiing drunkenly on feet that look too big for them, like frogman's flippers; their legs are set far back on their bodies, the better to paddle and steer with, and this makes them look so top-heavy and ungainly.

They have the reputation for being greedy — they eat up to a stone of fish a day. And cowardly, too; they will stand by helplessly while robber Gulls smash and eat their eggs. Their breeding ledges stink to high heaven — big, unwieldly nests covered with guano and rotting half-digested fish. Other birds don't care for them — only Guillemots consort with them on nesting-sites. With their long hooked beaks and cold emerald eyes, they look distinctly baleful.

But see them in close-up, and the whole conspectus changes. You see then that their plumage is dazzlingly beautiful — an iridescent glossy bluey-black, shot through with unexpected glints of rich colour, of bronze and brown and purple and green and silver, like petrol that has leaked into a puddle of water.

And in the sea itself, they're truly in their element. Master-fishermen all, diving like seals to catch their prey. If they catch a big, reluctant fish, they will beat it into submission by slapping it on the water before swallowing it whole. So expert are they at their craft that in some Asian countries they are actually used to catch fish for man, tethered by the neck and with their throats bound to stop them swallowing the catch.

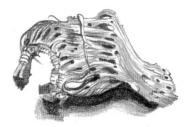

most beautiful and best preserved but the best documented of all Northumbrian manuscripts.

The *Lindisfarne Gospels* is now on permanent display in an exhibition case in the British Library in London. But there is a copy of the facsimile edition, made in 1956, on display in the parish church of Lindisfarne. This replica was presented to Lindisfarne by members of Rockford College Community in Illinois, U.S.A. — a munificent gift indeed, for fewer that 700 copies of it were printed. Also in the parish church is a sumptuous sanctuary-carpet based on the design of one of the great illuminated pages from the *Lindisfarne Gospels*.

For those who wish to learn more about this great masterpiece from the Golden Age of Northumbria, I would unreservedly recommend *The Lindisfarne Gospels* by Janet Backhouse, an Assistant Keeper in the Department of Manuscripts at the British Library (Phaidon, 1981). Lavishly illustrated and elegantly written, it does its great subject full justice.

Chapter 11 The Vikings

> *793. In this year terrible portents appeared over Northumbria, which sorely affrighted the inhabitants: there were exceptional flashes of lightning, and fiery dragons were seen flying through the air. A great famine followed hard upon these signs; and a little later in that same year, on the 8th of June, the harrying of the heathen miserably destroyed God's church on Lindisfarne by rapine and slaughter.*

That celebrated annal from the *Anglo-Saxon Chronicle* is always cited as marking the onset of the Viking Age: the very first recorded Viking raid on a western church. It was followed next year by a raid on Jarrow, Bede's old monastery, although the Vikings didn't have it all their own way there — one of their leaders was slain and several of their ships shattered by storms (the survivors were promptly killed as they struggled ashore). Also in 794, according to the *Annals of Ulster*, the island of Reachrainn (Rathlin?) off Ireland was attacked, and the Isle of Skye in the Hebrides. St Columba's monastery on Iona was assaulted in 795, and again in 802 and 806. Also in 795, the island monastic communities on Inisbofin and Inismurray off the west coast of Ireland were attacked, and the church on Lambay island near Dublin was burned down. In 799 the abbey of St Philibert on the island of Noirmoutier, near the estuary of the Loire, was plundered for the first time. The floodgates of pagan Viking violence had opened.

'Pagan Viking violence': it's an emotive phrase — the sort of phrase that has coloured historical thinking about the Vikings down the centuries. Pagan they certainly were at the time; but there is little evidence that they bore any specific hatred or malevolence towards Christianity or Christian churches. Their 'violence' was relative, too; a brief glance at the *Anglo-Saxon Chronicle* shows that Christians were being just as violent towards each other as the Vikings were. In 797, for instance: 'In this year the Romans cut off the tongue of Pope Leo and put out his eyes . . .' (in actual fact, we know from other sources that Pope Leo survived the assault with his sight and speech unimpaired, but the intention was certainly there).

The point is that violence (or tales of violence) was the stock-in-trade

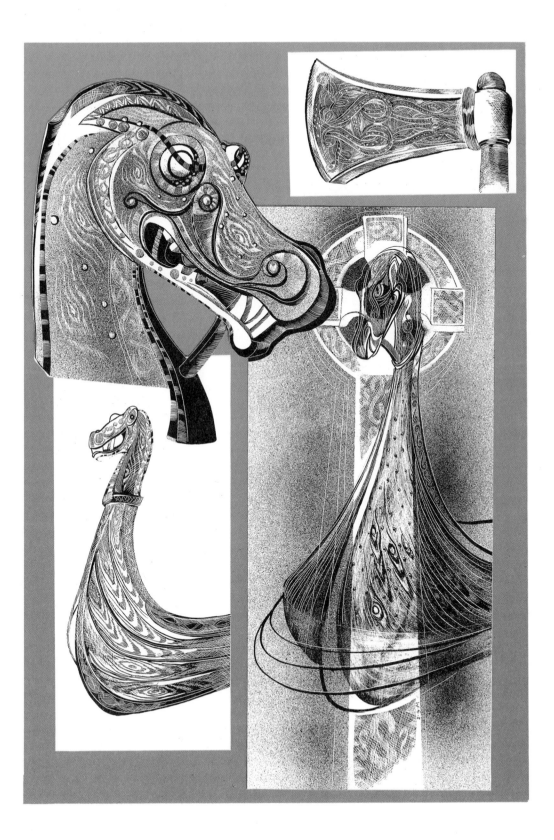

A TERRIBLE BEAUTY

W. B. Yeats, in his poem *Easter 1916* about the abortive
Rising in Dublin, penned this unforgettable couplet:

> All changed, changed utterly:
> A terrible beauty is born.

All beauty, whether terrible or not, is in the eye of the
beholder; and to my mind the Viking longship — long, lean
and predatory — was a thing of beauty. It may not have
seemed so to the monks of Lindisfarne when the first Viking
keels scraped noisily ashore on the shelving beach of Sandham Bay, or Lindisfarne harbour, or wherever else the Vikings landed for that historic raid in 793; but to me, the Viking
ships, like the Gokstad and the Oseberg ships (both now in
the Ship Museum in Oslo), are poems carved in wood.

What grace of line! What latent power in every curving
plank! Oak-hulled and pine-masted, they were built for
speed and strength. With their extraordinary shallowness of
draft — less than a metre even when fully laden — they could
steal up rivers and through channels where no warship had
ever gone before. They were endlessly versatile: they could
be sailed or rowed, they could even be dragged overland on
long portages, using wooden rollers under the hulls. It was
this versatility that gave them perhaps the most important
factor in warfare — the element of surprise — of shock,
indeed, as Alcuin so eloquently expressed it. In an age of
ocean cart-horses, the Viking ships were thoroughbreds.

Beautiful — and terrible. The image of terror was deliberate: dragon-prows, carved and gilded, snarling menace as
the ships skimmed into action. Princes loved them; poets
poured praise on them; peasants took profound pride in
them. They were ships fit for heroes:

> Men will quake with terror
> Ere the seventy sea-oars
> Gain their well-earned respite
> From the labours of the ocean.
> Norwegian arms are driving
> This iron-studded dragon
> Down the storm-tossed river,
> Like an eagle with wings beating.

(Snorri Sturluson: King Harald's Saga)

126

of the times. Seen in the perspective of history there was nothing special, or especially destructive, about Viking violence. Like other effective hunters, those Vikings who were raiders had a keen nose for the right prey — and churches and monasteries were the local banks of the time, crammed with wealth and totally undefended. The Vikings weren't committed sacrilegionists; they were after simple loot in the form of treasure, or coins, or livestock, or slaves to sell, or captives to ransom — and church-establishments, they knew from growing experience, were the best targets for quick returns. Also, all the accounts of the raids were written by the victims; the Vikings at the time were unlettered, whereas the clerics whose sanctuaries suffered were highly literate, with a vocabulary already fine-tuned to describe horror and suffering.

Furthermore, the stories of Viking atrocities lost nothing in the re-telling. The *Anglo-Saxon Chronicle* itself is not a contemporary account of these early and unco-ordinated raids; the *Chronicle* is actually a conflation of several lost chronicles, drawn together during the reign of King Alfred of Wessex in the 890s and 'topped up' annually from then on, with a notable bias in favour of the history of Wessex and a noticeable disregard for events in the north (the raid on Lindisfarne in 793, for instance, isn't mentioned at all in the main, or 'Parker' version of the *Chronicle*; it is only found in a secondary version, the 'Laud' *Chronicle*). It is always worth bearing in mind that for the first century of the so-called 'Viking Terror', the contemporary-sounding *Anglo-Saxon Chronicle* was written anything up to a hundred years after the events.

Two hundred years later, the story had been embroidered considerably and made even more lurid by the Northumbrian chronicler Simeon of Durham early in the 12th century:

> In the same year [793] the pagans from the northern regions came with a fleet of ships to Britain like stinging hornets; and spreading on all sides like dreadful wolves, they robbed, tore and slaughtered not only beasts of burden and sheep and oxen, but also even priests and deacons, and companies of monks and nuns.
>
> And they came to the church of Lindisfarne, laid everything waste with grievous plundering, trampled the holy places with polluted feet, dug up the altars and seized all the treasures of the holy church. They killed some of the brothers; some they took away with them in fetters; many they drove out, naked and loaded with insults; and some they drowned in the sea.

This generalised impression of grim Viking ferocity seemed to be powerfully reinforced by the celebrated Lindisfarne Stone, which was unearthed in the 1920s during restoration work around the ruins of the Norman Priory by the then Ministry of Works. The original, after being on loan to the British Museum for some years, is now back in the little site museum on the island. On one side it depicts a menacing file of seven warriors, wearing heavy jerkins and tight-fitting trousers, and brandishing swords and axes; the other side depicts two figures worshipping before a raised Cross which is flanked by the Sun and the Moon, with God's hands reaching in towards the Cross from the sides of the frame.

It was always automatically assumed that the Lindisfarne Stone was carved to commemorate that first Viking raid of 793. But that assumption has been called into question by recent scholarship. In particular, Richard N. Bailey, in his valuable book *Viking Age Sculpture in Northern England* (1980), has argued convincingly that the Lindisfarne Stone is an Anglian grave-marker, carved for a lay burial after the monastic community had abandoned Lindisfarne in the middle of the 9th century. Its theme is not the Viking raid, but one of the major preoccupations of medieval Christianity — the imminence of Doomsday, the Day of Judgement when the Cross would overshadow the sun and moon and the souls of all mankind; the procession of warriors represents the 'wars and rumours of wars' as one of the certain signs of the impending Doom (*Matthew*, XXIV, 6).

Lindisfarne may not have been the first target for Viking attack — our sources for the period are rather thin and selective; but it was regarded as the most significant, because of the significance of Lindisfarne as a major centre of Christianity, a crucial sanctuary of the spirit. The violation of a place of such hallowed associations sent the first shock-waves of alarm spreading throughout Europe. That alarm and horror was expressed in a series of letters from the distinguished Northumbrian scholar, Alcuin of York. Alcuin, who has been described as the most distinguished Englishman of his age and later became abbot of Tours, was at the Frankish court of the Emperor Charlemagne at the time of the Lindisfarne raid, and he responded to the news by firing off a positive barrage of five letters to England — to Bishop Higbald of Lindisfarne, to King Æthelred of Northumbria, and to a priest on Lindisfarne. A letter to King Æthelred contains a much-quoted passage:

> Lo, it is nearly 350 years that we and our fathers have inhabited this most lovely land, and never before has such a terror appeared in Britain as we have now suffered from a pagan race, nor was it

thought possible that such an inroad from the sea could be made.

Behold, the church of St Cuthbert spattered with the blood of the priests of God, despoiled of all its ornaments; a place more venerable than all in Britain is given as a prey to pagan peoples . . .

Who does not fear this? Who does not lament this as if his country were captured? Foxes pillage the chosen vine, the heritage of the Lord has been given to a people not His own; and where there was the praise of God, are now the games of the Gentiles; the holy festivity has been turned to mourning.

Shock and horror, yes; astonishment, yes, that such a crossing of the North Sea had been possible (people in the south were well used to attacks by coast-hugging pirates from Frisia); but above all, the raid gave Alcuin occasion for a blistering sermon — not against the Vikings, but against the English! The Viking attack, he claimed, was a direct visitation of divine wrath against the sins of the English — sins that included peccadillos like fornication, adultery, incest, avarice, robbery, injustice, luxuriousness, long hair, and flashy clothing.

Personally, I don't believe that the raid on Lindisfarne was nearly as destructive as the shrill jeremiads of the time would suggest. In his letter to Bishop Higbald, for instance, Alcuin offers sober help through diplomatic channels for the ransoming of 'the youths who have been led into captivity' (and at least one of them was ransomed later). The stories of indiscriminate slaughter of monks and nuns (Simeon of Durham) hardly ring true, for there were no nuns on Lindisfarne. Nor could the Vikings have 'dug up the altars and seized all the treasures of the holy church' (Simeon of Durham), because the shrine of St Cuthbert with all its treasures escaped intact — and that was lying just beside the altar. I think it was more a matter of disruption than real destruction.

Disruption there certainly was. We are told by Simeon of Durham that when the raid was over, Bishop Higbald and the surviving monks returned to the 'abbey' and 'continued for a long time to reside near the body of the blessed Cuthbert'. But for how long? The conventional wisdom, based on Simeon of Durham, is that the Lindisfarne community abandoned their island in the year 875, in the face of growing threats from a Danish army loose in Northumbria. It now seems much more likely, however, that Lindisfarne was deserted much earlier — during the time of Bishop Ecgred of Lindisfarne (830-845), in fact. According to the mid-10th century *Historia de Sancto Cuthberto*, Bishop Ecgred dismantled the church on Lindisfarne and rebuilt it at Norham, on the river Tweed (now the site of a formidable Norman keep); the body of St Cuthbert was translated thither as well — a suggestion confirmed by a text known as *List of Saints' Resting Places in England*, originally dating from the 9th century. The motive for this move to a more secure base inland could well have been provided by a resurgence of Viking activity on the Continent and in the south of England in the 830s. There had apparently been a lull in the raids after the first flurry of attacks in the 790s; but now whole fleets of Vikings from Denmark began to attack the cities and monasteries of the crumbling Carolingian empire. In 841, according to the *Anglo-Saxon Chronicle*, there were raids on East Anglia and Lindsey (the area south of the Humber), and this may well have been enough to persuade the Lindisfarne community to seek safety in flight.

It was in 875, however, that the major exodus began, whether from Norham-on-Tweed or from Lindisfarne. Ten years earlier, a large Danish army had landed in East Anglia intent on permanent conquest, not quick plunder. Within a year they had captured York and taken control of Northumbria, Mercia and East Anglia. Only Wessex held out. In 875 the Danish army divided; one half of it went south to try to crush Wessex once and for all (it failed to do so), while the other half, under their leader Halfdan of the Wide Embrace, concentrated on consolidating Viking power in the north. In the following year, 876, the *Anglo-Saxon Chronicle* tells us that 'Halfdan shared out the lands of the Northumbrians, and they started to plough and make a living for themselves'.

This was enough to send the Lindisfarne community into flight. For eight years, the 'Congregation of St Cuthbert', as it came to be called, wandered from one refuge to another. They were led by their bishop, Eardulf: a motley crowd of monks and priests, laymen and their families with a wagon for all their belongings, and seven specially-appointed young men who acted as bearers of St Cuthbert's shrine, now crammed with all the treasured relics of Lindisfarne. Simeon of Durham gives a splendid and highly-coloured account of their travels:

> They wandered throughout the whole district of Northumbria, having no settled dwelling-place; and they were like sheep flying before the face of wolves ...

They seem to have headed west, for what appeared to be the relative safety of Cumberland, somewhere in the neighbourhood of the River Derwent. At one stage, according to Simeon of Durham, they tried to reach Ireland; but the ship they had chartered ran into a fierce storm.

Three terrible waves struck the vessel and half filled it with water, which immediately turned to blood; and a copy of the Four Gospels, 'adorned with gold and precious stones', was swept overboard and lost. The voyage was abandoned, but Cuthbert himself came to the rescue; he appeared in a dream to one of the Bearers, a man called Hunred, and told him that the book could be found washed up, unharmed, on the sands near Whithorn in Galloway — and so, of course, it was. Simeon of Durham naturally identified this book as the *Lindisfarne Gospels*, but this is now discounted as pure legend.

Somehow, the 'Congregation' were able to cart their precious cargo the length and breadth of Northumbria without falling foul of the Vikings — which is odd, on the face of it, especially when we are told by Simeon of Durham that wherever they went, they were showered with gifts — money, treasure, fine garments, even grants of land. How was such a tempting and conspicuous prize able to escape the Vikings' predatory hands? Could it be that the alleged animosity of the Vikings towards the Christian church was much less virulent than later commentators would have us believe?

Indeed, it might well be that the Vikings gave their active protection to Cuthbert and his relics at this time. Remember, the Vikings were now settlers and colonists, not hit-and-run raiders. They had a stake in the land by then, a stake in its security and political future. They knew the power and importance of the church as a political factor; they had appropriated monastic lands and thereby cut off the sources of wealth that kept the monasteries alive — but they hadn't even attempted to destroy the structure and the hierarchy of the Church itself. Viking craftsmen, too, were only too eager to learn new skills from Christian English craftsmen; they themselves, although expert in metalwork and wood-carving, had never worked in stone in their homelands — but very quickly a new Anglo-Norse style of stone-carving arose, a happy cross-fertilisation of skills and motifs and aptitudes.

There is one revealing little story in Simeon of Durham which claims that, towards the end of their Wandering, the Lindisfarne community was busily involved in politics. By that time, the 'Congregation' had moved back into Yorkshire to Crayke, only a few miles from York, right in the Viking heartlands. After the death of Halfdan in 882, St Cuthbert is said to have taken a positive part in the choice of his successor: Cuthbert appeared to the Lindisfarne abbot in a dream, and instructed him to find and ransom a captive Danish Christian called Guthfrith, and make him King of Northumbria. His instructions were carried out, and Guthfrith acceded to the throne at a curious mixed Christian/pagan ceremony which apparently involved oaths sworn both over a sacred gold armlet or ring, and Cuthbert's body.

Little is known of this King Guthfrith, who reigned from about 882 to about 895. But Simeon of Durham says that the new king was so pleased that he gave the 'Congregation' a place to settle at the old Roman station of Chester-le-Street, where he built them a fine cathedral and richly endowed the shrine of St Cuthbert. But this was evidently not sufficient reward, in Cuthbert's eyes, for the saint promptly appeared in a vision to the abbot once again and demanded all the lands between the Tyne and the Wear as well — which King Guthfrith duly handed over.

Whether there is any truth in this account or not, it certainly casts the Vikings in a very different light. It shows the Vikings being pragmatic. They recognised that Cuthbert and his relics were, to put it crudely, the goose that laid the golden eggs for the Lindisfarne community, both literally and metaphorically; and if they couldn't beat him, they had better join him. It also shows the Lindisfarne community in a different light; with their lands already appropriated by earlier Vikings, they had moved in from the periphery of politics on Lindisfarne, right into the centre of the political arena, intent on rebuilding their landed wealth.

It was land that was at the heart of the Viking revolution, just as it was to be under William the Conqueror, and later under Henry VIII. Monasteries depended on gifts of land from grateful patrons. The relics of a successful saint, especially such a hugely successful saint as Cuthbert, were of inestimable value to the lucky church that owned them. And as the Cuthbert cult spread far and wide, because of the miraculous stories of the uncorrupted body in the coffin-reliquary, anyone who wanted to win the hearts and hands of the people had to show due reverence and deference to Cuthbert, just as Guthfrith did. So, too, in 934, did King Athelstan of Wessex, grandson of Alfred the Great, when he marched from the south to drive the Vikings out of York. The crown of Northumbria had by then reverted to pagan Viking kings who had strong connections with Dublin and were building a power axis across the north of England, and King Rögnvald of York had seized the lands of the Chester-le-Street church and distributed it, once again, amongst his followers. Cuthbert clearly afforded a powerful patriotic rallying-point against the 'alien' kings of York; so Athelstan made an ostentatious visit to Cuthbert's shrine at Chester-le-Street,

EGG-LARDERS ON BLACK LAW

It's odd, isn't it, that no one has a good word to say about Rats — even such tough, intelligent and enterprising characters as the common or Brown Rat (*Rattus norvegicus*). The trouble is that they're too clever by half for their own good, and so they have to be got rid of. The matter of the egg-larders on Black Law is a case in point.

Black Law is a small, islanded ridge of shingle and sand across the water from Lindisfarne harbour. It is an important ternery, offering sanctuary and comparative safety to all five species of Terns that breed in Britain — the Arctic, Common, Sandwich, Roseate (which is not very common) and Little (which is extremely uncommon).

It is difficult of access except by dinghy; but that's no obstacle to a vigorous swimmer like the Brown Rat. Once settled on Black Law, the rats evolved an ingenious system of hoarding eggs near their burrow-entrances, sometimes even hiding them in rough-and-ready stone caches. They preferred Eider eggs, since they were the largest, but any eggs would do — Terns' eggs, Ringed Plovers' eggs, anything that would provide nest-eggs for a rainy day.

But there are some things you simply cannot do with impunity on a National Nature Reserve, and stealing birds' eggs is one of them. The Reserve employs a part-time warden for Black Law, Robin Henderson, whose job it is to prevent sightseers coming ashore during the breeding season, and to discourage predators like Carrion Crows and Black-headed Gulls and Brown Rats. He is a cheery, apple-cheeked former Lifeboatman, now in his seventies, who freely admits to having been an ardent egg-collector himself in his youth.

His first priority was to exterminate the poacher rats. He tried laying down some tunnel traps, but the rats were much too smart to be caught that easily. In the end he resorted to poisoned bait placed by the rat-runs, and as usual these insatiable scavengers fell victim to their own greed, and succumbed.

The following year, the ternery on Black Law had its most successful breeding season ever . . .

and gave to it the most magnificent gifts — church plate, money, and the royal estate of Wearmouth. He also made several gifts which were found in the shrine when it was opened — some valuable vestments, including a stole and maniple of silk and gold thread now preserved in Durham Cathedral, and a copy of Bede's *Life of St Cuthbert*, complete with an illumination depicting Athelstan making the actual presentation (this book is now at Corpus Christi College, Cambridge). It certainly paid dividends: for as long as he lived, until 939, Athelstan was undisputed king of all England, including Cuthbert's Northumbria.

In 995, renewed Viking pressure prompted another Cuthbert evacuation, this time southwards to Ripon. The 'Congregation' stayed there for only four months, and then decided to return to Chester-le-Street. But they never got there. At some point to the east of Old Durham, the wagon bearing Cuthbert's shrine stuck in the road, and seemed to refuse to be moved. This was interpreted to mean that the saint was reluctant to return to Chester-le-Street; after three days of prayer and fasting, the brethren were vouchsafed the indication that he wanted to go instead to Durham — and now the cart moved off with the greatest of ease. When the 'Congregation' reached Durham, they settled on the naturally fortified plateau of land almost encircled by the River Wear, and there they proceeded to build a church to give Cuthbert's relics a permanent home. In September, 998, the White Church of Stone was consecrated, and the relics placed inside. Cuthbert's 250-year hejira was over at last.

There was to be one further disturbance. In 1069, the last Saxon bishop, Ethelwine, fled with the Cuthbert relics back to Lindisfarne for the winter, in fear of a punitive expedition to the north led by the new King of England, William the Conqueror. Come spring, with the danger past, the body of St Cuthbert and his relics was borne across the sands of Lindisfarne for the last time, and taken back to Durham. In 1093 the foundation stone of the huge Romanesque Cathedral was laid; and in 1104, Cuthbert's relics were solemnly translated to their present setting at the high altar. The coffin was opened for examination on that occasion and, according to Simeon of Durham's vividly detailed account, the saint's body was found to be still uncorrupt.

The coffin was opened yet again in 1537 by Henry VIII's commissioners at the time of the Dissolution of the Monasteries. Once again, the body of the saint was reported to be still intact; but many of the treasures — including, it is supposed, the *Lindisfarne Gospels* — were confiscated and removed to London. It was not until the formal investigation of the coffin and its contents in 1827 by Cathedral officials that the mortal remains of St Cuthbert had become just another skeleton in a winding sheet.

Chapter 12 The Priory Ruins

They have a resonance all their own, like the knell of history itself and the passing of time. On the outskirts of the village, in the lee of the Heugh, stand the sombre ruins of the medieval Priory Church, all weathered red sandstone and gravely Romanesque arches. Like so many ancient abbeys, Lindisfarne Priory has a stricken beauty in its desolation, profoundly poignant and evocative: 'How wondrous this wall-stone, shattered by Fate', indeed.

At first sight, the imagination runs riot: so this is what those dreadful Vikings did to the cradle church of Christianity in the north! That is certainly how Sir Walter Scott depicted it, in a positive orgy of romantic but totally inaccurate images, in Canto II of his *Marmion*:

> In Saxon strength that abbey frown'd,
> With massive arches broad and round,
>   That rose alternate, row and row,
>   On ponderous columns, short and low,
>   Built ere the art was known,
>   By pointed aisle, and shafted stalk,
>   The arcades of an alley'd walk
>   To emulate in stone.
> On the deep walls, the heathen Dane
> Had poured his impious rage in vain;
> And needful was such strength to these,
> Exposed to the tempestuous seas,
> Scourged by the wind's eternal sway,
> Open to rovers fierce as they,
> Which could twelve hundred years withstand
> Winds, waves, and northern pirates' hand.
> Not but that portions of the pile,
> Rebuilded in a later stile,
> Shewed where the spoiler's hand had been;
> Not but the wasting sea-breeze keen,
> Had worn the pillar's carving quaint,
> And moulder'd in his niche the saint,
> And rounded, with consuming power,
> The pointed angles of each tower:
> Yet still entire the Abbey stood,
> Like veteran, worn, but unsubdued.

S.G.M.

It's all too tempting to associate the ruins with that historic Viking raid of 793, as Sir Walter Scott did. But the Priory and Church whose remains we see today belong to a different and much later era, to the time of the attempted Norman revival of monastic life on Lindisfarne some 250 years after the original foundation had been abandoned.

For all these years, Lindisfarne seems to have been completely deserted. The accounts of the flight from the island, whether it was in the 830s or in 875, suggests that the evacuation was total, involving not only the monks but the 'civilian' population as well — the whole Congregation, in fact. There is no further mention of Lindisfarne in the historical record until the winter of 1069–70, when Bishop Æthelwine, the last Anglo-Saxon bishop of Durham, sought sanctuary there with Cuthbert's shrine and the guardian successors of the original Congregation. Æthelwine seems to have been as much concerned with his own personal safety as that of Cuthbert, for he had come out openly in support of a massive English uprising in Northumbria, supported by a huge Danish fleet, against the Norman conquerors; he had fled to Lindisfarne when King William came marching grimly north to teach the rebels a lesson, systematically and ruthlessly devastating the fertile lands of Yorkshire. Even while he was on Lindisfarne he had planned to make his escape permanent by seeking refuge with William's enemies in France; but the ship he had requisitioned at Wearmouth harbour to take him abroad was driven back by contrary winds. He was eventually taken prisoner by the Normans, still in possession of some of the treasures of Durham, and died in prison at Abingdon in 1071.

The harrying of the north, and the appointment of a 'safe' Flemish bishop, Walcher, to the see of Durham, wiped the page clean, as it were: Cuthbert's shrine was back in Durham Cathedral, saint and king were reconciled, the north was pacified, and Bishop Walcher was able to concentrate on building for the future. He was anxious to introduce into his diocese the revived Benedictine monasticism of the 11th century. The old foundations at Jarrow, Wearmouth, York and Whitby, long abandoned and derelict as a result of the Viking invasions, were now resuscitated; and before his death in 1080, Bishop Walcher had begun to erect new conventual buildings at Durham to house a reformed Benedictine community to look after Cuthbert's relics.

His successor was William of St Calais, the first Norman bishop to hold the see of Durham. He completed Walcher's plans by disbanding the members of the Cuthbert Congregation and replacing them with a new Chapter, consisting of 23 regular Benedictine monks drawn from

PRIORY AND PARISH CHURCH

Only about fifty feet to the west of the ruined Priory Church on Holy Island stands the parish church of the island — the Church of St Mary the Virgin. It, too, has had its ups and downs; for a time it was practically derelict; but today it is in splendid condition, the hub and focal point of religious life on the island for locals and visitors alike.

It, too, is very old, at least in its original form. The earliest parts of the present fabric (three Norman arches on the north side of the nave) date from the late 12th century — only about 100 years after the foundation of the Priory Church itself. The parish church was greatly enlarged in the course of the 13th century; this was when the fine chancel, lighted by eight lancet windows, was built.

But during the 16th and 17th centuries it began to suffer seriously from neglect. In 1646, the Parliamentary governor of the Castle made a determined effort to refurbish the interior and supply it with some furniture, such as a carved oak pulpit and some box pews. A little belfry was added in 1723. The progressive deterioration continued, however, and in 1836 ambitious plans were drawn up for a major 'spring-clean' and renovation. Unfortunately there was no money available; and by the time that the Victorian traveller, Dr George Johnston, penned his impressions of the church (*Our Visit to Holy Island in May 1854*), it was in pretty poor shape:

> The Church is cold, damp, and musty within; the walls covered with green mould, and 'sclaters' were crawling on the paved floor. The seats are unfitted for the service, so much só, that neither male nor female can kneel on any part of it. Every seat has a large brass plate on the door, engraved with the name of its proprietor: and the 'Border Brewery' has three seats to its share. The conduct of the service suited the Church; there were no responses made, and a very considerable proportion of the small flock had no books. Enough!

Dr Johnston would not recognise it as the same church today. The planned renovation was started in 1860, shortly after his visit, and further beautification of the interior carries on to this day.

140

Wearmouth and Jarrow, under their own prior. To this Chapter, Bishop William granted the church of Lindisfarne and some neighbouring mainland parishes, and it became the mother church of a district known as Islandshire.

The original independent see of Lindisfarne, that glowing lantern of the north, had now become a mere adjunct or out-house of Durham, a small and subordinate cell controlled by the prior of Durham, an isolated backwater on the periphery of affairs; indeed, there is some evidence that dissident monks were actually 'posted' to Lindisfarne, as if to some Siberia, as a punishment for misdemeanours. But the glory of Lindisfarne's past as the mother-church of Celtic Christianity in the north was commemorated in two ways, the one intangible, the other very tangible: the name 'Lindisfarne' was changed to, or superseded by, the title of 'Holy Island' in honour of its saints; and a magnificent new Priory Church was built on the site of the old monastic cemetery below the Heugh.

In August, 1093, Bishop William laid the foundation stone of the splendid new minster at Durham that houses Cuthbert's relics to this day; and at about the same time, work started on the building of the Priory Church on Lindisfarne.

It was a massive, Romanesque construction, entirely Norman in inspiration and execution, closely related to Durham Cathedral in architectural style and to Whitby Abbey in design. It was an extraordinarily grandiose building for such a small island; it must have been intended as a cult centre for pilgrimage, for its lands were quite insufficient to support an enterprise on such an ambitious scale.

All the building stone was carted across the sands from the mainland, chiefly from Goswick, and we are told that 'the men of the neighbourhood willingly lent a helping hand'. The church was cruciform in shape, with a long, six-bayed nave, a stubby transept, and a short chancel ending in an apse (this early chancel was subsequently replaced, in the second half of the 12th century, by a square-ended presbytery of three bays — the only structural change ever made to the church).

There was a splendid ceremonial entrance through the west front of the church leading into the nave. This elaborate round-headed doorway, pure Norman in style, is still an impressive sight; it now has an ornamental wrought-iron gateway, which was installed by the then Lord of the Manor in 1840 when enlightened land-owners were beginning to take a responsible interest in the ruins on their estates.

The west face, which fronts the back of the parish church of St Mary the Virgin, still has the remains of one of the twin towers that originally flanked it.

Most of the nave is now gone. The north wall (on the left as you enter through the ceremonial west doorway) still stands to some extent — the two east bays are still there; but the south wall is no more, where it once adjoined the small rectangular cloistered courtyard of the priory itself. One can still see the stumps of some of the massive piers. alternately cruciform and round (as in Durham Cathedral), that once supported the vaulted stone roof. All that remains of the vaulting now is a spidery rib, still with its keystone, arching diagonally across the transept and known locally as the Rainbow Arch; it was on top of this that the massive central tower of the church once sprouted. Much of the walling of the chancel at the east end of the church still stands.

The priory buildings, or their remains, are all to the south of the church, on ground that slopes gently downhill. The priory seems to have been almost an afterthought, tacked on to the church and built in a contrasting grey stone. There was a cloister of sorts, but the community of monks was never very large and their original accommodation seems to have been purely domestic. There is little evidence of a school, or a scriptorium; Lindisfarne no longer aspired to the cultural heights and deeply religious activities of the original Celtic foundation. The cloister walks were just covered corridors, rather than places for study or contemplation; after the door in the south wall of the nave leading to the cloister area was blocked up, they were useless for processions as well. The buildings which accreted round and beyond the cloisters were as much to do with trade and commerce as with spiritual matters. By the 14th century, the annual accounts of the Priory show the handful of monks busily engaged in organising coal-mining, quarrying, brewing, baking, lime-burning, farming, fishing and a brisk trade in cloth and iron and kelp.

The accounts, which run in an almost unbroken sequence from 1326 until the Tudor Dissolution of the Priory in 1537, make fascinating reading. The brethren lived well: 7 chaldrons (tons) of salt, 7,800 red herrings, 198 codlings — £16 13s 6d. Two pounds of sugar of Cyprus, 16d. Two boxes of ginger, 20d. Four pounds of saffron, 8 lbs of pepper, 60 lbs of almonds, 16 lbs of rice, 7 flagons of olive oil, and one basket of figs — £4. Beer for the table of the monks for a year — 23s 10d. Gift of wine to the brethren of Durham — 26s 6d. Meanwhile, William the Mason earned 43s 10d for 57 weeks' work, John the Clerk earned 4s for

142

shaving the monks for a year, and painting the image of St Cuthbert cost 53s 4d. The prior did himself well — 5s for two pairs of boots, 2s 2d for his expenses for a funeral (including six pairs of gloves), 26s 2d in expenses for attending the fair at Darlington, and 14d to the Skinner for repairing the fur of the prior's hoods and tunics. The tailor got 7d for making seven pairs of breeches for the monks, the cowherd got 3d for watching the prior's cows, the minstrels of 'divers Lords' cost 6s 8d, while the monks lashed out 39s 7d for linen for themselves, and 17s for a table-cloth, with towels, to cover their groaning board. Building a new ship and boat cost £17 11s, and buying a sloop laden with oysters from 'a certain Scotchman' cost 100s. The purchase of six herring nets cost 107s 8d.

In stark contrast to this busy inventory of entrepreneurial activity is the meagre list of books that were in the Priory library in the year 1367, for instance:

> Two illuminated missals, one quarto containing the rule and regulations of St Benedict. Two small red books. The book of St Cuthbert which fell into the sea; one book of sentences belonging to the priory of Coldingham; many pamphlets on divers subjects.

And that was the sum total of scholarly reading available to the monks of Lindisfarne in 1367 — all five of them! The reference to 'the book of St Cuthbert which fell onto the sea' is intriguing, because it suggests that the *Lindisfarne Gospels* may have returned to the island, at least temporarily; if that was indeed the case, the *Gospels* soon returned to Durham, according to an item in the Durham Cathedral relic list of 1387.

Even in the 14th century, when Northumbria suffered remorseless raiding from across the Border during the Scottish wars, Lindisfarne itself escaped damage except for one occasion around 1326, when a band of Scottish Borderers led by William de Prendergast looted the bakehouse and the brewhouse. The church estates on the mainland, however, whose tithes and supplies helped to maintain the Priory community, were laid waste with monotonous regularity; the annual accounts reveal alarming fluctuations in the revenues — 'No tithes this year, for the Scots have it taken'. An old rhyme reflects the frustration the monks must have felt:

> From Goswick we've geese; from Cheswick we've cheese;
>   From Buckton we've venison in store;
> From Swinhoe we've bacon, but the Scots have it taken,
>   And the Prior is longing for more.

It's little wonder, perhaps, that the monks of Lindisfarne ran the priory more as a commercial enterprise than a centre of piety — they were obsessed with the worldly problems of economics and making a living. Farming and fishing were the mainstay, but any speculative ventures that might show a profit were undertaken — even investments in foreign trade. It was during the priory days that the foundations for the economic patterns of Lindisfarne's livelihood were laid. The nucleus of a small indigenous population began to form: fishermen who worked the priory boats, farm-workers who ran the farms owned by the priory, growing hay, flax, hemp, beans, onions and leeks, and pasturing livestock. Farm tenancies and market gardens were leased out, priory properties were rented out, huts and cottages were built for letting as lodgings. There was a market on the island, and a safe haven for ships in all weathers — as well as lucrative pickings from ships that didn't make the harbour in time and were wrecked on the wicked rocks and sand-banks all around.

Despite the ever-present risk of raiding parties of Scottish reivers, the island began to prosper. New buildings were added to the south of the original cloisters, the prior built himself a handsome new lodging in the middle of the 14th century, and fortifications were added, with a barbican between the cloisters and a new outer courtyard to the south. Lindisfarne Priory ceased to be a Benedictine monastery in all but name, and became a fortified church of strategic importance locally. The monks became more and more worldly, too, frequenting taverns, playing dice, telling dirty jokes and swearing — just like any junior business executives today.

In 1537, as part of the great national take-over bid by King Henry VIII known to history as the Dissolution of the Monasteries ('privatisation', as it would be called today), the Priory of Lindisfarne was dissolved. The 59th and last prior, Thomas Sparke, was pensioned off as suffragan bishop of Berwick; his golden handshake was a life-time lease of the site and buildings and other priory properties on the island. Soon afterwards he sub-let it to the King's surveyor of victuals at Berwick, who promptly turned the Priory Church into a storehouse. By 1550 the buildings were said to be in very poor condition, and masonry from 'the olde abbey lately dissolved' was used to build a fort on the commanding crag of Beblowe (cf ch 13).

After Bishop Sprake's death in 1571, ownership of the property became a vexed issue between the Dean and Chapter of Durham, who had been granted the lands of Holy Island at the time of the

Dissolution, and various other claimants to whom the King had made grants or leases of church properties in the north-east. Eventually, in 1613, Lord Walden (later the second Earl of Suffolk) cut the Gordian knot by stripping the priory buildings of their lead roofs and the church of its bells. The spoils were carried off by ship, but, with poetic justice, the ship foundered in a storm on its way south, with the loss of all its cargo.

Thus brusquely bereft of its roof, the dilapidated Priory Church became an overnight ruin, sinking further into dereliction with each passing decade. It was not until the 19th century, with the growth of interest in the 'Gothick' aspect of gloomy ruins, that any attempt was made to tidy the Priory site and render it safe. It was excavated in 1888 by the then owner of Lindisfarne, Major-General Sir William Crossman, who also made a plan of the ruins. In 1913 the ruins were transferred to the old Office of Works (later the Ministry of Works, now subsumed into the Department of the Environment), and further remedial excavations were carried out in the 1920s.

The remains were extensively restored and stabilised. The artefacts unearthed — mainly carved stone grave-markers, pillow-stones, old coins and sherds of medieval pottery — were stored in an outhouse (the drying-room) of the old Manor House, just beside the gate leading into the churchyard of St Mary the Virgin. After the last War, this shed was converted into a little site museum in which the artefacts, including the so-called 'Lindisfarne Stone', are now on display. The museum, which attracts some 50,000 visitors a year, is open all year round apart from Fridays in winter. It has been supervised since 1982 by the custodian, Fred Rose, and his wife; Mr Rose is a Tynesider who came to the island when he retired from the RAF. The museum and site now come under the newly-formed Historic Buildings and Monuments Commission, and a proper Visitor Centre complete with offices and toilets is to be built there soon.

So the old Priory Church, Walter Scott's 'frowning abbey', has been given a dignified rehabilitation. But it has been a sorry tale of indecent diminution, of greatness brought low, of grandeur made desolate by callous neglect. The only redeeming feature, paradoxically enough, is that the imagination can now invest these gaunt and lifeless ruins with a respect and regard that the living buildings themselves had failed to inspire.

13 'A Daintie Little Fort'

SGM

They call it, rather grandly, Lindisfarne Castle; but in truth it is only a fort, albeit a highly romantic fort. It perches like an eagle's eyrie on the highest point on Holy Island, a cone-shaped eminence, 100-foot high, known as Beblowe Crag — a splendidly conspicuous pinnacle of rock formed when molten dolerite forced its way through a wide fracture in the basic sandstone.

It has the kind of fairy-tale quality associated with a story by Hans Christian Andersen or a Walt Disney fantasy. This has attracted a number of film-makers to use it as a backdrop for feature films and dramatised documentaries — particularly Roman Polanski, who embellished the old fort with fibre-glass turrets and plywood towers for his productions of *Cul-de-Sac* and *Macbeth*. Much more substantial and enduring embellishments were carried out at the start of this century by the architect, Sir Edwin Lutyens, who converted the fort into a comfortable country house without losing any of its visual grandeur. Lindisfarne Castle is now owned by the National Trust, and has become one of the island's major tourist attractions.

It stands there as solid and uncompromising as a block-ship carved in stone, superintending the sea-approaches to the island, left high and dry by the ebb of historical events that caused its construction. It grew out of the turbulence and tensions of the Reformation that debased the Norman Priory and Church to the status of store-houses. Politically and militarily, the North of England and the Scottish Borders — the physical and psychological borderline between Scotland and England — were in turmoil. Scotland had been at war with England, intermittently, since 1286 — more than two centuries of conflict highlighted by fearful battles like Bannockburn in 1314 and Flodden in 1513 — and her 'auld ally' during all that time was France; but in the 1530s, Henry VIII's rejection of Papal authority and his championship of the Protestant Reformation created another potentially explosive situation in international relations throughout Europe.

Henry VIII and his nephew, King James V of Scotland, were deeply embroiled in political intrigues and counter-intrigues involving France, the Holy Roman Empire, and the Pope: an extraordinary chess-game of shifting moves bringing kings and queens and bishops and knights and castles into menacing interplay. Pawns like Scotland were as likely to be sacrificed without compunction one day, as strenuously courted and protected the next.

In the North of England the series of risings in 1536 known as 'The Pilgrimage of Grace', followed by the Yorkist rising in 1538, coupled with endemic trouble in Ireland and Henry's excommunication by the Pope in December 1538, made the danger of an invasion of England itself seem very real. Scotland in that case could well provide a hostile base for English dissidents and French ambitions; so in 1539 an Order in Council was issued which ordained that 'all Havens should be fensed with bulwarks and blockehouses against the Scots'.

Nothing came of that particular crisis. As well as planning 'bulwarks and blockehouses against the Scots', Henry VIII courted his nephew James V assiduously in the hope of ensuring Scotland's alliance, or neutrality at least, while he prepared for war or wars elsewhere. France countered these blandishments by proposing a joint Franco-Scottish crusade against England; but all that came of it was an abortive solo Scottish invasion of England in November 1542, a half-hearted affray that ended in humiliation at the Rout of Solway Moss in Dumfriesshire. In the following month (December 1542) King James V of Scotland died at Falkland Palace; on his deathbed he was brought the news that a child had been born to his French consort, Mary of Guise (Lorraine). This was the future Mary Queen of Scots — and at once the patterns of the murderous political chess-game changed.

Henry VIII saw in the birth a chance of a 'final solution' to the Scottish problem: he had a five-year-old son and heir, Edward (the future King Edward VI, the last Tudor king of England, offspring of his third marriage, to Jane Seymour), and now the kingdom of Scotland had a baby Queen. What better than a marriage-alliance that would unite the two Crowns for all time? There was a pro-English, pro-Reformation party in Scotland that was in powerful support of such a policy of lasting reconciliation; but there was an equally strong pro-French, pro-Catholic party that preferred to rely on the 'Auld Alliance' with France. At first the pro-English party was in the ascendancy, and in July 1543 the Scottish Parliament agreed to a treaty of marriage whereby Mary was to marry Edward when she was eleven years old. But this hope was immediately confounded by the powerful

Cardinal Beaton of St Andrews, and the infant queen's mother, Mary of Guise, as well as by a widespread popular belief that what King Henry really wanted was to make himself master of Scotland, and Scotland a mere province of England. So the Scottish Parliament did a rapid U-turn and repudiated the marriage-treaty with England.

Henry's fury knew no bounds. He despatched Prince Edward's uncle, Henry Seymour, the Earl of Hertford, on a punitive expedition against the Scots — a two-year campaign of devastation that came to be known as the 'Rough Wooing'. That autumn, Lord Hertford moved north towards Berwick-upon-Tweed; on his way he landed on Holy Island, 12 miles to the south, with 2,200 troops, bringing ten English line-of-battle ships to anchorage in the harbour. By then, in accordance with the Order in Council of 1539, two bulwarks had been built on Lindisfarne by Robert Rooke of Berwick, the one to command the road and the other to defend the island:

> There is stone plentie and sufficient remayning of the olde abbey lately dissolved there to make the bulwark that shal defend the eland all of stone if it maie so stand with the good pleasure of the kinges said majestie.

Lord Hertford must have been impressed with the military possibilities of Lindisfarne as a naval base as he moved on; it enabled him to fall upon Edinburgh like a bolt from the blue in May 1544, burning it to the ground (he was to repeat the treatment the following year, when he devastated the Lowlands again and burnt the abbeys of Kelso, Melrose, Dryburgh and Eccles). In 1544 the Privy Council discussed repairs to the bulwarks; and in 1548-9 Sir Thomas Holcrofte and an engineer were directed 'to view the place by the churche, what hill or grounde were mete for fortification there'.

Construction work must have started immediately. In 1550, Sir Robert Bowes reported in *A book of the state of the Frontiers and Marches between England and Scotland*:

> The Fort of Beblowe, within the Holy Island, lyeth very well for the defence of the haven theire; and if there were about the lowe part thereof made a ring, with bulwarkes to flancke the same, the ditch thereabout might be easily watered towarde the land. And then I thinke the said forte were very stronge, and stood to great purpose, both for the defense of the forte and annoyance of the enemies, if they did arrive in any other parte of that Island.

The proposed moat was never built. But the Bowes Report echoed Lord Hertford's opinion of Lindisfarne's strategic importance:

The Holy Iland is also a place much necessarye to be defended and preserved, for there is a harboroughe sufficient for a great navye of shippes to rest safely in, and very aptlye for the warrs towards Scotland. And in that Island be both store howses, brewe howses, and backe howses, to conserve and prepayre victualls sufficient to furnish the said navye withall; which storehowses must either contynuallye be kept in reparations, or ells they will shortelye decaye.

And the greatest decaye that appeareth in them is the South-east wall of the brewhowse which standeth uppon proppes, like to fall, and would with expedicion be made upp with stone.

A piece also of the roofe of the great storehowse that was the Churche of the Priory, was the last yeare, in a great winde, broken downe by a parcell of the imbattlement of the same howse, that feel thereuppon, which would be repayred with expedicion, or ells the weat discending thereby will cawse great decaye in the floores of the said storehowses.

Although Lindisfarne was thus thrust once again into the forefront of history, it was seldom to be in the front-line of events. The fort on Beblowe never had a very large garrison. In 1559, for instance, it consisted of a captain (non-resident), two master gunners (at 1s per day), a master's mate (10d per day), and twenty soldiers at 8d per day. For armament, the fort was equipped with culverins (large long-barrelled cannons) and demi-culverins, sakers and falcons (light ship's cannons).

Apart from the fort, community life on Lindisfarne was at a depressingly low ebb. A Survey made for the Crown in 1561, the third year of Queen Elizabeth's reign, paints a desolate picture:

The Holy Iland . . . hath in the same a little borowgh towne, all sett with fishers very poore, and is a markett town on ye Satterday, howbeit it is little vsed, and yit by reason thereof all the townes of Norham and Ilandshyre ought theire to receive y^r measors and wights, and are in all things to be directed by thassisse of the said towne of Iland.

And there was in the same Iland one Cell of Monks of the house of Durham, which house hath the personage of the said parish as before is declared, which mansione howse was build in fovre square of two Courts, as appeareth by the platt theirof, and nowe the same howse is the Quene's Maties storehouse, and also another howse in the towne called the Pallace, which is the newe brewehouse and bakehouse, and other offices in the same for the said storehouse . . .

The moreparte of the towne is nowe decayed in howses, and yit the tofts and crofts where the howses did stand remayne, of which the burrowe rent is nowe for the most part collected and raysed . . .

149

In 1603, with the death of Queen Elizabeth, Henry VIII's old dream of a Union of the Crowns came true (albeit a generation later) when Mary Queen of Scots' son, James VI of Scotland, succeeded to the throne as James I of England as well; and with that, Lindisfarne lost even its strategic importance. The garrison was kept on, however; and before long there was to be occasion for the fort to be repaired and improved as King Charles I's troubled reign moved onto a collision course with his Scottish subjects as well as his Parliament in England.

Ironically, in view of the early history of Lindisfarne, it was religion and ecclesiastical dissension that brought the island back into brief prominence. Charles I was determined to impose upon Scotland a form of Episcopal (some said Roman) worship and church order that offended against Scotland's Presbyterian forms. Both sides were wilful and uncompromising, and it soon became clear that only an eventual recourse to force of arms would resolve the issue.

Before that came about, however, we get a glimpse of Lindisfarne in the journal of Sir William Brereton, a gentleman of Cheshire who would later distinguish himself during the Civil War as a Parliamentary Commander-in-chief. In 1634-5, he made an extended tour of Britain and the Low Countries; and in June 1635 he paid a brief visit to Lindisfarne, which he reported in *Notes on a journey through Durham and Northumberland in 1635*, published by the Surtees Society in 1914. What seems to have impressed him most was not so much the fort as the physiognomy of its governor, Captain Robert Rugg (of whom much more anon):

> In this island, in a daintie little fort, there lives Capt: Rugg, Governor of this fort: who is as famous for his generous and free entertainment of strangers, as for his great bottle nose, which is the largest I have seen. This is a daintie little fort built towre-wise uppon the toppe of a little round hill, which is a rocke...
> There are neate, warme and convenient roomes in this little fort.

Four years later, in 1639, the religious antagonism between Charles and his Scottish subjects came to a head. Both sides gathered an army, and in the spring, King Charles led his forces northwards to Berwick-upon-Tweed, using Lindisfarne as a naval staging-post. Twenty ships under the command of the Marquis of Hamilton, the king's commissioner for Scotland, anchored in Lindisfarne harbour and landed two regiments of foot, which marched off towards Berwick, while Hamilton himself was to sail further north with 5,000 troops to menace Aberdeen.

150

One of the king's suite, John Aston, another gentleman of Cheshire, took the opportunity of paying a quick visit to Lindisfarne from the royal encampment at Goswick. He noted his impressions in his *Journal* (also published by the Surtees Society):

> There is a pretty fort in it, which upon this occasion was repaired and put into forme. There are 2 batteries on it, on the lower stood mounted 3 iron peeces and 2 of brasse, with carriadges and platformes in good order. On the higher was one brasse gunne and 2 iron ones with all ammunition to them. There are 24 men and a captain kept in pay to man it, the common souldiours have 6d per diem. The captain at our beeing there was Captain Rugg, knowne commonly by his great nose.

Nothing came of the 1639 showdown with King Charles. Both sides were reluctant to cross the Tweed, and backed off without coming to blows. Meanwhile, Captain Rugg's spectacular proboscis continued to excite amazed comment from all who beheld it. In 1643, Father Gilbert Blakhal, 'a priest of the Scots Mission in France, in the Low Countries, and in Scotland', was storm-driven into Lindisfarne harbour, providentially escaping shipwreck by a hair's-breadth; a Yarmouth vessel that tried to follow them into harbour was dashed against the rocks, with all hands lost. There followed an unseemly brawl amongst the islanders as they looted the stricken ship. Father Blakhal later visited the fort ('which is no strength at all') and met Captain Rugg — 'a notable good fellow, as his great read nose ful of pimples did give testimony'; and in his rather engaging account of his travels (*A brieffe narration of the services done to three noble ladyes, 1631-49*, published by the Spalding Club in 1844), Blakhal relates what Captain Rugg told him about the islanders' attitude to ships in mortal peril:

> He was a very civil and jovial gentleman, and good company; and, among the rest of merry discourses, he tould us how the common people ther do pray for shippes which they sie in danger. They al sit downe upon their knees, and hold up their handes, and say very devotely, Lord send her to us, God send her to us. You, said he, seing them upon their knees, and their hands joyned, do think that they are praying for your sauvetie; but their myndes are far from that. They pray, not God to sauve you, or send you to the port, but to send you to them by shipwrack, that they may gette the spoile of her. And, to show that this is their meaning, said he, if the shippe come wel to the porte, or eschew naufrage, they gette up in anger, crying, the Devil stick her, she is away from us.

How Captain Rugg managed to afford all the hospitality that gave him both his nose and his reputation for conviviality is a mystery, because King Charles was always chronically short of funds, and Captain Rugg was owed several months' arrears of pay. In May 1643 he sent a jocular rhyming letter to the Royal Paymasters asking for his overdue pay:

> The greate Commander of the Gormorants,
> The Geese and Ganders of these Hallowed Lands,
> Where Lindisferne and Holy Iland stands,
> These worthless lines sends to yor worthie hands.
> To one or all the fower, I care not whether,
> Gib: Jack: Hob: James, when you meete together,
> Send in my disbursements, made out by direction
> From my good lord; sirs, hasten my collection.
> For want of pay, and prest soe sore by cravers,
> My soules p'plexed, then blame I the receavers.
> Layinge the fault on those that should releeve me,
> And soe to doe doth not a little grieve me.
> I owe for bread, beere, beefe, in sundry places;
> The cuntrie calls upon me with disgraces;
> Sorry in towne, ashamed to see there faces,
> Yett not afeard of Serjants, Maiors, or Maces.
> This is a missery, but here's the thinge,
> Because I am protected by the Kinge.
> I know not if these lines stand with your likeinge;
> I have a conscience none can toss a pike in.
> Lett me have what is ordered to be given,
> I will doe wrong to noe man livinge.
> I wrote so often prose that I was weary,
> I would tell all my vices were I neere you;
> In such a straine I should expresse my sorrow,
> I sure would gett my owne, or sure would borrowe,
> To my fast freinds I thinke enough is spoken,
> Although my meanes be meene my hart's not broken;
> I wish I had wherewith for to interr me;
> Thus to yor best discressions I reffer me,
> And that greate God that houlds the Devell in fetters,
> Blesse good Kinge Charles, myselfe, and you my debters.

Not even this poetic appeal for back-pay sufficed to loosen the purse-strings, however; and that may well have induced Captain Rugg to hand over the fort to the Parliamentary forces during the Civil War of the 1640s. In 1645, we find that Parliament decreed that all arrears of garrison pay at Lindisfarne should be paid, and that Captain Rugg, who had retired by then, should receive £100 'for his relief, he having first rendered it into the hands of Parliament'. But Parliament proved no more open-handed than the King; when Rugg died in 1646, his will included a legacy to his daughter of the £100 still owed to him by Parliament.

During the Civil War, the fort came under occasional sustained pressure, particularly after Berwick fell to the Royalists in 1647; the island was blockaded for lengthy periods, and supplies sometimes ran perilously low, but relief always arrived in the nick of time. With the return of peace and the Restoration of the monarchy, Lindisfarne settled into its backwater again, and the garrison was gradually reduced to a complement of seven.

In the 1670s, however, there was need of further defensive reinforcement of Lindisfarne during the Dutch Wars, and in 1675 a second small fort, described as a 'Plattforme and Redoutte', was built at the Steel End (the eastern end) of the Heugh. It was designed and made by Daniel Collingwood and Robert Trollope; Trollope was a northern architect of some note, and was responsible for the Exchange and Guildhall in York. His secondary fort at Lindisfarne was designed to command the harbour more closely than Beblowe; it comprised a diamond-shaped walled enclosure with three gunnery turrets, placed on an outer crenellated platform, with a central tower of several storeys. Today, the Steel End has the truncated remains of this or some other strong-point, thoughtfully provided with bench-seating which offers shelter from the wind.

There was to be only one final moment of drama in the military story of the fort on Beblowe Crag; it happened in 1715, during the abortive Jacobite Rising in Scotland in support of the 'Old Pretender', James Stewart, only son of the exiled King James II. On October 10, a certain Lancelot Errington, 'a man of an ancient and respectable family in Northumberland', seized the Castle briefly on behalf of the Jacobites. The story, a swashbuckling tale of derring-do if ever there was one, corroborated by the son of an eye-witness, is delightfully told in William Hutchinson's *The History and Antiquities of the County Palatinate of Durham*, Vol. III (1794):

> At this time the garrison consisted of a serjeant, a corporal, and ten or twelve men only. In order to put this scheme in execution, being well known in that country, he went to the castle, and after some discourse with the serjeant, invited him and the rest of the men, who were not immediately on duty, to partake of a treat on board of the ship of which he was master, then lying in the harbour: this being unsuspectedly accepted of, he so well plied his guests with brandy, that they were soon incapable of any opposition.
>
> These men being thus secured, he made some pretence of going

on shore, and with *Mark Errington*, his nephew, returning again to the castle, they knocked down the sentinel, surprised and turned out an old gunner, the corporal, and two other soldiers, being the remainder of the garrison, and shutting the gates, hoisted the Pretender's colours as a signal of their success, anxiously expecting the promised succours.

No reinforcement coming, but on the contrary, a party of the king's troops arriving from Berwick, they were obliged to retreat over the walls of the castle among the rocks, hoping to conceal themselves under the sea weeds till it was dark, and then by swimming to the main land, to make their escape; but the tide rising, they were obliged to swim, when the soldiers firing at Lancelot, as he was climbing up a rock, wounded him in the thigh; thus disabled, he and his nephew were taken, and conveyed to Berwick goal, where they continued till his wound was cured.

During this time, he had digged a burrow quite under the foundations of the prison, depositing the earth taken out, in an old oven. Through this burrow, he and his nephew, and diverse other prisoners escaped; but most of the latter were soon after taken. The two Erringtons, however, had the good fortune to make their way to the Tweedside, where they found the custom-house boat; they rowed themselves over, and afterwards turned it adrift. From thence they pursued their journey to Bambrough castle, near which they were concealed nine days in a pea stack; a relation who resided in the castle supplying them with provision.

At length travelling in the night by secret paths, they reached Gateshead-house, near Newcastle, where they were secreted, till they procured a passage from Sunderland to France. A reward of £500 was now offered to any one who would apprehend them; notwithstanding which, Lancelot was so daring, as soon after to come to England, and even to visit some of his friends in Newgate. After the suppression of the rebellion, when everything was quiet, he and his nephew took the benefit of the general pardon, and returned to Newcastle, where he died about the year 1746, as it is said, of grief at the victory of Culloden.

It is a story worthy of Sir Walter Scott himself, and there is no doubt where William Hutchinson's chivalrous sympathies lay: 'In which exploit, such policy and courage were exerted, as would have done them much honour, had they been employed in a better cause'.

After this last flurry of alarums and excursions, the garrison relapsed into its customary torpor, until it was finally withdrawn in 1819. The castle was variously used for a time as a coastguard station, and as the headquarters of a detachment of the Northumberland Artillery Volunteers. By the end of the 19th century, Lindisfarne Castle had fallen into disuse and was in a sorry, if not actually ruinous, state; but it

SET A CRAB TO CATCH A RABBIT

One of the most bizzare stories you may hear on Lindisfarne is the alleged island habit of using Edible Crabs (*Cancer pagurus*) as a substitute for ferrets, to bolt rabbits out of their burrows — by candlelight!

The story was given currency by the eminent naturalist Richard Perry in his book *A Naturalist on Lindisfarne* (1946). On page 38 he quotes a 19th century traveller (apparently Dr George Johnston, author of *Our Visit to Holy Island in May 1854*), although I cannot trace the paragraph in the original publication):

> [The islanders] have a curious use for crabs. A strong large dog-crab is selected, and a piece of tallow candle, about an inch long, is stuck on the back of the crab. A rabbit hole is then selected, the candle lighted, and the crab sent on this travels down the hole with his light. The rabbits bolt out into a net, as if a ferret had been sent in!

I was absolutely fascinated by this tale, and made a point of asking every old-timer I met if they had ever seen it done, or even done it themselves. Well, no, not actually — but they all seemed to know of someone who knew someone else whose cousin used to do it.

Only one of my informants claimed to have tried it for himself: fisherman James 'Clinker' Brigham, whose father, 'Clinch' Brigham, was a professional rabbit-catcher for many years — using snares, not crabs. Clinker says he heard the crab-story when he was a boy, so he and his pals decided to conduct an experiment. They picked a sturdy red-backed crab, melted some wax on its shell, and jammed a stub of a candle onto it. The theory was that the heat of the burning candle would galvanise the crab into a brisk canter down the burrow, and the light would strike dread into the heart of any rabbit holed up inside.

Alas! It didn't work. These crabs cannot breathe in air, and are only mobile on land for a couple of hours. Clinker's crab resolutely refused to go in, and the rabbits refused to come out.

Ah well. It was a good yarn while it lasted. But as Clinker is the first to tell you, you should always take his stories with a pinch of salt, to help you swallow them.

156

was then, when it seemed to have lost all its usefulness, that it was given a new and splendid lease of life — as an Edwardian live-in country house: a dainty little fort, indeed.

The man behind the transformation was one of the great unsung patrons of English architecture: Edward Hudson (1854-1936), the founder and presiding genius for nearly 40 years of *Country Life*, the weekly illustrated magazine that became, in the words of the 1st Viscount Runciman, 'the keeper of the architectural conscience of the nation'. Hudson was a wealthy connoisseur of *objets d'art* who took over the family printing firm at the age of 21. He launched *Country Life Illustrated* (as it was first called) in January 1897 — and thereby found not only his life's work but also the ideal vehicle of expression for his own shy, inarticulate passion for artistic perfection and ordered romanticism.

In 1901 he was touring Northumberland with his editor, Peter Anderson Graham, looking for country houses worthy of being featured in the magazine. They popped over to Holy Island for a quick look round; and there Hudson caught sight of the Castle for the first time. Graham told the story in an article in *Country Life* in June 1913 (later published in book form as *Lindisfarne or Holy Island*, 1920):

> He knew nothing about it or its story, for he had never been on the island before; but, finding it empty and apparently abandoned, scaled the wall and entered.
>
> Few men in the conditions under which he found it would have conceived the idea that it might be transformed into a thing of beauty. The last to reside in it had been the coastguards, and any features of good building which the Castle might originally have possessed were certainly not enhanced by their treatment.
>
> At the best there is something forbidding and desolate about the inside of a house that has been vacated, but this case was much worse than the ordinary. The coast-guards had evidently regarded the fortress merely as a rough barracks and nothing more. As if to increase the forlorn squalor, lying about were the *disjecta membra* of such furniture and utensils as they had not thought it worth while to take away.

The Castle was Crown property at the time. Hudson began immediate negotiations for its purchase, and in January 1902 he sent to his friend 'Ned' Lutyens, the foremost young country-house architect in Britain, a dramatic telegram: 'Have got Lindisfarne'.

Edwin Landseer Lutyens (1869-1944, knighted in 1918) was then 33 years old. He has been hailed as the greatest English architect since Christopher Wren — the pioneer of what contemporaries called 'the

English Wrennaissance'; indeed, much of his inspiration was drawn from Wren's interpretation of Roman classicism. Today he is best remembered for Hampstead Garden Suburb, the Cenotaph in Whitehall, the Viceroy's House in New Delhi (and New Delhi itself), the British Embassy in Washington, and the (unbuilt) first design for Liverpool Roman Catholic cathedral. At the time of the telegram from Edward Hudson he had just designed the British Pavilion for the Paris Exhibition of 1900, and had established a considerable reputation among the *cognoscenti* for designing and renovating picturesque country houses like Munstead Wood in Godalming, Surrey, the home of Miss Gertrude Jekyll (1843-1932), the outstanding garden-designer of her time. It was through Miss Jekyll that Hudson first met Lutyens in 1899; this led to an immediate commission to design Hudson's country house, Deanery Garden in Sonning — and to a lifelong and devoted friendship.

The commission to convert Lindisfarne Castle into a country dwelling presented Lutyens with a perfect challenge to his fertile and romantic imagination. No one in England was more in sympathy with the Tudoresque Revival style that Lindisfarne Castle called for. Lutyens loved working with natural local materials, and had a rare feeling for texture, harmony and history; and in Edward Hudson he had the ideal patron. They shared the same meticulousness of taste, the same regard for integrity in buildings. As Peter Anderson Graham put it in his *Country Life* article:

> It was not the first time Mr Hudson and Mr Lutyens had worked together, and to their combined taste and judgement is due the fine building that sits as naturally on the Beblowe rock as a sea-bird on its nest.
>
> The rock and dwelling do not stand apart like hostile neighbours, but cling to one another like twin brethren. The outline and composition of the group of buildings and the choice of right materials and their appropriate treatment make the work of man look like a continuation and completement of that of Nature.
>
> Outside and in, the effect is obtained not by ornament and elaboration, but by form, proportion and attention to the texture and colour of the structural features. The fact that it was a solid practical building set up for defence and not for beauty has not been lost sight of; yet the general result is beautiful.

The basic physical structure of the ramparts was still solid and substantial; Lutyens subtly improved the external appearance by removing the crenellations and rounding the edges, thus simplifying the silhouette and emphasising the impression of a stone sea-bird crouching on its nest of rock, just like the Fulmars (*Fulmarus glacialis*) which nest on the ledges of the crag. In spring and summer the rock-face is starred with vivid colour: tall Red Valerian (*Centranthus ruber*), Stonecrop (*Sedum acre* — also called Wall-pepper from the acrid taste of its leaves), spikes of vivid blue Viper's bugloss (*Echium vulgare*).

The entrance to the fort was approached by a gently sloping ramp traversing the southern flank of the crag. Lutyens retained this approach, but he removed the stone balustrade and laid the shallow-stepped ramp with cobbles in herring-bone pattern (almost a Lutyens trademark, that), now dusted with purple creeping Wild Thyme (*Thymus drucei*). The old portcullis guarding the entrance-door is still visible in its overhead slot, its winding-machinery still in working order in what used to be a look-out post in the old Fort but is now the scullery.

The fort entrance is not the entrance to the Castle proper, however. It leads only into a small vestibule, with a dark stone stairway leading upwards to the right, at the top of which the visitor is unexpectedly thrust out into the bracing air and splendid panoramic views of the open Lower Battery. The gun emplacements (but not the guns) are still there, commanding the main channel into the harbour towards the south-east.

What Lutyens did with the interior was to rationalise and join up the haphazard collection of buildings that constituted the old garrison quarters, to make an impressive if somewhat austere family home with nine bedrooms and some very striking public rooms: a steeply vaulted Dining Room with a fine wide fireplace, a barrel-vaulted Drawing Room (once an ammunition store, now known as the Ship Room because of the splendid scale model of the Dutch vessel *Henrietta of Amsterdam*, made in 1840, that Lutyens suspended from the ceiling), a Long Gallery linking the former east and west buildings, and a noble pillared Entrance Hall.

The rooms were equipped with furniture and fittings specially designed by Lutyens, like the ingenious wooden door-catches and bolts, the dresser and refectory table in the Kitchen, and the oval oak dining-table in the Dining Room; but for the most part, the Castle was furnished with handsome antiques of English or Flemish 17th century make. Everywhere there is a sturdiness of stone pillars and arches, curving staircases and cavernous fireplaces, mullioned windows and embrasure-seats and herring-bone brick floors. It could be a cold, dank place, and one early house-guest, the historian Lytton Strachey, found it appalling: 'Very dark, with nowhere to sit, and nothing but stone under, over and round you, which produces a distressing effect'. But a hardy stoicism was the order of the day for most of these literary, romantic Edwardians who liked to renovate and live in old castles.

To complete the picture, Edward Hudson commissioned his old friend, Gertrude Jekyll, to design a garden for the Castle. He originally envisaged a water garden in the Stank, a marshy hollow to the north of the crag, with a tennis court or croquet lawn; but this proved impractical, and in 1911, Miss Jekyll devised a scheme for a small walled garden on a southward facing slope some 500 yards to the north, utilising an existing quadrilateral field-enclosure. It provided a sheltered oasis of colour with a handsome view of the Castle. The original planting plans, recently discovered in the Beatrix Farrand Library of the University of California at Berkeley, have enabled the National Trust to re-create the Castle garden as far as possible in accordance with Gertrude Jekyll's intentions.

For many years, Lindisfarne Castle was Hudson's pride and joy. The first weekend party was held in September, 1905, and from then on it became famed for its celebrated visitors — the Prince and Princess of Wales (later King George V and Queen Mary), Lord Baden-Powell, Asquith and his daughter Lady Violet Bonham-Carter, J.M. Barrie, Sir Malcolm Sargent, Dame Alicia Markova, and, above all, the Portugese cellist, Guilhermina Suggia, to whom Hudson gave a Stradivarius and for whom, I suspect, the bachelor Hudson (he only married, late in life, in 1929) harboured a more than musical but secret passion.

After the First World War, 'the island', as Hudson always called it, became too remote for him to visit regularly. He was then in his late sixties, and in 1921 he sold the Castle to a London banker, Oswald Falk; Falk soon sold it to the distinguished London merchant banker, Sir Edward de Stein, who used it with his sister Gladys as a family holiday home for friends and relatives — especially their flock of young nephews and nieces. Sir Edward was a noted philanthropist who dabbled successfully in water-colours and light verse. In 1944 he gave Lindisfarne Castle to the National Trust, although he remained its tenant until his death in 1965; thereafter his sister Gladys took over the tenancy until her own death in 1968.

The National Trust has embalmed the Castle as a monument to Sir Edwin Lutyens and his exercise in Edwardian nostalgia. Apart from renovating the walled garden, the Trust has also renewed the set of store-sheds at the base of the Castle; they are, literally, 'boat-houses', in that they were originally a Norwegian fishing boat used on the celebrated 'Shetland Bus' escape route across the North Sea from occupied Norway during the Second World War. The vessel was brought down to Lindisfarne and sawn into three sections, and then installed upside-down as a row of sheds — a felicitous echo of the motif of boat-sheds down by the harbour.

Since 1980, the administrators of the Castle on behalf of the National Trust have been Michael and Patricia Hepworth, who occupy the private flat above the Entrance Hall and Kitchen. They can call upon half a dozen part-time stewards-cum-guides to help out during the summer months; most of them live on the mainland, but one of them, Ernie Evans, now in his sixties, is a retired Further Education Adviser from Tyneside who now lives on the island after holidaying there for some twenty years, and who also conducts a weekly Local History Walk round the island. Some 50,000 visitors (the number is growing each year) come to the Castle each summer, to admire the 'daintie little fort', Tudor-built with stones from the Norman Priory, that the Edwardian age endowed with timelessness and romance.

S.G.M.

14 The Nineteenth Century

It was not until the end of the 18th century that Lindisfarne shook itself free from the insular apathy that had set in after the Dissolution of the Monasteries and the building of the fort on Beblowe Crag in the 16th century. The intervening years had been bleak indeed for Holy Island. It became not so much an island sanctuary as an island of poverty. The houses were little better than hovels, the population sank to a mere forty families. There had been a brief revival in the middle of the 17th century, when the fishing was good and there was money to be made from gathering seaweed and burning it in pits to make fertiliser and soda. But this brief burst of prosperity, during which the population rose markedly, soon petered out. The 18th century was marked by a return to grinding poverty, to emigration, to lawlessness, and to falling population figures.

But then, with the onset of the Industrial Revolution, the tide began to turn again. Under the Enclosure of the Common Land Act of 1793, the agricultural potential of the land was released, and its value was estimated to have increased eightfold. William Hutchinson, writing in his *The History and Antiquities of the County Palatine of Durham* (1794), was there to see the signs of revival:

> The village consists of a few irregular houses; two or more of which are inns, one appertains to a farm-hold, and the rest are inhabited by fishermen: it has been improved of late years by the building of several new tenements . . .
>
> The fishermen, in the winter season, are employed in catching lobsters, which are sent in great quantities to the London market. Ten or twelve, three- or four-men boats are used in the summer, fishing for cod, ling and haddocks, which abound on the coast.

Hutchinson also gives us a glimpse of the first stirrings of activity on the industrial front, involving the island's natural mineral resources:

> On the north part of the island, there is abundance of limestone; and a small seam of coal, never much worked, on account of the water, and other difficulties. There is plenty of iron ore in a bed of black shiver or slate . . .The Carron company have men getting iron ore, but they are obliged to work at the ebbing of the tide, as the ore lies within high water mark.

162

JETTY TO NOWHERE

On the foreshore just to the east of the Castle, near the Riding Stone, stand the remains of what was once a bustling jetty. Today, the group of gaunt sprouting timbers looks like a modern sculpture — of a First World War battlefield, perhaps; but a century ago these stark, rotting piers supported a wooden jetty that was the outlet for a major industry on Lindisfarne — lime-working.

Limestone had been quarried in modest quantities and burnt for lime on Holy Island since the Middle Ages (the Benedictine monks of Lindisfarne Priory had found it a useful addition to their revenues). Early in the 19th century, when the Industrial Revolution was creating extensive new markets, the quarrying of limestone on a large scale at several sites on the island became a commercially viable proposition. In the 1860s a Dundee company started work in a quarry at Ness-end, in the north of the island. It built massive new limekilns near the Castle, and created a raised embankment to take a tramway down the east coast of the island to bring the quarried stone to the kilns. And it built a spanking new pier for exporting the lime to the mainland.

It was big business. Something like 20 percent of the adult male population (the total population was then at a peak of 600) were employed in lime-working and carting. Five ships plied their trade between Lindisfarne and Dundee, carrying away cargoes of lime and bringing back coal. The Dundee company also erected two slender obelisks on Old Law, due south beyond the sandbanks on the mainland, as navigational aids to help their ships find the deep-water channel into the haven.

But the business didn't prosper for long, alas. At about the time that Edward Hudson was prospecting the possibilities of Lindisfarne Castle as a country house, in 1901, the ovens of the handsome limekilns nearby were being banked for the last time. The tramway embankment was grassed over, the waste-dumps by the kilns became inscrutable archaeological mounds, the wooden jetty that now led nowhere was abandoned. But the limekilns with their splendid stone arcades still stand, and have been taken over by the National Trust as a mute monument to Lindisfarne's brief decades of industrial enterprise.

164

The amenities of the island were improving, too. Although there had been a teacher on the island for most of the 18th century, it was not until 1796 that a National School, with a schoolmaster's house, was built by public subscription on land set aside under the Enclosure Act. The population was on the increase; by 1797 it had risen to 364. Lindisfarne was even becoming a sort of spa, according to Hutchinson:

> The shore of this island is, in many parts, excellent for bathing, and the situation is at once healthy and romantic: it is, of late years, become a place of great resort; and much praised for the beauties that grace its solemn walks.

The first half of the 19th century brought a spectacular revival of prosperity for the island. The annual birth rate soared, and incomers started to flow across the sands. By 1841 there were 497 people on the island; ten years later, 553; and in 1861, a peak of 614. Two industrial factors were chiefly responsible — the growth of the mining and quarrying industry, and a tremendous boom in the herring fisheries.

The lime-quarrying, which had been going on desultorily for centuries, was at the heart of Lindisfarne's little Industrial Revolution, although it was not to last into the 20th century. Apart from the Dundee-based enterprise which has left the fine lime-kilns near the Castle there was a complex of kilns with adjacent workmen's cottages at the south-western part of the Links run by the Kennedy Lime Works, which imported Irish labour for the task; and a network of raised embankments to take horse-drawn wagons on rails seamed the island.

Nodules of ironstone were gathered commercially by the mighty Carron Iron Company, near Falkirk on the Firth of Forth, which started operations in 1760 and quickly became the major iron-producing operations in Britain (it even gave its name to a light cannon, the carronade, which was much used in Nelson's navy). But Lindisfarne was too meagre a source to satisfy the hungry furnaces on the River Carron.

Various attempts were also made to get at the coal seams that underlie parts of the island. A coal mine was in existence on the Snook by 1791, and other experimental borings were sunk elsewhere. But the major attempt to exploit the coal resources was made in 1840 by the Lord of the Manor, Mr Selby, in 1840. It does not appear to have been very successful, and by 1875 it had been abandoned; but at least it has left us with the most enigmatic monument on the island: Snook Tower. No one seems to know why it was built. Some people think it must have been a winding-tower for the coal-mine, but there is no sign of a shaft, and no winding-gear within the Tower, and no sign of subsidence anywhere around. There is a staircase inside, leading up to the roof, with a flag-pole on top, and on an old chart the Tower is listed as a flag-signalling station. But why such an elaborately-built miniature medieval Tower? It's a mystery — yet another Folly from an age much given to Follies of various forms.

But the dominant feature of island life in that buoyant era was fishing. William Hutchinson had noted 10 or 12 small boats operating in 1794; in 1826 there were 13 island boats engaged in the burgeoning herring fisheries — smallish boats with crews of four men and a dozen nets which they shot off the Farne Islands. White fish and lobsters were also being taken, for export to London where cod fetched 8s a score and lobsters 12s a score. By 1840 there were 15 boats at the fishing, including some big boats with 37-ft keels. By the middle of the century, half of the adult population was occupied in fishing and allied trades. There were now 36 large boats, each with a crew of 5 or 6, engaged in fishing for both herring and whitefish, as well as lobsters and crabs. The island was — quite literally — humming, as Dr George Johnston of Ilderton, one of the founders of the Berwickshire Naturalists' Club, described in *Our Visit to Holy Island in May 1854*:

> A stroll through the village disclosed very sensibly the nature of the principal occupation of the natives. In every street heaps of the shells of the mussel and limpet are collected before the doors, and mixed with the refuse of the fishing lines, and with the household ashes, etc. They do send forth a most foul and fishy smell, evidently agreeable to the senses of the house-holders. Men, and more women, were sitting in the sun, at the doors, occupied in baiting the lines for the morrow . . .
>
> A number of skates were laid on the tiled roofs of many of the houses, to be dried by the sun. They were not ornamental, and sent forth a pungent smell. When fully dried they become a favourite relish to the fishermen when drinking their ale; and I was told that they were much in demand by the sailors of the Scotch vessels that are driven here for the shelter. They are eaten without preparation, or simply toasted at the fire.

Another visitor in the 1850s, Walter White, a gentleman hiker who wrote many books on his rambles through Britain, has left us a vivid picture of the herring bonanza in his *Northumberland, & The Border* (1859):

> We saw 'the town' under its busy aspect, preparing for the herring fishery; nets lay in heaps, or stretched out fifty or sixty yards, while men and boys disentangle their mazy folds and tie the

166

loops; around almost every door lies a heap of floats, and lines, and queer-looking oil-skin garments, and ample sou'westers hang on the walls . . .

We passed the beach where the fishing-boats come in, and saw the huge wooden vat — if vat it be — round which the women stand to clean the herrings, and on the other side of the road fourteen hundred herring-barrels in piles and rows, and two men industrious over their preparation. 'There wouldn't be any too many', they said, 'nor yet half enough, if the boats did but have luck' . . .

While recrossing the herring beach, we had a pretty sight in the departure of a number of the boats. The tide served, evening was coming on, and one after another they hoisted sail, stood out of the bay, made a tack, some two tacks, and then away to the open sea, perhaps for five-and-twenty miles.

At the height of the season, in the 1860s, when the entire herring catch was bought by two local curers for the Stettin market in the Baltic, it is said that a man could walk on upturned herring-barrels for half a mile along the green above the harbour beach from the Ouse to the lime-jetty below the Castle. Beside the Ouse, the impressive three-storeyed Herring House with its handsome red-tiled roof, which used to be the hub of the curing industry, has now been converted into a block of modern dwellings. Indeed, several delightful old buildings have now been renovated. The Old Granary in St Cuthbert Sq was one of the first to be converted into a comfortable home (by the professor of architecture at Newcastle University). Three whitewashed old Coastguard cottages in Sandham Lane have been modernised. The old *Iron Rails* Inn, probably named after the wagon-way for the lime traffic that ran nearby (or the distinctive railings at the entrance), is no longer a pub — it was converted into a dwelling-house by Mine Host, George Moody, in 1976 by the simple expedient of making the saloon bar a sitting-room; but a fine old herring smoke-house behind the *Iron Rails*, complete with racks of nails from which the herrings hung while they were being cured, has recently been beautifully transformed into two holiday homes.

These renovations, blending discreetly into their context, have done much to help conserve the vernacular flavour of the village buildings, and to remind us of the more rumbustious days when Lindisfarne was like a Wild West frontier Roaring Town: the days when there were no fewer than 10 pubs in the village (the *Ship Inn*, the *Britannia*, the *Fisherman's Arms*, the *Selby Arms*, the *Plough Inn*, the *Iron Rails*, the *Northumberland Arms*, the *Castle Hotel*, the *Crown & Anchor*, and the

167

Cambridge House), when the pub-doors opened at six o'clock in the morning for whiskey at 3d a half and rum at 4d a noggin. Fights and brawls were commonplace, there was no doctor, and no policeman could be induced to stay for any length of time. One night in February, 1889, after a good-going riot, a certain PC Johnston (nicknamed Constable Joe Smoke) was rash enough to clap one of the island fishermen into the lock-up. This so incensed the islanders that they wrecked the police station on the Market Square, forcing the wretched constable to take to the roof of the gaol and seek refuge with the vicar, the Rev W.W.F. Keeling, author of a delightful little book on *Lindisfarne or Holy Island* (1883). Next day it took a contingent of 20 mounted police from Berwick to come riding across the sands, like the U.S. Cavalry, to restore order. The last resident constable on the island left in 1923.

By the time of Constable Joe Smoke's discomfiture, the fishing industry had already passed its peak. By 1875 the herring boom was beginning to dwindle, and only sixteen boats were still fishing from the island, compared with about 500 from Eyemouth and North Sunderland. The tide was on the ebb again. In an attempt to keep up with the times, two of the boats were of the decked type, with a 55 ft keel and a crew of nine or ten men. But the herring and the men who hunted them — fickle creatures both — were now giving Lindisfarne a wide berth; landings on the island fell while landings on the mainland soared. The advent of the first steam-driven drifters in 1907, followed by the even more efficient motor-driven drifters, finally killed the inshore fishery trade. One by one the big sailing boats — useless hulks now — were upturned on the beach by the Ouse with their bows sawn off; tarred and weatherproofed, they made good store-houses for the fishing-gear, as they do to this day, looking just like a scene out of *David Copperfield*. The large boats were gradually replaced by 25 ft paraffin-driven flat-bottomed cobles, which needed far fewer crewmen and were used for line-fishing and lobsters. The last large boat was laid up in 1914. It was the end of an era.

But it was also the start of another era — the Age of Tourism. As long ago as 1794, William Hutchinson had noted that Lindisfarne had 'of late years, become a place of great resort'; but little progress had been made in that direction by 1859, when Walter White noted in his *Northumberland, & The Borders*:

> It is said that if good lodgings were available, the Island would be more visited than it is by sea-bathers; but the difficulty of access

and the want of pleasant scenery are perhaps the chief reasons against immigration.

But Lindisfarne, throughout the 19th century, was a place of considerable resort for field-naturalists — men like C.M. Adamson who visited Holy Island every year from the 1830s to the 1880s and eventually published four books on the island's birds, and the ornithologist Prideaux J. Selby of Twizell who catalogued the birds of the region in the 1830s and 40s. In the second half of the century, gun-toting naturalists like Abel Chapman were blazing the trail for an increasing number of Victorian sportsmen, and the railway revolution, which brought rail traffic to Lindisfarne's doorstep with the opening of Beal Station in 1847, made access to the island considerably more easy for new generations of the leisured rich.

Travel-writers had frequently made mention of Lindisfarne as a place of quaintness, at least. But it was two books published in 1883 that really started the 'mass market' appeal of Lindisfarne. One was by the island vicar, the Rev W.W.F. Keeling (*Lindisfarne or Holy Island*, Newcastle 1883), which was the first real guide and history, written with great charm and affection. The other was *Medical Guide to Health Resorts of Northumberland, Durham and their Borders*, by R.A. Ellis. Dr Ellis is fulsome in his appreciation:

> The island is frequented in the season as a health resort, but it deserves to be better known. The author has paid it several visits, and his family have stayed there, and, with others recommended, have derived much benefit from their sojourn. It will undoubtedly become more popular when the transit from Beal is improved. The establishment of a sanitarium or boarding-house with a resident medical man, and provision for hot sea-water baths, would, in the interest of invalids, and indeed of the island, be very desirable.

And what were its main therapeutic advantages?

> One feature of Holy Island is, that even in the height of summer, the air is always pleasant and fresh, and never overpowering, and that languid sensation and exhausting heat felt in large towns is never experienced. It must be remembered that the air of the island is not polluted by mill or factory chimney, and it has from the west the pure air of the Cheviot and Kyloe Hills; from the sea, by which it is twice surrounded in the twenty-four hours, a life-giving amount of ozone, a super-charge, so to speak, approaching most in their conditions to an ocean voyage, which seems to strengthen and nourish as inhaled.

He couldn't recommend Lindisfarne for cases of asthma, bronchial irritation, or consumption. But for practically every other ailment imaginable, Lindisfarne was a panacea:

> Debility, especially that of the jaded brain of town dweller and worker; nervous debility, leading to hysteria and depression of spirits; spinal weakness and sleeplessness; scrofulous complaints, including enlarged joints, weak joints, and relaxation of the joint ligaments in children; ricketts and its consequences; enlarged and stiff joints left by rheumatism . . .loss of appetite, and a condition of the system [similar] to that produced by blood poisoning, from living in an impure and vitiated atmosphere, notably the sick-chamber, from prolonged nursing, and where, although there may be no wound, the blood is as certainly poisoned as if inoculation had taken place.

The list also includes 'some of the pelvic diseases of women', and being generally 'out of sorts'. Finally:

> The place is adapted to restore the system where it has been poisoned by excess in, and prolonged abuse of, alcohol.

Dr Ellis's reference to the desirability of 'improved transit from Beal' could well be a veiled reproof to the islanders themselves, who in the 1860s had vigorously resisted a proposal to connect the island permanently to the mainland — they preferred their demi-insularity, and were determined to preserve it. An even more visionary scheme to build a railway branch-line from Beal across the sand to the island, ending in a jetty and pier with promenades — a sort of Blackpool of the east coast — had also come to nothing.

In Dr Ellis's time, and for centuries before that, the only way to reach Lindisfarne overland, at low tide, was by horse-drawn cart, or on Shanks's pony. The latter was not to be recommended; Walter White noted rather sourly, in 1859, that 'walking on plashy sands is not agreeable, especially with nothing to interest you on the way' (he was obviously not an ornithologist!). If you went by horse-cart, there was a choice of two routes: one was the 3-mile Pilgrim's Way, running directly across the sands from Beal Road end to Chare Ends on the island, crossing the stream called the Lough — the traditional route, well marked by a long row of 270 tall posts with barnacles up to the high-water mark and two lofty Refuge Boxes for heedless travellers trapped by the tide. The other route went directly across the sands the shortest distance to the Snook, shepherded by a line of 100 posts, about a mile in length, and then skirted the inside curve of the island along the firm sands to Chare ends.

One of the islanders, Mrs Eleanor Garvin (née Bell), who now lives on the mainland at Wickham but who comes back with her husband every weekend to the old family home, still remembers with nostalgic pleasure the days of the horse-carts. Her family ran the Post Office, with its mail contract, for generations; they had a farm, and did a bit of coal-mining, and ran the bakery, her father ran the *Castle Hotel* and worked at the fishing, her uncle had the *Northumberland Arms*; and in those pre-war days, 'tourists' were visitors, usually somewhat elderly visitors, who came to stay for a week or a resolute fortnight.

Eleanor had to go to school in Berwick for her secondary education, and had to catch the 8.20 a.m. bus from Beal. The horse-and-trap was better than a car for this purpose, because it could get through deeper water if necessary. Eleanor remembers the horse frequently having to swim for it, with the trap awash and her school case with her clean clothing for a week practically a-float.

Taxis had come to the island in the 1920s, a fleet of battered old Model T Fords. They had high-slung engines, but even so they couldn't go through more than a foot of water; they had broad running-boards, and if the water threatened to come over the running-boards, they had to turn back. By 1939 there was a fleet of 11 taxis, which could be summoned by telegram to meet the train at Beal Station. One of the early taxi-drivers was Eleanor's aunt, Eleanor Bell, known to everyone as 'Lal'. The taxis had no brakes to speak of, and hardly any clutch (the bottom gear served as the brake), but they could cram an astonishing number of passengers into and onto it, ten people at a pinch, with luggage strapped in layers all round the car.

Mr Garvin's widowed mother, Mrs Isabel Garvin, remembers her honeymoon in August 1922, which was spent in the Manor House Hotel. The hotel sent a horse-trap to meet them at Beal, and they were driven across the Pilgrim's Way to Chare Ends. Because a honeymoon on the island was such a rare event, some of the island fishermen took the horse out of the trap and manhandled it themselves, and the whole island, it seemed, turned out to greet them and practically filled the trap with rice and posies of flowers. Those were the days!

It's all very different now, of course. The horse-traps are all gone, along with the old Model T Fords. The short route from Beal shore to the Snook is now a metalled Causeway, which has revolutionised access to the island. Short experimental sections were constructed on the Beal side, first in 1929 and then again in 1949; the road surface was seen to stand up very well to the action of the tide, and in 1954, a further 1,420 yards, including the 50-yard bridge across the Lough, were built, linking Beal shore directly with the Snook. The 2-mile section of metalled road linking the Snook along the curve of the island to Chare Ends was completed in 1966.

And so, a hundred years after the proposal to 'connect the island permanently to the mainland' had first been mooted, and quashed, Lindisfarne now had easy access assured. It still needs care, however; despite the prominently-sited boards giving the tide-tables and suitable warnings, incautious day-trippers still get trapped by the incoming tide and have to huddle in the Refuge Boxes until rescue arrives, or the tide goes down. Indeed, in January, 1978, a brand-new Vauxhall Viva with four airmen from the base at RAF Boulmer was trapped during an exceptionally high tide. The men managed to reach a Refuge Box, where they had to stay for nine hours; but the Vauxhall Viva was never seen again . . .

S.S.M.

15 Wildfowl in Reserve

In 1964, in a bold attempt to reconcile the wants of waders and wildfowl with those of wildfowlers and weekenders, much of Lindisfarne and its environs was established as a National Nature Reserve. It seems, with hindsight, such an obvious thing to do, but it was none the less welcome for that. The blessed isolation of Lindisfarne was in danger of being overwhelmed by visitors, and the wildlife was increasingly threatened by indiscriminate and uncontrolled shooting.

Lindisfarne has always been a natural sanctuary — 8,000 acres of some of the finest dune-land and saltmarsh and mud-flats in all Britain, host-land to huge numbers of winter migrant birds that have made it a site of truly international ornithological significance. It's an unbelievably busy, teeming place, a microcosm of the whole wide world of Nature in the endless revolutions of its cycles. Everything that lives is food for other life, everything that dies is transmuted to other use. The tireless sea scours and refreshes and enriches: mud and sand, grasses and seaweeds, sedges and rushes, shellfish and worms, all things that creep and crawl and hide and feed and grow — they all act and interact incessantly in the beautiful, endlessly intricate miracle of replenishment, the eternal surge for life. All this makes Lindisfarne a paradise for birds in all their seasons — and most particularly for waders and for wildfowl.

And yet — they shoot the wildfowl on Lindisfarne still. And the question has to be posed: just how, on a sanctuary island like Lindisfarne, in a National Nature Reserve at that, can one possibly justify the killing of hundreds, nay thousands, of wildfowl for sport when the creatures home in on Holy Island to seek winter refuge from the hunger and hazards of their Arctic breeding grounds? Because that is what happens: every autumn at the end of the close season on September 1, after the teeming hordes of summer tourists and trippers have gone, there is another and very different influx of visitors to Lindisfarne. They come laden with guns and shooting gear — and this to a hallowed island which had been declared a kind of unofficial bird sanctuary by St Cuthbert more than a thousand years ago.

It would seem, on the face of it, that conservation and killing — killing for sport — are totally irreconcilable, mutually incompatible. So why is it condoned, on Lindisfarne of all places?

'You have to take the emotionalism out of it,' says David O'Connor, Warden of the Reserve. 'You have to look at it the way it actually is. You have to be sensible about it, rather than sentimental. In the first place, wildfowling is a traditional pastime that has been associated with Lindisfarne for ages and ages, something to which the islanders have long felt they had an inalienable right. In the second place, the National Nature Reserve here was established by the Nature Conservancy in 1964 precisely *because* of the wildfowling, in order to control it, and thereby provide safeguards for the birds and their habitats.

'The fact is that wildfowling is not only a perfectly legal pursuit; from the point of view of managing this Reserve properly it's a positively useful pursuit, just so long as it is as strictly controlled and monitored as it is at present. Enormous numbers of wildfowl arrive here every autumn — something like 20-30,000 Wigeon, a thousand Mallard, hundreds of Teal, and many Common Scoter, Pintail, Pochard, Scaup, Goldeneye, Long-tailed Duck, and, of course, thousands of Eider all the year round — Lindisfarne's own special duck because of its traditional associations with St Cuthbert.

'We also have thousands of Greylag Geese, making Lindisfarne one of their major wintering sites in Britain; and in particular, we give sanctuary to an extremely rare sub-species, the Pale-bellied Brent Goose, which breeds in Spitzbergen and overwinters only here and at a site in Denmark. They are on the list of Protected Birds, of course. We also get one of the largest wintering herds of Whooper Swans in England — more than 400 in some years — as well as a few Bewick's Swans and dwindling numbers of Mute Swans.

'And all that isn't taking into account the myriads of waders — Dunlin, Knot, Sanderling, Bar-tailed Godwit, Grey Plover, Redshank, Oystercatcher and so on — which are protected now, and which most true sportsmen never regarded as quarry, anyway.

'All of these birds descend on Holy Island each autumn and winter. Lindisfarne is a sort of avian Crewe Junction of the migration routes, and with over 8,000 acres of saltmarsh, mud-flats and dunes in the Reserve, it's a pretty tempting place for weary and hungry birds.

'Shooting is simply another management tool; but it's a tool we use with great care. We issue some 600 seasonal permits a year (although

'THE DREADED SPARTINA'

David O'Connor always refers to it as 'the dreaded *Spartina*': *Spartina townsendii*, familiarly known as Cord Grass, an alien denizen of the Wetlands that was deliberately introduced to the area in 1929 by the farmer of Elwick Farm at Fenham, on the mainland opposite the island. The farmer had an erosion problem, and had read about the way *Spartina* had been used in Holland to stabilise and reclaim inter-tidal areas. So he bought 28 stone of seedlings and planted them along the estuary. They 'took' all too well, and stands of *Spartina* started developing strongly up and down the mainland shore.

It's an immensely vigorous plant, with tough reed-like stems about 2-3 ft high and a tenacious rhizome system of underground roots. It creates a dense sward that traps silt drifting down with the current at high tide; and because of its density and height, the substrate below it becomes starved of oxygen (anaerobic) and no longer teems with worms, shell-fish and many other invertebrates — thus reducing the area of mud-flats useful to waders and certain wildfowl for their daily food requirements.

Worse than that, it is invading and smothering the *Zostera* meadows. *Zostera*, or Eel Grass, the only flowering plant that grows completely submerged in the sea, provides an almost exclusive diet for the Pale-bellied Brent Goose (*Branta bernicla hrota*), which breeds on the island of Spitzbergen, 1700 miles north-east of Holy Island. Lindisfarne, and a site in Denmark, provide the only winter-grounds for this endangered race; there are only some 2,000 of them remaining, and that is one of the reasons why Lindisfarne was one of the 'elite' sites designated by the Government at an international convention at Ramsar, in Iran, in 1971.

So the Nature Conservancy Council declared war on the dreaded *Spartina*, to save the geese. After much experimentation a herbicide, Dalapon, was found which knocked even the obdurate *Spartina* on the head. So now the further spread of *Spartina* will be contained, at least, and the winter *Zostera* diet of the Pale-bellied Brent Goose — and the huge population of Wigeon (*Anas penelope*) — has been saved. But *Spartina* will not be totally eradicated — just controlled. Even enemy aliens have a right to sanctuary in a sanctuary.

not all of them are used much, if at all) to *bona fide* sportsmen, who are required to report the numbers of visits made and birds shot, so that the hunting pressures can be closely monitored. The number of birds shot in any one season — about 2,500, largely made up of Wigeon — is only a tiny proportion of the total wildfowl population. There is another limitation as well. Shooting is only permitted on certain areas of the Reserve — basically, the central area of flats and sands directly between Lindisfarne and the mainland. This shooting zone is flanked by no-go areas — Goswick Sands to the north, and Ross Back Sands and Budle Bay to the south — as sanctuary proper, to which the birds can move to feed and roost undisturbed.

'The point I want to stress is that there is no evidence that shooting causes significant damage to the wildfowl stock; only those birds whose numbers are sufficient to withstand this annual harvest, like Wigeon and Mallard, are taken; all threatened species are totally protected, of course. No, there's no danger to the bird populations involved, or to the future of Lindisfarne as a National Nature Reserve'.

In order to see 'the way it actually is', as David O'Connor puts it, we have to delve for a moment into the history of wildfowling itself; and here I am indebted to books like *The New Wildfowler* (1979) and Eric Begbie's *Modern Wildfowling* (1980).

The pursuit of wildfowl for the pot is as old as mankind itself, for *Homo sapiens* has always been a hunter. Before the advent of the gun, man would exercise all his considerable ingenuity in devising methods to catch and kill his quarry: trapping them on the ground, netting them in flight, rounding them up during the brief moulting period in the late summer when they shed all their flight feathers simultaneously and become flightless for a few weeks. But for these early hunters, the birds weren't 'game', with all the unfortunate connotations of that word; wildfowling in primitive times wasn't done for 'sport' or for 'recreation' (and there's an even more unfortunate irony in the basic meaning of that term). Wildfowling for leisure and pleasure only came in with what we are pleased to call civilisation.

Ancient Egyptian wall-paintings in tombs depict elegant young men of doubtless noble blood, hunting ducks and geese with S-shaped throwing-sticks (early boomerangs?), using cages or spreading clap-nets (spring-loaded hoops with nets attached), or even fashioning decoy ducks made of feathers and mud: the ideal Pharoah was just as much a sporting enthusiast as King Edward VII was, for instance. Wildfowling was an aristocratic pursuit in the ancient regimes of

China, just as it was in the days of the Roman Empire.

In medieval England, wildfowling in aristocratic circles was considered a sporting challenge to the archer's skill: to bring down a bird on the wing with a long-bow arrow fledged with goose-feathers was an achievement worthy of a gentleman.

The advent of the muzzle-loading flintlock gun in the 17th century brought a totally new dimension to the sport of wildfowling, and a new vocabulary: certain firearms, which had been developed since the 14th century as exclusively military hardware, became known as 'fowling-pieces'. It was the long-barrelled 8-bore fowling-piece — the so-called 'marsh-rail' with its 60-inch-long barrel — which made both professional and sporting shooting a practical proposition by the end of the 18th century; that, and the introduction of the mighty 2-inch swivel gun, mounted on a skiff or punt, which could decimate a flock of birds as easily and devastatingly as the 'whiff of grapeshot' with which Napoleon Bonaparte, according to Carlyle, dispersed the Vendémiare counter-Revolution in the streets of Paris in 1795.

For the professionals who stalked the winter saltings it was a rough tough life, perpetually soaked, facing gale-force winds, ruthless frosts and ragged seas. For the gentry and the burgeoning upper-middle-classes who were taking up the sport with boundless enthusiasm, it was a no less hardy business — but at least it was a self-imposed penance. Some people might call it a godless activity, in the colloquial sense — getting up at godless hours and going out in godless weather: an activity only for masochists. But the aficionados insist that it is only for poets and romantics. J. Wentworth Day put it handsomely in his *Wild Wings and Some Footsteps* (1948):

> The true philosopher of the gun is the wildfowler, for he must have the sensitive eye of an artist, a love of solitude and lonely places. He measures beauty by the flash of a bird's wing, by the glint of dawn on sliding waters, by the march of slow clouds. He is the son of solitude, the lonely one.

The scale of the slaughter, as recorded in day-to-day sporting diaries, was staggering in the early days; pioneers of the sport, like Colonel Peter Hawker (1786–1853, author of the first comprehensive treatise on the subject, *Instructions to Young Sportsmen*, 1814), exulted as gleefully over the size of the 'bag' as of the dire hardships they had endured to achieve it. Victorian sportsmen-naturalists like the eccentric Irishman, Sir Ralph Payne-Gallwey (1848–1916) and that indefatigable trophy-hunter, Abel Chapman (1851–1929), came into their own with

OWL-POSTS

A few years ago there was a move to create a Nature Trail, suitably sign-posted, to channel visitors across the dunes of the National Nature Reserve on Lindisfarne. Warden David O'Connor was uneasy about the idea, fearing that it might distort the island ecology if too many people were focussed into too few areas. However, the project seemed certain to get the go-ahead, so he started putting up the posts that would way-mark the Nature Trail.

Eventually, however, the proposal was abandoned. All that was left of it were half a dozen enigmatic timber posts sticking up here and there in the middle of nowhere.

It so happened that David O'Connor was engaged at that time in a study of Short-eared Owls (*Asio Flammeus*). They are an increasingly familiar sight nowadays, hunting in broad daylight and dusk, quartering the dunes with their slow, flapping, heavy-headed flight. The 'ears' of its name aren't ears at all — merely small tufts of feathers for display purposes. The short-eared owl feeds mainly on field voles, and its distribution is largely decided by the availability of this particular food supply.

David O'Connor wanted to know more about the diet of the short-eared owls which spend the winter on Lindisfarne. To this end, he was studying their 'pellets' — the regurgitated packets of undigested fur and bones of the owl's prey, which is normally swallowed whole. Usually, this would mean scouring the area to find the perching-places which the owls used for their post-prandial digestion.

And then, to David's delight, it turned out that those abandoned Nature Trail posts were exactly what the short-eared owls liked to perch on, thereby providing him with a set of ready-made and easy-of-access regurgitories.

Very accommodating of them, to be sure.

180

the advent of the breech-loading shotgun.

There were massive social changes going on, too. The rapid development of railway transport and other modern means of communication brought the once-lonely estuaries within easy range of the townsman, and made expeditions to remote fenlands and saltings much more feasible. The growth of the rising middle classes created a new reservoir of would-be sportsmen, eager to indulge themselves in what had formerly been the preserve of the privileged few. By the end of the 19th century, the indiscriminate mass-killing of ducks and geese, swans and waders, and rare species like the Bittern *(Botaurus stellaris)*, the Avocet *(Recurvirostra avosetta)*, and the Ruff *(Philomachus pugnax)*, was becoming a desperately serious menace to the future of many species — birds whose traditional estuarine habitats were already under threat from equally indiscriminate urban and agricultural expansion.

Lindisfarne was no more immune to the Transport Revolution than anywhere else. Once the old North Eastern Railway opened a station on the Tweedmouth-to-Chathill reach at the hamlet of Beal in 1847, roughly a mile from the coast directly opposite the Snook of Holy Island, traffic to Lindisfarne grew rapidly. The railway station eventually closed in January, 1968; but by then, there was a brand-new metalled Causeway over the sands, prompting a growing flood of visitors, both armed and unarmed.

By the turn of the century the carnage of British wildfowl species and winter migrants was becoming a scandal, and public opinion was making itself heard with demands for the total protection of the birds and the outlawing of guns from their preserves. The more far-sighted sportsmen, even fanatical shots like Stanley Duncan (1878–1954) and Sir Ralph Payne-Gallwey, came to realise that wildfowling as a serious sport was itself under threat. The outcome of their concern was the formation in 1908 of the *Wildfowlers' Association of Great Britain and Ireland* — now the *British Association for Shooting and Conservation* — which has grown into an effective pressure group actively involved in protecting the interests of wildfowlers and wildfowl alike.

It is noticeable that public opinion against wildfowling has gained in impetus after each of the World Wars in this century. Perhaps it has been a reflex reaction against the whole idea of further killing — killing anyone or anything, killing *per se*. Perhaps it has to do with the profound economic shake-up, the social levelling that followed in the wake of each war. In the 1930s the professional fowler was virtually squeezed out of business as the prices of Wigeon and Mallard dropped steadily;

at the same time, Whooper Swans and Brent Geese were practically put out of business, too, when a world-wide fungal disease all but wiped out the mainstay of their diet — the bitter-tasting Eel-grass (*Zostera*).

In the aftermath of the Second World War, the outcry for national legislation grew louder. After prolonged and often heated debate in Parliament, and intense lobbying by WAGBI and other interested parties, the *Protection of Birds Act, 1954,* eventually reached the Statute Book, to be followed by another Act in 1967 to consolidate it; these Acts made it an offence to kill, injure, or take *any* wild bird (and its eggs), apart from those specified in Schedules to the Act which withdrew protection outside the close season for most of the recognised 'sporting' wildfowl. These Acts have now been incorporated into the all-encompassing *Wildlife and Countryside Act, 1981.*

The purpose of the early Acts was to provide legal protection for birds against excessive human predation, with the emphasis on 'excessive'. That was the underlying philosophy, the compromise if you like, that enabled the lions of WAGBI to lie down with the lambs of the naturalist and conservation societies, and start working together towards the joint aim of safeguarding their common heritage of wildlife. And it was this willingness to co-operate that led directly to the establishment of the National Nature Reserve at Lindisfarne in 1964, after a joint approach to the Nature Conservancy by all the interested parties involved.

But there was one further piece of proposed legislation that failed to reach the Statute book, mainly because of ferocious opposition from the WAGBI parliamentary lobby — an attempt in 1967 to ban for all time the exotic sport of punt-gunning . . .

Punt-gunning was practically invented by Sir Ralph Payne-Gallwey and Abel Chapman, those big-shots of the Victorian age who wrought such carnage in the ranks of the world's wildfowl.

For me, the whole concept of punt-gunning holds a kind of morbid fascination. I find the very idea incredibly bizarre: two men stealthily stalking a wary flock of birds in a camouflaged kayak, or punt, with a monstrous cannon on the bows to blast the wretched creatures out of the skies with a huge home-made cartridge the size of an artillery shell, crammed with $1\frac{1}{2}$ lbs of AA or BB shot — more than ten times the average load of both barrels of a 12-bore shotgun. Words almost fail me; the mind almost boggles. But it happens — oh, yes, it happens all right, although not to the same extent as in the past. There are signs today that on Lindisfarne, at least, the practice is dying a quiet and natural death. Where there were five or six gun-punts on the island a few years ago, now there are only two.

The punt itself is 16 or 17 ft long, with a draught of only a few inches. Amidships there is a long, narrow well, or cockpit, in which the hunters lie prone, usually soaked to the skin. The craft is painted light grey, to blend with the pewter colour of water on a dull day; the foredeck slopes down towards the stem, to soften the outline and make the punt as unobtrusive as possible. Mounted on a block of wood set into the keel behind the bows is this massive piece of artillery, with a bore of up to $1\frac{3}{4}$ inches (the legal maximum now) and a barrel anything up to 11 ft long. It is anchored by a stout rope sling which absorbs much of the recoil when the gun is fired; even so, the boat is propelled smartly backwards by the force of the discharge. The gun points straight ahead; it cannot be swivelled, although it can be elevated or depressed by means of a movable bridge near the bows — so the whole boat has to be aimed at the target, like a torpedo, in order to get in a withering shot.

The boat is propelled — 'stocked', as they say — by the man in the rear. His is the more delicately expert task. He uses either a paddle or a variety of punt-poles to cope with different sea-bed conditions. With one arm trailing surreptitiously over the side, he has to manoeuvre the punt to within 70 or 80 yards of the wary quarry. This, apparently, is the breath-holding climax of the operation, the thrill of the stalk, the nerve-racking excitement of those last vital yards to get within range of perhaps a hundred pairs of alert, suspicious eyes. When the puntsman thinks the punt is perfectly sited, perfectly balanced against the wind and current, he gives the side of the boat a sharp rap with his knuckles, the flock springs up in raucous alarm, the gunner pulls the lanyard and — BANG! The birds fly straight into a lethal pattern of shot about 12 ft in diameter, and ten, twenty, perhaps thirty of them may be brought down, dead or wounded. The largest shot ever recorded at Lindisfarne was a lucky freak that claimed no fewer than 116 birds, in the mid-1960s; it was made by island mussel-fisherman George 'Steptoe' Kyle and the late 'Big' Bob Alison. It may well be a world record, for all I know.

Then comes the business of collecting the 'bag'. There is no room for a dog in the punt, so it has to be done by hand. Before running the boat aground and stepping out in their waders and oilskins, the men put on wooden mud-shoes, or 'pattens', and go floundering over the mud and ooze to pick up the dead birds. They also carry an old 12-bore shotgun ('cripple-stopper' is the brutally expressive term for it) with which to despatch injured birds. It is a matter of honour to recover every single bird that has been downed, even if it means a laborious chase for hundreds of yards. David O'Connor confirms that he and his colleagues very, very seldom find dead or injured birds washed up on the high-water mark following a punt-shot.

So what is David O'Connor's official attitude to all this?

'For the present at least we can see no cause to intervene. It's a traditional pastime, sanctioned by law. The annual haul made by punt-gunning nowadays is about 500 birds; the average bag per outing is about 25 birds. That's not enough to have any injurious effect on the overall wildfowl stocks.

'Most shoulder-gunners don't like it because they think it gives the puntsmen an unfair advantage; it's rather like the rivalry between anglers and salmon-netters. In actual fact our statistics show that the average bag of the 10 most successful shoulder-gunners is similar to the average obtained by punt-gunners.'

But what has caused the decline in interest amongst the local puntsmen? I talked to a number of island veterans of the sport — men like salmon-fisherman James 'Clinker' Brigham and fisheries expert 'Wee' Ralph Wilson; and it emerged that as they grew older, they gradually came to question the ethics of it (just like Sir Peter Scott, who began to feel remorse at the slaughter he had inflicted on wildfowl in his younger days and atoned for it by establishing the Wildfowl Trust and its celebrated sanctuary at Slimbridge on the Severn in 1946).

Clinker told me: 'I just went off punt-gunning because I began to feel sorry for the ducks. It's so indiscriminate. Shoulder-gunning is much fairer, and it's much more fun than punt-gunning, which is sheer hard labour'.

Wee Ralph told me: 'I used to do a lot of it, just as my father did. It's a young man's sport, really, although my father was at it until he was about 70; but when he'd come home, he'd say, "Ach, it's a damn shame to shoot them anyway". And many a time I would think, "Well, why are we doing it, then? Why should we be doing it this way?". And then I sort of stopped it too, in a way, gradually. It was just something at the back of my mind that said, "Ralph, you've had your share, forget about it". Basically, I just started feeling sorry for them.'

But there's more to it than that, I think. I think it has a lot to do with a devastating tragedy that happened the day after New Year's Day in 1971, when one of the younger members of the Brigham family, Charles

HUNT THE FOX

Holy Island is normally a fine sanctuary for Foxes (*Vulpes vulpes*). The old Marram grass of the sand-dunes provides cosy winter lies, and there is a varied diet on tap: apart from rabbits and voles and young birds, there's a good sea-food menu on offer down by the shore — shell-fish, mussels, small crabs and carrion of all kinds.

In the old days, life wasn't quite so easy-going. The islanders used to organise mass fox-drives at high tide, when the foxes couldn't escape across the mud-flats. All the children would be mustered to beat the island from the Snook end towards a line of waiting guns at the narrow waist, and up to half a dozen foxes would be accounted for each time.

The fox-drives have almost stopped now. But on three recent occasions the Lindisfarne foxes have been rudely disturbed by a pack of hounds and huntsmen in full cry. The first hunt since pre-war days took place on January 24, 1977. The small North Northumberland Hunt, which hadn't met since the 1930s, were invited across by the island farmers on the eve of the lambing season. Since a National Nature Reserve was involved, it attracted enormous publicity, as well as a field of 42 mounted huntsmen and hundreds of foot-followers.

The Warden and a colleague spotted seven individual foxes on the island that day. Of these, only two were run down and killed by the hunt. But the Nature Reserve itself took a terrible pounding, with 40 horses and all those foot-followers crashing around all over the fragile sand-dunes.

The hunt has been back on only two occasions since then, in 1980 and 1981, but under strictly controlled conditions. Only six mounted huntsmen were allowed. There was no pre-publicity. The hunting was excellent, but there were no kills. Further requests to hunt over the island have been politely refused.

But the foxes cannot rest entirely easy. They still have to be kept under control, especially in winter when sheep are at their most vulnerable.

'Twinnie' Brigham, was fatally injured in a punt-gunning accident on the day after his 29th birthday. It seems that the gun misfired; the cartridge didn't discharge, but the black powder in the cartridge, which had probably become damp, started smouldering secretly in a delayed-action combustion, instead of exploding immediately on the impact of the hammer. This is what is known as a 'hang-fire'. After a misfire the gunners wait for a time — about two minutes — in case there is any chance of a hang-fire; then they unscrew the breech and replace the defective cartridge with a fresh one. On this occasion, however, something went apallingly wrong; just as Charlie Brigham was unscrewing the breech, after allowing the appropriate time to elapse, the powder suddenly exploded, blowing the breech backwards with terrible violence . . .

When a death occurs on Lindisfarne, especially one so poignant and shocking as this one, the whole island mourns. The family's loss is everyone's loss. The grief is shared, deeply felt, almost tangible in its sombre all-pervading presence.

And with that, I believe, the former innocent pleasure of punt-gunning, with all its perversely satisfying hardships, simply evaporated. All the joy went out of it. The price of sporting pleasure had, at one cruel stroke, become too high.

The islanders do not talk about it much, especially to strangers — they prefer to keep their innermost feelings to themselves. But I believe the trauma of that tragedy is still with them.

All the island punt-gunners I met are also expert shoulder-gunners; and with only one notable exception, that of Selby 'Sparrow' Alison, they all claimed to prefer the 12-bore to the punt-mounted blunderbuss. But the manner of the shoot is every bit as weird and wonderful, to the layman at least, as punt-gunning. Their happy hunting ground is a wide stretch of saltings and mud-flats in the heart of the Holy Island Sands, between the Snook and the mainland — an area known locally as the Swad (probably a corruption of 'sward').

This is the favourite winter feeding-ground of the Wigeon and the Mallard, and the strictly protected Pale-bellied Brent Goose from Spitzbergen. Hither they come in their hundreds and thousands to partake of the principal mainstays of their diet — the lank and languid Eel-grass, its threads streaming gently in the water of the channels like Ophelia's hair, and the alga *Enteromorpha*.

From a distance, the vast wide-open sands look as level as a billiard table, devoid of any human presence. But go closer, and you almost stumble into the permanent shooting-butts of the island shoulder-gunners, dug into the sea-bed; and what extraordinary butts they are! Some are sunken half-barrels (for sitting upright in); others are simply wooden boxes. But the height of luxury is an old cast-iron bath to lie full-length in — without taps or plug-hole, of course. The doyen of the bath-butts belongs to salmon-fisherman Tommy 'Tinko' Douglas; it's been there for twenty years or so now, but others have now started to sink their own tubs.

And so, at the appointed hour when the conditions look favourable, the men drive out to the Snook track, where they park their cars and then go trudging a mile or so across the flats to their boxes, with waders, oilskins, guns, a bucket and a fertiliser-bag stuffed with straw for comfort. When they reach their own boxes, they bale them out with the bucket, deposit the sacks of straw to sit or lie on, and then settle down to await the pulse-quickening sounds of the packs of Wigeon flighting in.

Some use wigeon-whistles to try to call the birds in. Some fashion decoys out of heaps of mud to lure the wildfowl to the guns. Others disdain all such artificial aids, relying entirely on skilled marksmanship and absolute stillness instead. All of them, as far as I could gather, ignore the pious advice of the text-books to wear a white surplice if it's snowing — despite the island's reputation for holiness!

On an exceptionally good night, a skilful shot can bag as many as twenty birds — almost entirely Wigeon, for Wigeon are *the* sporting ducks of these shorelands. But it's seldom as good as that; half a dozen is considered a satisfactory night's work. In a season of occasional outings, the Lindisfarne locals are content with a total bag of 50 birds, just for the pot and for their friends. Duck, they all say, is the finest meat you'll ever taste.

But the one bird that is absolutely sacrosanct is the Pale-bellied Brent Goose. A Greylag or a Pinkfoot they would take, if one came within range — but never a Pale-bellied Brent. All of them know that it's an endangered species; they feel that Lindisfarne is privileged to be its only winter sanctuary in Britain, and they're proud of the fact. And so they will let the Brents paddle heedlessly around them, no matter what the temptation to loose off a couple of errant barrels.

Now *that's* what I call true sportsmanship.

16 Rabbits Galore

In the autumn of 1978, a young ecology lecturer from the Zoology Department at Newcastle University arrived on Lindisfarne to stake out a claim — a land-claim. He wanted to study rabbits; and the best place for him to study them was in the National Nature Reserve on Holy Island. For Dr Peter Garson (instantly nicknamed 'Peter Rabbit' by the islanders, of course), it was to be the start of a six-year study project that would overturn many of our most cherished preconceptions about the social and domestic behaviour of that exasperating, lovable, cuddly and destructive creature, the wild rabbit (*Oryctalogus cuniculus*).

Rabbits aren't native to Britain. They were introduced to the British Isles by the Normans soon after the Conquest, in the late 11th century, to be kept and cropped, like any other farming resource, in special areas called Warrens. On Lindisfarne, a Warren was established on the dune-lands of the Snook and seems to have contributed to the revenues of the island in medieval times. In the 18th century, however, progressive farmers in England began to break up the old Warrens and convert the land for supposedly more profitable arable or forestry uses; the effect of this was to increase the areas of farmland for rabbits to forage in — and by the beginning of this century they had become a serious agricultural pest. Professional rabbit-trappers attempted to keep the rabbit populations in check, but the phenomenal breeding potential of the animal, perhaps up to 35 young per female per year, ensured not only its survival but its continued increase.

The most spectacular example of rabbit-damage occurred in Australia. In 1859, homesick settlers took a small shipment of rabbits to Australia and released them on a livestock farm near Geelong in Victoria. Within 40 years they had caused a devastating ecological disaster. The lush forage for sheep (at that time the mainstay of the Australian economy) was wiped out. Pasturelands were turned into dust-bowls. Native browsing species like jumping mice were driven to extinction. And there was no way of stopping it. When fences were erected, waves of migrating rabbits would form a ramp of dead bodies over which others would swarm.

It was not until 1950 that the rabbit-plague was halted. In that year, Australian farmers, after years of fruitless field-trials and experimentation, successfully introduced the *Myxoma* virus, after scientists realised that it could be carried from rabbit to rabbit by the blood-feeding female mosquito in the damp season. The result was electrifying. The rabbits died in their millions, the grasslands revived.

In cooler European climates the most important carrier was found to be the rabbit-flea (*Spilopsyllus cuniculi*). In 1952 a certain Dr Armand Delille introduced the *Myxoma* virus to his estate near Paris. The effect was equally phenomenal. The disease spread through France like wildfire, killing 99% of the rabbit population (in the 1340s, by comparison, the Black Death, which was carried by rat-fleas, killed about 50% of the human population). In the autumn of 1953 the disease came across the English Channel to Kent. From there it spread rapidly throughout the country, often by the deliberate introduction of diseased rabbits (despite the Pest Act of 1954, which makes this illegal even today). By the end of the ghastly winter of 1955–6, when millions of rabbits lay dead and rotting all over the countryside, the problem of rabbit infestation seemed to have been solved at a stroke — and at no cost whatever.

Myxomatosis had proved itself a brilliantly effective means of extermination. Economically, it saved the agricultural industry a staggering £50 million (£250m at today's prices) a year in crops which would otherwise have been ravaged. But there were many who were aghast at the horribly visible scale of the slaughter — although, as John Sheail remarks in his *Rabbits and Their History* (1971), 'If the animal had been the rat, [myxomatosis] would have been treated as a godsend'.

By the 1970s, however, the rabbit population had made a noticeable recovery. It became apparent that rabbits were developing a degree of inborn, genetic immunity to the effects of the virus — and that, simultaneously, the virus was evolving numerous new strains whose effects are much less severe than the original type. So it looks as if the old traditional forms of rabbit-control — shooting, gassing and ferreting — are coming back into favour. But a farm-worker's time is no longer cheap; it is obviously best to make a rabbit-cull a quick and efficient business designed to have the maximum long-term effects.

So, in order to control the rabbit efficiently and economically, it is necessary to know what makes the rabbit tick: how it lives, how it breeds, how it spreads, where and how it feeds. And that's where Dr

RABBIT PUNCH

It was Beatrix Potter who popularised *Oryctolagus cuniculus* as a cuddly, lovable little creature called Peter Rabbit. But rabbits aren't always so cuddly or so lovable — especially towards each other.

Dr Peter Garson, who is working on the social behaviour of rabbits on Lindisfarne, has observed a large number of encounters between male rabbits, many of them evidently over a female. Buck rabbits are often possessive over females, and spend a lot of time 'mate-guarding' — feeding rather intermittently while keeping close to a female, and obviously alert to the approach of other males. If an intruder comes too close, the guarding male makes a series of subtly threatening gestures — raising his head, sitting up on his forepaws, taking a few steps towards the interloper. If the hint isn't taken, a chase ensues, with the two males jinking and jumping up and down the sand-dunes and racing across the 'slacks'; sometimes the pursuer tries to grab the pursued by the scruff of the neck with his teeth, making the fur literally fly.

A rabbit's main weapons are its hind legs, which are extremely powerful with long and very sharp claws; and if the dispute is still not settled by the chase (which is usually brief, but can cover 100 metres or more), the combatants square up briefly before starting a series of 'jumping passes'.

It's as formal as a medieval tourney, and almost balletic in its ritualistic agility. The two males confront each other, a metre or two apart, and then almost simultaneously spring high into the air past each other; and as they cross, they rake at each other's bellies with those wickedly piercing claws. As soon as they land they turn in a flash and do it again, perhaps six times in all, before the chasing is resumed.

Dr Garson has never witnessed a fight to the death, but several of his resident rabbits have torn ears and scarred faces — presumably injuries sustained during these extraordinary jousts or the accompanying chases.

It adds a new dimension to the idea of the rabbit punch.

Peter Garson, 'Peter Rabbit' himself, comes in.

Until now, most rabbit studies have been based on the behaviour of 'captives' in relatively small enclosures, like Ronald Lockley's detailed revelations in *The Private Life of the Rabbit* (1964), which formed the biological basis for Richard Adams' enchanting best-seller, *Watership Down* (1972). But for a phenomenally fecund animal like the rabbit, to be enclosed creates gross overcrowding that will inevitably distort its normal behaviour and probably make it neurotic, even psychotic. Only by studying rabbit behaviour and ecology in the wild — especially when the rabbits are not seriously affected by myxomatosis — will we be able to predict the economic consequences of rabbit-control measures with any precision.

So Peter Garson sought, and received, permission to work on the dunes in the National Nature Reserve. His study area covers some 10 hectares (25 acres) at the ballooning western tip of the island known as Snook Point. It is an area of very large sand-dunes, some of them 45 ft high, which provides good natural vantage points for positioning observation hides. The sandy soil is excellent for burrow-making (a new burrow can be dug in a couple of days). There are also large areas of low-lying 'slacks' and saltmarsh which provide lush green vegetation in the growing season. The burrows adjacent to these feeding-grounds are obviously the prime sites; the hinterland of dunes is less appealing to rabbits (or at least it contains far fewer burrows), for the main vegetation there is the tough Marram Grass *(Ammophila arenaria)* that gives the dunes their stability but is fibrous and indigestible.

Rabbits lead extraordinarily precarious lives. They are beset by powerful and clever predators — especially man. They persist, despite the attentions of man, foxes, buzzards and stoats, only because of their remarkable fecundity. On Lindisfarne, female rabbits (does) have two or three litters a year, but in arable farmland they can manage six or more. The gestation period is four weeks; and no sooner has the doe given birth than she comes on heat and is mated again. The young (kittens) are born naked, deaf, blind and helpless; they are suckled for 3 to 4 weeks in the nesting-burrow, visited only once a day, for their own safety, by their mother. Then, about when the next litter is due, they are left to their own devices in a strange and perilous world.

When Dr Garson first came to Lindisfarne in 1978, the rabbit population was at a low ebb, but was about to start booming again. There had been a devastating outbreak of myxomatosis in the mid-70s, followed by a widespread dune fire at the Snook end of the Reserve during the hot summer of 1976. The vegetation was just recovering from the blaze and was growing more strongly than ever on soil that had been fertilised by ash. In the autumn of 1978, the study area contained only 62 burrows, and perhaps 20 adult rabbits. By the end of the following summer there were 210 burrows, and 137 rabbit kittens (about 90% of all those which emerged after weaning) had been live-trapped for marking; the adult population had more than doubled. A year later, in the autumn of 1980, the number of burrows had gone up to over 500, and the total population of adults was over 100.

Since late 1981 there have been about 700 active burrows in the study area, and the adult population has stabilised. At the start of the population explosion, the mortality rate among the young rabbits was relatively low. But over the period 1979–82 the juveniles gained weight more slowly, and became progressively lighter for their size, in each successive summer; the slacks and saltmarsh were grazed very close, a sure sign that food was in short supply for everyone. Not surprisingly, given the length and bleakness of the Lindisfarne winter, youngsters in poor shape or of small size are less likely to survive; the exceptionally high survival rate of 40% noted in 1979–80 has now come down to the more normal rate for populations of small birds and mammals in general, of some 5%. The annual adult mortality is usually more moderate, at perhaps 50%, so that a few individuals live to be 4 or 5 years old — the rabbit equivalent of our own three score years and ten.

It's that first year which is, quite literally, the killer. And already Dr Garson has identified some at least of the factors that will decide a young rabbit's chances of survival in those first few critical months. In the first place, a rabbit born early in the spring has a better chance of survival than a summer kitten. This is because it has a better chance of reaching full adult body weight, and perhaps putting on a bit of spare fat, before the vegetation dies back at the start of the long winter.

Another factor is *where* it's born. The best nesting-burrows are those which are within easiest reach of the lush feeding areas — in the slacks and on the saltmarsh. When young rabbits first emerge at the age of 3-4 weeks, they only range out about 15 metres from the burrow-entrance for feeding; if you are born on the wrong side of the tracks, up in the marram dunes, you have a pretty poor diet to start with, and a much longer and therefore more perilous journey to get to the richer feed. Young rabbits are rather unco-ordinated; they haven't yet grown the long tibia in the hind leg that gives them their fast, bucketting run — they can only scamper, and often fall over themselves when they bolt in

RABBIT PLAGUE

When the first terrible outbreak of myxomatosis swept through Britain in the mid-1950s, not even a semi-island like Lindisfarne could provide sanctuary. The wild Rabbit (*Oryctolagus cuniculus*) on Holy Island was practically wiped out. In medieval times, the Warren on the island had provided useful revenues; but latterly the rabbit had become an expensive and destructive pest.

How the disease, *Myxomatosis cuniculus*, first reached Holy Island across the sands is a matter of conjecture. Rabbits can swim well, if they have to; but there is no evidence of regular rabbit-traffic between the mainland and the island.

Myxomatosis isn't a contagious disease. In Europe it is carried and spread by the blood-feeding Rabbit-flea (*Spilopsyllus cuniculi*), which is a remarkably tenacious creature. It leaps at its host in a spinning jump that gives it an instant grip on the rabbit's fur instead of bouncing off.

For fifteen years after the 1950s epidemic the rabbit population in Britain stayed well below pestilential levels. However, today's rabbits have some measure of inherited, genetic immunity to the *Myxoma* virus. Immune females can pass on useful antibodies to their kittens, giving protection for 10 weeks after birth. As the population recovers, however, it loses this acquired immunity and a new outbreak of myxomatosis may occur. There have been two recent outbreaks on Lindisfarne, in the mid-1970s and again in 1982; on each occasion, an estimated 90% of the rabbit population died. But how did the outbreaks occur? Many islanders believe that the disease crossed the Causeway accidentally — perhaps brought by fleas lurking in the fur of mainland ferrets that had been used in infected burrows. *But* — rabbit-fleas stick exclusively to rabbits (luckily for Peter Garson).

During the last outbreak, however, there *was* sanctuary for rabbits on Holy Island — in Dr Garson's study area, which he has turned into a no-go area for myxomatosis, in order to protect his study population. He does this by vaccinating as many rabbits as possible with a vaccine called Weyvak, and by de-fleaing the burrows; for this he uses talcum powder mixed with a trace of an insecticide called Permethrin, which he blows down every burrow periodically with a stirrup-pump.

S.G.M.

panic. It makes them easy meat for foxes and weasels. So, females which have early litters in burrows beside good feeding-grounds will normally be those leaving the most descendants.

There are many questions still to be answered. But already it is apparent that not all rabbits in the wild behave in the same way as rabbits kept for observation in enclosures do (or, indeed, as rabbits in Beatrix Potter do!). In the wide-open spaces of a coastal dune habitat like Lindisfarne, Dr Garson has found no evidence of a dominant 'Chief Bunny' which tyrannises a colony. Nor do his rabbits live in 'warrens' in controlled groups. Nor do they defend carefully defined territories — although bucks can be distinctly antagonistic towards one another. And although there are indications from elsewhere that females, even in the wild, may kill other does' young, there is no evidence for this practice on Lindisfarne. It seems clear that the kind of rabbit behaviour observed by Ronald Lockley and immortalised by Richard Adams is not typical for a habitat like Holy Island, where there is no shortage of underground living-space but periodic severe limitations on food-supplies: when competition becomes too intense locally these rabbits are able to disperse to seek new accommodation and feeding-grounds elsewhere, an option not available either in medieval warrens or Robin Lockley's experimental enclosure.

From the point of view of the Nature Conservancy Advisory Panel, Peter Garson's research project could provide valuable new insights into how best to manage a duneland Nature Reserve with a wild rabbit population: how the rabbits can be controlled, how fragile flora can be protected, whether particular areas should be 'rabbit-rotated' like fields that are allowed to lie fallow between crops — or whether rabbit populations should, in the common interest, simply be exterminated once and for all. And if so — how?

Meanwhile, Peter Garson's rabbits can enjoy a measure of safety in their sanctuary on Holy Island — protected from man, at least, protected from myxomatosis, protected from everything except Nature and their own voracious appetites.

But their days may well be numbered.

S.G.M

197

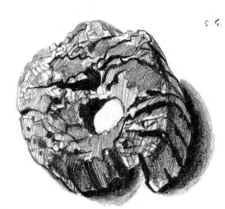

17 Salmon-fishers

The early morning is dank under a hazy sky. There's a bit of a swell, quite choppy in the channel, the sea a sullen grey, not hostile but not particularly friendly either. The coast is just a distant smudge.

The engine of the *Lona M* makes an agreeably busybody sort of noise, self-important and bumbling, all 29.9 horsepower of it; it bobbles, rather than chugs. The conditions are quite good for salmon, says the skipper, Jimmy 'Clinker' Brigham. You get three or four heaving swells in succession, followed by calm water for a few minutes while the sea holds its breath; but on a far shore the breakers are gleaming white when the sun struggles through. It might be quite a good day, he says. Or it might not. You never can tell.

The *Lona M* (registered in Aberystwyth, AB112), is a Treave 25, a lobster boat with a big well amidships still equipped with a lobster-pot hauler for the autumn and winter fishing. Clinker adapted it himself for the spring salmon-fishing. It's a bit rusty, and extremely untidy, the open well cluttered with mounds of candy-floss netting. Nobody goes around with a vacuum cleaner on this boat, although Clinker admits to emptying the ashtray over the side now and again.

It's a homely, tubby little vessel. The engine needs a lot of tender loving care, which it gets at frequent intervals. The throttle arrangement is original and eccentric: the throttle in the engine box is attached by a piece of string to a length of blue rope which leads through the wheel-house window and is tied to a heavy bar of steel that looks suspiciously like a length of British Railways track, perching on the helmsman's throne. When more throttle is required, the steel bar is shoved unceremoniously off the seat, acting as a weight to pull open the throttle; to close the throttle, the bar is lifted onto the seat again. By then, however, the cover of the engine box has invariably snagged the rope, so the lid has to be jiggled a bit to release the rope, which slackens the throttle, which eventually slows us down. Heath Robinson would have been proud of it.

Clinker is at the helm, turning the boat in a slow semi-circle to create a patch of clear water in the choppy sea for the *Lona M* to start shooting

DUCKLING FOR DINNER

Infectious myxomatosis, that terrible scourge of rabbits throughout Europe since the disease was first deliberately introduced into France in the early 1950s, has had an unexpected side-effect on one of Lindisfarne's most colourful birds — the boldly-plumaged Shelduck *(Tadorna tadorna)*, Britain's largest sea-duck.

At its height in the mid-1950s, the myxomatosis epidemic exterminated 99% of Britain's rabbit population of over 60 million. And when a rabbit population is all but wiped out, it poses a major problem for its major predator — the fox. Where can a hungry fox expect to find a square meal when there aren't any rabbits around for the taking? Answer: try the nearest rabbit-burrow nonetheless — not for rabbits, but for Shelducks.

The Shelduck's plumage is strikingly conspicuous. Both male and female birds display a handsome arrangement of black and white, with a chestnut band spreading across breast and shoulders, and a red beak. A ground-nesting bird would be, literally, a sitting duck for predators; so, for protection, the Shelduck nests in a rabbit-burrow or hollow tree, or in the close shelter of boulders or bushes. Inside the burrow the female lays a clutch of about 10 creamy-white eggs, which she incubates alone for about a month (although her mate calls every evening to take her out for dinner).

When the eggs are hatched she leaves the nest with her brood almost immediately, waddling down to the inter-tidal mud and pools to search for molluscs and shrimps and insects. It takes two months for the young to learn to fly — looking more like geese than ducks with their slow wing-beats and wedge-shaped formations.

Foxes were quick to adapt to this new delicacy for their table. Statistics show that in the late 1940s, more than 100 pairs of Shelducks nested in the Lindisfarne area; today, the nesting population has been reduced to about 15 pairs — although there is still a large migrant population, with some 700 visitors wintering in Budle Bay.

S.G.M

its nets across the tide — 600 yards of gossamer monofilament mesh made in Japan. In the stern of the boat the two members of the crew — Mrs Quita Jenkinson and young Kyle Luke — are standing by to pay the net out over the starboard quarter. Quita has already poured a small libation of whisky over the side — an age-old ritual of propitiation. Perhaps it's because she's Welsh, a Celt from Llanelli. Clinker scoffs at such foolish superstitions; it's just a waste of a good dram, he says. But Quita still does it. And she still refers to the sea, respectfully, as 'she'; Clinker just says 'it'.

'Throw her over!' — and over goes the *duka*, the blue marker flag at the start of the net. The flag-pole is embedded in a plastic pellet like a football, daubed with the owner's name or initials. The forward motion of the boat unravels the net smoothly from the tangle in the well, 40 meshes deep (about 20 feet), with a green cork every fathom (6 feet) or so. It takes only a few minutes to shoot the whole length of net; then the *Lona M* turns and idles for half an hour, waiting for the tide and the current to nudge an unwary salmon into the nets on its way through Budle Bay. A lone Fulmar glides past, stiff-winged, on a cursory reconnaissance, but finds nothing of interest to detain it. A flock of pied Eider Drakes are having a stag party away in the distance. A couple of Shags go scooting past. Now is the waiting time, as the nets drift slowly southward in a ragged line . . .

Clinker Brigham is one of only four fishermen on the island now licensed by the Northumbria Water Authority to net salmon in the area: licence no. 75, costing £306 a year (with an additional £50 for the sole rights in Budle Bay). Other inshore licences are issued on the recommendation of the Northumberland Sea Fisheries Committee, which is charged with the protection and preservation of fish-stocks within the 3-mile limit. All inshore boats have to be licensed, in order to protect the nursery areas of the smaller fish and the ground-gear of the lobster and crab fishermen. Bottom-trawling is forbidden except for boats under 38 feet in length.

At present there are nine boats operating from Lindisfarne. One of them is owned by the chairman of the Sea Fisheries Committee, islander 'Wee' Ralph Wilson, who is now in his sixties and is also the island Harbourmaster. There has been no spectacular decline or increase since Ralph started fishing on his father's boat, the *Reliance*, in the 1930s; anyway, the harbour cannot accommodate bigger boats, or cope with bigger landings. Ralph Wilson tried a larger vessel himself some years ago, a 46-ft stern trawler called *Silver Echo*, built in

Eyemouth, but it could only land at the little jetty for about half an hour right at the top of high water, and had to lie out in the harbour on a big mooring. It wasn't really a practical proposition for Lindisfarne, and he sold it after a while. Now he and the other island fishermen soldier on quietly at the salmon in spring and summer, the lobster and crab in autumn and winter. There are a few youngsters growing up who will want to take over with or from their fathers in the future. For the time being, the fishing industry on Lindisfarne seems to have found its right level . . .

On board the *Lona M* the waiting time passes quickly, with coffee and idle gossip. We talked about fishermen's superstitions, which are dying out nowadays. Certainly, Clinker seems impervious to them. For instance, in the old days a fisherman would never willingly take a woman or a clergyman on a fishing-trip; and no fisherman would ever mention the word 'pig', even though many of the islanders themselves keep pigs, and there is no taboo about eating pork. Instead they would call them 'articles' or 'yon things' or 'gadgies' or 'grumfits'. Selby 'Sparrow' Alison, now in his seventies and former Mine Host at the *Crown & Anchor*, had told me that in his childhood, the village boys would sometimes try to cheek the fishermen by shouting 'Pigs, pigs, pigs!' at them; the fishermen would instinctively touch cold steel to ward off any possible evil influence and chase them for their lives, brandishing their razor-sharp fish-knives. Although the superstition about naming 'pigs' is widespread throughout fishing communities, some Lindisfarne islanders trace it back to a specific incident when a boat with its crew of four was lost at sea after one of the men had tripped over a 'grumfit' lying on the road in the early morning darkness. It was a Friday the 13th, too.

But one particular tradition dies hard: to this day, the fishermen still sit in splendid isolation in the north aisle of the parish church, for formal services anyway — their wives and children have to sit separately, in the centre aisle.

It's time to have a look at the nets now. Salmon-fishing is an unpredictable business: some days you catch nothing at all, not a fin, not a scale, all morning, in three or four hauls. Other days you might get 40 fish, even 50 if you're lucky.

Quita and Kyle have got their yellow oilskins on now — *dopers*, they call them on the island. The boat-hook plucks inboard the marker buoy at the end of the net, and Quita and Kyle start pulling the net in, rhythmically and steadily, heavier work than it looks. Clinker tries to

BY THE GRACE OF . . .

Not many Grey Seal pups that lose contact with their mothers can expect to survive. But there's one young lady living amongst the Farne Islands, looking very complacent and well-fed, who not only lives but positively thrives on having been orphaned.

You see her hauled out contentedly on the rocks beside the landing-stage on Longstone. Principal lighthouse-keeper John Malcom Macpherson and his colleagues befriended her when she was still a pup, motherless and helpless, and fed her with fish until she was old enough to fend for herself. But acquired habits die hard, and the Longstone seal keeps coming back for more.

She adds another dimension to the lustre of Longstone as a place of rescue; because it was from the Longstone lighthouse that young Grace Darling and her father launched their frail coble to rescue nine survivors from the paddle-steamer *Forfarshire*, wrecked in a cruel autumn gale in 1838.

Grace Darling was 22 years old at the time. She was living in the lighthouse with her father William, the principal keeper, and her mother, who was then in her sixties. At 4.45 in the morning of Friday, September 7, 1838, Grace Darling woke up in her third-floor bedroom to a day that would bring her imperishable fame. Through the window, out in the raging darkness, she spotted the *Forfarshire* aground on the wicked Big Harcar Rock, half a mile away. When she and her father saw movement on the rock, two hours later, they manhandled their 20-foot rowing-boat across the island with the mother's help to a sheltered cove called Sunderland Hole, and from there the father and daughter rowed it through the fearful seas to the Big Harcar. It took two trips to rescue all nine survivors (eight men and a woman) from the rocks and bring them to shelter in the Longstone lighthouse.

The heroism of the Darlings, and particularly of daughter Grace, excited public attention to a degree unparalleled in the annals of Trinity House. Grace Darling became an instant national heroine, and £800 was raised for her by public subscription (but only £270 for her father). To this day, the Longstone lighthouse is officially open to visitors who want to make pilgrimage to the Darling shrine.

S.G.M.

lessen the strain by nudging the boat slowly along the bobbing line of corks. The net comes out smoothly, scattering drops of iridescence, breaking the water gently as a ripple, almost as if the sea itself were being drawn aboard — the sea made net, as it were. Sometimes the net comes out festooned with streamers of orange jellyfish like marmalade — *Cyanea lamarcki*, Clinker says it is, or 'swithers'. They can give you a painful sting, particularly if you rub your face with your hands after handling the net. At other times, the net may come up covered with a brown film of plankton, which makes the mesh all too visible to salmon and has to be washed off right away.

The net is empty. Six minutes of hard, unremitting labour to haul it in, and both Quita and Kyle are momentarily exhausted. There is a big hole in the net at one point, a reminder of the kind of damage a predatory seal can do when it rips a trapped salmon from the mesh. It's hardly worth repairing now.

We shoot the nets again, just for fun. But it's not a day for salmon, after all. It's been more of an excursion for my benefit than a serious fishing-trip, anyway. Clinker lets me line up the homeward bearing on the two beacons on Old Law; I shove the iron bar off the seat, and the *Lona M* surges ahead on full throttle, courtesy of British Rail. We must be doing all of 7 or 8 knots, but it feels like doing 70 on the motorway: exhilaration and contentment together, the wind in our hair and the sea chattering crossly against the bows.

No wonder Clinker wouldn't change his island way of life for anything.

S.G M

205

18 The Old Course at Lindisfarne

St Andrews in Fife is not the only place that can boast an Old Course for golfing enthusiasts; Lindisfarne has one, too — or at least it used to have one until it sort of petered out in the early 1950s.

It was situated on the Links (where else?), which lie to the north of Chare Ends. And it was laid out by one of golf's all-time greats, the immortal James Braid, the first man to win the Open five times (between 1901 and 1910), and four times winner of the Professional Match-Play Tournament between 1903 and 1911. He was the son of a ploughman/forester in Fife, took to golf early, and came into his own when he was apprenticed to a joiner in that Mecca of golf, St Andrews. He turned professional in 1893, first at Romford and then, from 1904 until his death at the age of 80 in 1950, at Walton Heath. According to the *Golfers' Handbook 1983* he was 'a tall, powerful player who lashed the ball with great fury'. He was the prototype of the taciturn Scot, a man of few words and even fewer smiles — it was said of him that 'nobody could possibly be as wise as James Braid looked'! He knew a thing or two about golf courses, too — he helped to plan the two magnificent courses at Gleneagles in Perthshire.

Such was the man who was approached by Edward Hudson, the new owner of Lindisfarne Castle, to lay out a nine-hole course on the island early this century. It was completed and ready for play by Easter, 1907, and according to a contemporary newspaper report, Braid himself apparently felt it was 'next to a little golfing Elysium'. He expressed himself even more fulsomely in some publication allegedly called *Golf in Queer Places* (which I confess I have been unable to trace in any library catalogue — I am taking the word of the author of an enchantingly period *Guide to Holy Island* by W. Halliday, Esq., in 1909):

> The new course, one of the wildest and most natural to be found anywhere, will furnish fine golf that will gladden the hearts of the players of the heroic school. On Holy Island the making of bunkers is a business of the utmost simplicity. You just remove the top turf, and the wind does the rest, scooping out the sand and shaping the bunker in the proper way, proving once again how golf, of all games, is most akin to simple nature.

The original subscriptions for playing over this golfing Elysium were as follows: Residents — 2/6d per annum (at the Lord of the Manor's behest); Non-residents — gentlemen 15/-, ladies 7/6; Visitors — 5/- per month, 2/6d per week, or 1/- per day. Sunday golf was expressly forbidden.

Today, the course that James Braid built is only a fading memory. The Clubhouse, which stood at the end of Golf Course Road just where the surface demotes itself into a grass track, has long since been demolished. Only the faintest traces of the lay-out of the course can be detected — just a shadow of an old green or a hint of an old tee, although it is said to be more easily discernible from the air.

One of the island's mussel-fishermen, George 'Bash' Moody, remembers the club in its declining years; he was part-time assistant green-keeper there after the last War. There were practically no members left by then, and barely enough money to pay his token wages. The original course as described by the estimable W. Halliday, Esq., which had required a good deal of 'scaling heights, topping sandhills, etc', had been chopped and changed around a lot over the years to make it play more easily: Lindisfarne's Old Course had proved too heroic even for golfers of that heroic island school.

I cannot resist ending this brief Note on the Old Course at Lindisfarne with a story for the nineteenth hole.

It is the story of the putt that would not drop, of the shot that got bunkered, of the drive that got shanked — or, to put it another way, of the research effort that fell upon stony ground. It is the story of my abortive attempt to rewrite the earliest annals of the royal and ancient game of golf, to the greater glory of Lindisfarne — by proving that no less a personage than holy St Cuthbert himself played golf, some seven centuries before the huge stained-glass Perpendicular window was installed in Gloucester Cathedral to commemorate Edward III's victory at the Battle of Crécy in 1344. This magnificent window was commissioned by Sir Thomas Broadstone in pious memory of fallen comrades; and one of these comrades is clearly depicted *swinging a club at a ball*: playing golf, in fact.

It was another stained-glass window that set me off on the trail of golfing history; and once again, it was the good W. Halliday, Esq., who teed me up. In his *Guide to Holy Island* (p 60), he suddenly blurts out this extraordinary aside:

> Referring to golf, the question arises, 'Did the Monks of Holy Island, in those remote times, play golf?'

The only approach to a solution of this problem is the fact that in St Cuthbert's Church, Philbeach Gardens, Kensington, one of London's most beautiful churches, dedicated to St Cuthbert, there is a beautiful stained glass memorial window depicting the Saint in the act of striking the ball with a club, very similar to the present-day driver.

Who could resist the challenge of such a bizarre question? What enthusiast could overlook such an opportunity to make his mark on the record books? Ignore the fact that all the golfing text-books tell you that the first written reference to 'gouf', as they called it then in Scotland, was in 1457, when King James II, the spoilsport, had the temerity actually to ban the game by an Act of Parliament. No matter that learned Dutch scholars have impiously claimed that the game had its origins in Holland, not Scotland, away back in 1296, and that the very name is derived from the Dutch word *kolv*, meaning 'club'. Golf encourages all sorts of mental aberrations in otherwise perfectly normal people. Philbeach Gardens in Kensington was about to change everything.

St Cuthbert's Church is a large red-brick building in Victorian neo-Gothic, standing in the shade of the Earl's Court Exhibition building. It was built in the 1880s as a by-product of the Tractarian movement in Anglican High-Church circles towards a primitive sacramental Catholicism; and its provenance is sardonically underlined by a contemptuous carving of the face of the virulent, anti-Romanist, Protestant agitator, John Kensit, on one of the misericords in the chancel — on the underside of the hinged seat of the vicar's own pew in the choir stalls: it portrays him with ass's ears, and braying like an ass. Kensit had earned himself this dubious distinction after staging a noisy demonstration denouncing 'idolatory' at a Good Friday service in the church in 1898. He was convicted on a charge of 'behaving in a riotous and indecent manner', but acquitted on appeal; but he later got his come-uppance, poor fellow, when he was fatally injured during a religious riot in Liverpool in 1902.

It is a highly ornate church, crammed with the tangible effects of Kensington fervour and devotion to the cause of the Catholic Revival: jewels, carvings, paintings, inlay work, and a large number of stained-glass windows. One of the windows in the south aisle is unequivocally labelled thus in the church guide-book:

> *St Cuthbert playing a game:* St Cuthbert is depicted as a boy playing golf with his friends. In the background can be seen Melrose Abbey, and in the inset above Prior Boisil, whom St

Cuthbert was later to visit.

The window was designed by a local London artist, Charles Edward Tute, who had worked as a draughtsman in the studio of Charles Eamer Kempe. The date is now indecipherable — the window was damaged by bomb-blast during the War, and somewhat clumsily repaired across the Roman numerals; but it is a reasonable assumption that it originally read 1884, the year in which the Foundation Stone of the church was laid A.M.D.G. – *Ad Majorem Dei Gloriam*, 'To the greater glory of God'. That Foundation Stone had been laboriously quarried on Lindisfarne, by the vicar of Holy Island himself, the Rev W.W.F. Keeling; on its journey along the Pilgrim's Way across the sands to the mainland, the cart broke down and the stone fell off into the wet sands, with the tide beginning to rise. Only by the most frantic of efforts was a new cart procured and the stone rescued in time to catch the London train from Beal for the inaugural ceremony . . .

In the stained-glass window, the haloed Saint is depicted wearing a garnet-red, knee-length, long-sleeved tunic with gold-embroidered cuffs and hems, and cute little lace-up ankle-boots. The white ball is clearly visible at his feet, and the club is held high at the top of the swing.

Now, the appearance of a seventh-century St Cuthbert teeing off at Melrose Abbey on a nineteenth-century stained glass window in London does not prove *ipso facto* that the real St Cuthbert actually did play golf, whether at Melrose or over some Older-than-oldest Course on Lindisfarne. It would merely indicate that Charles Edward Tute, at least, thought he did; and Mr Tute might well have had access to golfing secrets that are no longer available to mere hackers like myself. He might even have seen it in a vision, to adumbrate the construction of the Lindisfarne Old Course. Stranger things than that have been reliably reported from Lindisfarne.

Be that as it may, a long cool look at the window in question brings the whole edifice of excited surmise tumbling to the ground. The thesis is absolutely tenable, apart from one ugly little fact: the so-called 'driver' is quite patently not a driver at all, *pace* W. Halliday, Esq. — not even a prehistoric proto-driver. It is nothing more nor less than an ancient hurling-stick (the Gaelic form of hockey played in Ireland to this day): St Cuthbert is merely having a free swipe at the ball during one of those 'manly' games in which, as he used to suggest to his monastic friends in later years, he had shown no little prowess as a youth.

Ah well! The *Guinness Book of Golf Facts and Feats* (2nd edition) won't need to rush into a 3rd, corrected edition yet a-while, alas. Not on St Cuthbert's account, at any rate. Anyway, Cuthbert was a left-hander, as we know (*cf* ch 7) — but the telltale window in Philbeach Gardens, Kensington, shows him addressing the ball right-handed.

S.G.M.

THE WOMBLES OF LINDISFARNE

Lovers of Kenneth Grahame's enchanting *The Wind in the Willows*, the children's classic that first came out in 1908, will be delighted to know that Ratty is alive and well, and flourishes on Lindisfarne. But he's got a new name now: on Holy Island, he's called a Womble.

Grahame's original Ratty wasn't a rat at all. He was a water vole (*Arvicola terrestris*), which is often confused with the brown rat, another good swimmer. So Kenneth Grahame wasn't alone in his mistake.

The water vole is a relatively large creature, about eight inches long — considerably larger than the more common field short-tailed (*Microtus agrestis*). It is an excellent swimmer, especially underwater, and usually lives in burrows in river-banks, with the entrance often just below the surface of the water. But on Lindisfarne it has become a landlubber. The steep side of the Heugh is honeycombed with small burrows, the entrance hole about 3 inches in diameter. This is a major swarming ground for the water voles, which started coming ashore in the 1960s, moving inland from the Lough and up the open field drains. They came in positively plague proportions, nibbling busily at plant stems and roots, and becoming garden scavengers as well. Anything that grows underground, like potatoes and onions, are a luxury, as well as windfall apples.

Children romping on the Heugh were delighted to find water voles starting up almost from under their feet. The island dogs found a new and exciting pursuit. And because the plague began when the Wombles of Wimbledon were taking the country by storm in the record-shops and toy-shops, the Lindisfarne water voles were promptly nicknamed Wombles, too.

And is anyone worried about having wombles at the bottom of their gardens? Not a bit of it. With their tiny ears, blunt snouts and long tails, the Wombles of Lindisfarne are considered sweet little creatures — especially by anyone who was brought up on *The Wind in the Willows*.

212

S.G.M.

19 The living of Lindisfarne

Today, there is a famous Tyneside pop group, formed in 1970, which calls itself, for sentimental reasons, *Lindisfarne*. There is a small society in San Francisco called the Lindisfarne Club. A new Island Class fishery protection vessel is named HMS *Lindisfarne*. There is a Co-operative Wholesale Society, founded in Edinburgh in 1859, called St Cuthbert's (now subsumed into the Scottish Midland Co-operative Society); it was named after the parish church near their original shop in Ponton St, and has won wide renown for providing magnificent coaches for Royal state occasions — and the handsome coach-horses, promoted from their daily milk-rounds. There are still innumerable churches the length and breadth of Britain dedicated to the memory of St Cuthbert and, to a lesser extent, St Aidan.

The cult associations of the island are still extant in many different ways. But what about on Lindisfarne itself?

I went to ask the present vicar of Holy Island, the Rev Denis Bill, of the parish Church of St Mary the Virgin. He has been on the island since 1954, when 'the bishop sent me', as he puts it. He had expected to be posted to a tough area of Newcastle; instead he was entrusted with the gentler, more contemplative living of Lindisfarne.

He speaks of Aidan and Cuthbert with affection, like old friends. Would he have actually *liked* them, I asked?

'I think I would have *loved* them. And that's a very considered answer. Cuthbert was a wonderful person. He loved God very much, that was obvious. And he loved people very much. He had a great gift of prayer — he had a relationship with God which he was fortunate enough to be able to express in prayer with people. Cuthbert's relationship with God I would liken to having a good marriage: it's a satisfying thing, a deepening thing, which should be one's whole life. Aidan had this, too.

'I think I would have *liked* both of them, too. We know that Aidan was gentle and discerning, and detached enough to rebuke if he had to. There are other Celtic saints whom I might not have liked at all; but Aidan and Cuthbert, yes, certainly.'

And was Holy Island still a holy place, to him? Words can be misleadingly inadequate, and he pondered his answer carefully:

'I am personally very conscious that this is a holy place. I believe in the communion of the saints, as a matter of reality and of fact as opposed to historical legend. I believe that we share a fellowship with the saints, and that in this very particular place one is very conscious of the fact — especially at the altar. I'm not talking about anything emotional, or psychic. It's simply that it is here.

'It's very difficult, and I can't really describe it. But I feel that I'm standing with the saints; there isn't any time-lag. It's the overall impression I get from my whole life on Lindisfarne: I can look back and think, yes, there is this fine simple feeling of growth and reality.

'Lindisfarne wasn't *the* starting-place, but it was *a* starting-place, and I believe it is still a starting-place for quite a number of people who come here to find something. And find it they do.'

They find it most noticeably, perhaps, on formal pilgrimages which continue and commemorate a tradition that began even in Cuthbert's own lifetime. In 1887, for instance, there was a massive Roman Catholic pilgrimage on the 12th centenary of Cuthbert's death. The year 1951 provoked another mass pilgrimage to commemorate the 13th centenary of Aidan's death. The Tenth Lambeth Conference of 1968 occasioned a Newcastle Diocesan Pilgrimage; and in 1983 there was another mass influx to celebrate the centenary of the Newcastle diocese itself. Nearly every year, indeed, there are groups to be found, both large and small, treading the ancient Pilgrim's Way across the boundless sands (some of them with staves and sandaled (*cf* ch 1) feet), for an open-air Eucharist or a special service in the parish church.

The islanders themselves wouldn't claim to be a particularly 'religious' community; but they enjoy perpetuating old traditions associated with religious ceremonies. At weddings, the bridal pair are greeted after the event by an honour guard of island shot-gunners firing ragged volleys; and the churchyard gates are tied until a substantial 'toll' is paid for the gunners' refreshment. A plate of wedding-cake is hurled over the bride's head (it has to break to bring good luck), and wedding guests' hats are often used for target practice. The bride herself is expected to step or jump over the so-called 'Petting Stone' (the socket of the old village Cross on the green, now sited behind the church); she is supported by two of the oldest inhabitants, and to negotiate the Stone without stumbling is considered an omen of good fortune and fertility.

The six Sundays of Lent and Easter are dimly remembered, but barely observed nowadays, in accordance with the old north-eastern Lenten rhyme:

Tid, Mid, Miserae,
Carling, Palm, and Paste-egg Day.

'Carling' is a dialect word, probably derived from 'Caring', as in 'Caring Sunday', and it is applied in the north-east to the parched black peas that were eaten on the eve of 'Caring Sunday' (a fortnight before Easter); the 'carlings' were steeped and boiled, and then served with a 'gravy' of sweetened rum in the island pubs on Carling Saturday. 'Paste-egg Day' for Easter recalls an old but now abandoned tradition of going round the village and collecting hard-boiled eggs in a basket, for rolling (or 'bowling') down the Easter Field beside Jenny Bell's Well.

New Year's Day (Ne'er Day in Scotland) is conducted with all due ritual. All the males of the community have to 'first-foot' every household, usually in strict rotation working from the south of the village. In recent years a rival, or retaliatory, custom has developed, called Ladies' Day, on January 2, when the roles are reversed and the ladies do the socialising.

In all these jollifications, the emphasis is on community. Ultimately, that is what the Lindisfarne experience is all about: the spirit of community, of self-help combined with concern for one's neighbours, of shared joy and shared grief. And from this sense of community there comes a sense of certainty, of steadfastness. In his marvellously evocative chapter on Lindisfarne in his book *Some Lovely Islands* (1968), Leslie Thomas caught it and expressed it memorably:

It has that quality of remoteness, the feeling of being beleaguered by God in a far sea, a rocky independence, and a lasting quietness, and these are the treasures of such places.

Yet this is not a community that feels beleaguered, by God or anything else. It is an island which is also demi-isle. Once the tide comes in, the island retreats into its own enchanted isolation, like some off-shore Brigadoon.

It has its own largely unspoken community law, which suits its way of doing things. The islanders know what is best for the island; they cherish its insularity, its integrity, not jealously but carefully. In the 1880s, a Victorian entrepreneur wanted to build a railway line across the sands, with jetties and piers and all the garish trappings of an amusement arcade; the islanders quashed it. In the 1980s, another

215

entrepreneur wanted to build another amusement arcade on the island; that too was quashed. So was the proposal to build a camping and caravan site on the Links.

Incomers aren't resented or cold-shouldered. But in a subtle way, there seems to be a sort of unwritten apprenticeship to be served first; people don't buy or build a house in the village until they have been hardy-annual visitors for many years, staying in the same cottage, perhaps, and always with the same family. Only then does it become apparent whether they are for the island, and the island is for them. And those who do come in, like the Rev Denis Bill, always feel a sense of privilege — the high privilege of living on Lindisfarne, the cradle island of so much that is precious to our heritage.

S.G.M.

Acknowledgements

Writing this book has given me nothing but pleasure; and this has been largely due to the warm support and enthusiastic help I was given by the people of Lindisfarne and a host of others associated with it.

First and foremost I wish to thank my two collaborators — the artist, Sheila Mackie, and David O'Connor, Warden of Lindisfarne National Nature Reserve, who is billed as 'Consultant' to the book but was in reality much more than that. Their profound affection for the island was a constant inspiration to me.

There are so many others I wish to thank for their individual contributions: Selby 'Sparrow' Alison; Lindsay Allason-Jones, of the Museum of Antiquities of Newcastle University; Margaret Anderson, of the Scottish Midland Co-operative Society; John Bainbridge, of Sunderland Museum and Art Gallery; the Rev Denis Bill, of the Church of St Mary the Virgin; Dr Ian Boyd, of the Natural Environment Research Council; Jimmy 'Clinker' Brigham and the crew of the *Lona M*; Robert Cartwright, of Robert Thompson's Craftsmen Ltd; Professor Rosemary Cramp, of Durham University; Col Humphrey and Lady Rose Crossman (Lord of the Manor); Mrs Betha Douglas; Stan and Dorothy Dover; Ernie and Connie Evans; Dr Peter Garson, of Newcastle University; Mrs Eleanor Garvin; Chuck and Pat Hannant; Peter Hawkey, Warden Naturalist of the Farne Islands; Henry Heaney, Librarian of Glasgow University; Robin Henderson; Michael and Pat Hepworth, administrators of Lindisfarne Castle; Jim Hislop, Joint Master of the North Northumberland Hunt; Professor George Jobey, formerly of Newcastle University; George 'Steptoe' and Barbara Kyle; Mrs Carol Luke; Mrs Barbara Marram, for help with the typing; Ian MacGregor, sub-postmaster; John Malcolm Macpherson, principal keeper of the Longstone lighthouse; George 'Bash' Moody; The National Trust; The Nature Conservancy; Roger Norris, of the Dean and Chapter Library, Durham; Miss Kathleen Parbury; the Venerable Michael Perry, Archdeacon of Durham; Fred Rose, custodian of the Priory Museum; Kate Tristram, of Marygate House; Anthony Tynan, curator of the Hancock Museum, Newcastle; Father Alban Walker;

John Walton, Warden on the Inner Farne; 'Wee' Ralph Wilson; Dr Christopher Young, of the Department of the Environment; and Dr Robert Young, of St David's University College, Lampeter.

And finally, for his saint-like patience, my publisher, Bruce Allsopp (who is also the specialist question-setter on architecture for *Mastermind*). This book was his suggestion to me, and I thank him for it most sincerely.

Magnus Magnusson,
February 1984.